Foodi Multi-Cooker Cookbook for Beginners :
600 Delicious and Time Saving Foodi Multi-Cooker Recipes to Cook Mouth-Watering Meals By

Julia Stella

Copyright 2019 @ Julia Stella
ISBN: 9781081717636

Copyright 2019 by Julia Stella @ All rights reserved.
ISBN: 9781081717636

All rights Reserved. No part of this publication or the information in it may be quoted from or reproduced in any form by means such as printing, scanning, photocopying or otherwise without prior written permission of the copyright holder.

Disclaimer and Terms of Use: Effort has been made to ensure that the information in this book is accurate and complete, however, the author and the publisher do not warrant the accuracy of the information, text and graphics contained within the book due to the rapidly changing nature of science, research, known and unknown facts and internet. The Author and the publisher do not hold any responsibility for errors, omissions or contrary interpretation of the subject matter herein. This book is presented solely for motivational and informational purposes only.

Table of Contents

5 INGREDIENTS SNACK AND APPETIZER RECIPES 23

FISH BALLS 23	ACORN SQUASH SIDE DISH 46
BABY CARROTS SNACK 23	BRUSSELS SPROUTS AND BROCCOLI APPETIZER SALAD 46
ITALIAN MUSSELS 23	CRUNCHY BRUSSELS SPROUTS SALAD 47
CLAMS APPETIZER 24	BRUSSELS SPROUTS AND APPLES APPETIZER 47
GREEK MEATBALLS 24	SWEET BRUSSELS SPROUTS APPETIZER 48
COCKTAIL BOILED PEANUTS 25	BEETS CAKES 48
CHINESE STYLE PEANUTS 25	MANGO SALSA 49
SOUTHERN PEANUTS 26	BROCCOLI APPETIZER SALAD 49
RED PEPPER HUMMUS 26	CREAMY BROCCOLI APPETIZER 50
ASIAN WINGS 27	BROCCOLI AND BACON APPETIZER SALAD 50
BEET APPETIZER SALAD 27	CHEESY BROCCOLI APPETIZER SALAD 51
ONION DIP 28	MUSHROOM DIP 51
MEXICAN CORN ON THE COB 28	CAULIFLOWER DIP 52
BBQ SQUARE RIBS 28	TOMATOES APPETIZER SALAD 52
GRATED CARROT APPETIZER SALAD 29	KALE AND CARROTS SALAD 53
GREEN BEANS APPETIZER SALAD 29	KALE AND WILD RICE APPETIZER SALAD 53
MUSHROOMS AND ROSEMARY 31	MINTY KALE SALAD 54
CHESTNUT MUSHROOMS 31	BRAISED COLLARD GREENS 54
WATERCRESS APPETIZER SALAD 31	COLLARD GREENS AND PEAS 55
HAM AND CHEESE DIP 32	PINTO BEAN DIP 55
SCALLION SPREAD 32	LIGHT LEMON DIP 55
CRAB SPREAD 33	GREEN OLIVE PATE 56
CHILI DIP 33	SHRIMP AND TOMATOES APPETIZER MIX 56
CORN DIP 33	RED PEPPER DIP 57
CREAMY ENDIVES APPETIZER SALAD 34	ARTICHOKES SPREAD 57
ZUCCHINI SPREAD 35	CHICKEN DIP 58
CABBAGE ROLLS 35	BLUE CHEESE DIP 58
TOFU APPETIZER 36	CHUNKY WARM SALSA 59
LEMONY ENDIVES APPETIZER 36	CUMIN DIP 59
ENDIVES PLATTER 37	TORTILLAS 59
MAPLE ACORN SQUASH DISH 38	WHITE BEANS DIP 60
RED ONIONS AND APPLES MIX 38	BLACK BEAN SALSA 60
CASHEW SPREAD 38	RANCH SPREAD 61
MUSHROOM APPETIZER SALAD 39	SPINACH AND SALAMI 61
LENTILS PATTIES 40	CREAMY SPINACH 62
BLACK BEANS PATTIES 40	CHICKEN APPETIZER SALAD 62
VEGGIE DUMPLINGS 41	OCTOPUS APPETIZER 63
TOMATOES AND GARLIC DIP 41	ORANGE AND BEET APPETIZER 63
CHICKPEAS APPETIZER 42	HULLED BARLEY APPETIZER 64
MUSHROOM CAKES 42	GARLIC GREEN BEANS 64
APPETIZER EGG SPREAD 43	KALE SAUTÉ 65
POTATOES AND SHRIMP APPETIZER SALAD 43	WHEAT BERRIES APPETIZER 65
STUFFED BELL PEPPERS APPETIZER 45	VEGGIES AND WHEAT APPETIZER SALAD 66
BRUSSELS SPROUTS AND POTATOES APPETIZER SALAD 45	BULGUR APPETIZER 66
CHINESE MUSTARD GREENS 46	SUMMER LENTILS APPETIZER 67

Green Beans and Cranberries Side Dish	67
Green Beans and Blue Cheese	68
Pork Burritos	68
Beef Sandwiches	69
Carrots Mix	70
Minty Carrots	70
Turnips Spread	70
Calamari Salad	71
Carrots and Walnuts Salad	71
Sweet and Sour Side Salad	72
Cauliflower Salad	72
Chicken Sandwiches	73
Pearl Onions Side Dish	73
Haricots Verts Side Salad	74
Lamb Ribs	74
Pork Cakes	75

BREAKFAST RECIPES 76

Espresso Steel Cut Oats	76
Chocolate Oatmeal	76
Ham And Egg Casserole	76
Egg Bake	77
Peaches Oatmeal	77
Apple Steel Cut Oats	78
Breakfast Meat Soufflé	78
Cheddar Quiche	79
Western Omelet	79
Pepper Frittata	80
Mexican Breakfast	80
French Toast	81
French Eggs	81
Eggs and Bacon Breakfast Risotto	82
Burrito Casserole	82
Spanish Frittata	83
Blueberry Breakfast Bowl	84
Quinoa Bowls	84
Breakfast Oatmeal	85
Scotch Eggs	85
Quinoa Breakfast	85
Breakfast Cake	86
Cornmeal Porridge	86
Breakfast Rice Pudding	87
Pumpkin Oatmeal	87
Buckwheat Porridge	88
Breakfast Tortillas	88
Pancake	88
Squash Porridge	89
Breakfast Banana Bread	89
Millet and Oats Porridge	90
Sweet Potato Hash	90
Blueberry Breakfast Delight	91
Breakfast Bacon Potatoes	91
Potato and Spinach Hash	92
Breakfast Banana Bread	92
Veggie Breakfast Casserole	92
Peach Breakfast	93
Bread Pudding	93
Egg Muffins	94
Chocolate Bread Pudding	94
Fruit Cobbler	95
Buckwheat Porridge	95
Squash Porridge	95
Espresso Oatmeal	96
Breakfast Rice Pudding	96
Apple Butter	97
Veggie Quiche	98
Strawberry Quinoa Bowl	98
Cornmeal Porridge	98
Breakfast Cobbler	99
Tofu and Sweet Potato Mix	99
Breakfast Apple Dish	100
Brown Rice Mix	100
Quinoa and Tomatoes Breakfast Mix	101
Breakfast Rice and Chickpeas Medley	101
Quinoa Salad	101
Breakfast Beans	102
Breakfast Arugula Salad	102
Cranberry Beans Salad	103
Wild Rice Breakfast Salad	103
Rice and Black Beans Breakfast Dish	104
Pineapple and Peas Breakfast Curry	104
Brussels Sprouts and Potato Bowls	105
Parsnip and Quinoa Breakfast Mix	105
Potato Salad	105
Italian Eggplants Bowls	106
Cauliflower and Barley Bowls	106
Breakfast Egg Salad	107
Strawberry Jam	107
Celeriac Breakfast Mix	107
Turkey Breast Breakfast Mix	108
Fresh Peach Jam	108
Breakfast Orange Marmalade	109
Pomegranate Oatmeal	109
Cheesy Cauliflower Bowls	109
Breakfast Potatoes	110
Sweet Potatoes Casserole	110
Swiss Chard Salad	111
Beets Spread	111
Millet Porridge	112
Quinoa with Sausages	112
Avocado Spread	113
Pinto Beans Breakfast Salad	113

Breakfast Chickpeas Spread	113
Breakfast Cheese Spread	114
Creamy Squash Bowl	114
Italian Eggplant Breakfast Mix	115
Breakfast Butter	115
Breakfast Apple Dumplings	115
Carrot Breakfast Salad	116
Tapioca Pudding	116
Breakfast Chestnut Butter	117
Breakfast Couscous Salad	117
Couscous and Mint	117
Quince Jam	118
Veggie and Couscous Breakfast	118
Potato and Salmon Breakfast	119
Rhubarb Breakfast Spread	119
Strawberry and Rhubarb Breakfast Compote	120

MAIN DISH RECIPES 121

Chicken Curry	121
Beef Stew	121
Juicy Roast	122
Mac and Cheese	122
Vegetarian Lentils Soup	123
Crispy Chicken	123
BBQ Ribs	124
Chili Beef	124
Rice and Beans	125
Turkey Meatballs	125
Shredded Chicken	126
Beef Stew	126
Cinnamon Pho	127
Black Bean Soup	127
Pork Chops and Tomato Sauce	128
Chicken Dish	128
Chickpea Curry	129
Beef Dish	129
Beef and Broccoli	130
Fast Salmon	130
Coconut Quinoa	131
Chicken Wrap	131
Steamed Tilapia	132
Lemon Pepper Salmon	132
Tikka Masala	132
Lemon and Olive Chicken	133
Fish Soup	134
Chili Mahi Mahi	134
Chicken and Tomatillo Salsa	134
Chicken with Dates	135
Cod and Orange Sauce	135
Garlic Shrimp	136
Beef Curry	136
Beef and Artichokes	137
Shrimp Boil	137
Fast Shrimp Scampi	138
Pork Roast	138
Pork and Pineapple Delight	139
Delicious and Simple Octopus	139
Teriyaki Scallops	140
Squash and Apple Soup	140
Chicken and Veggie Soup	141
Mussels and White Wine Sauce	141
Beet Soup	142
Chicken and Kale Soup	142
Chicken and Fennel Soup	143
Onion Cream	143
Black Bean Soup	143
Onion Soup	144
Chicken and Red Cabbage Soup	144
Minestrone Soup	146
Swiss Chard Soup	146
Turkey Soup	146
Red Pepper Soup	147
Broccoli and Cheese Soup	147
Potato Soup	148
Potato Soup	148
Meatloaf	149
Cream of Spinach	149
Soup	150
Bean Casserole	150
Flavored Pasta	151
Mussels Bowls	151
Artichokes and Citrus Sauce	152
Beans Chili	152
Pasta and Spinach	153
Chicken and Potatoes Mix	153
Cajun Sausage Mix	153
Pea and Ham Soup	155
Lamb Casserole	155
Turkey Mix	155
Chicken Fall Stew	156
BBQ Ribs	156
Jambalaya	157
Pork and Lemon Sauce	157
Fennel Cream	158
Cod and Beer	158
Salmon with Lemon	159
Cauliflower Salad	159
Collard Greens Stew	160
Chinese Fish	160
Salmon and Risotto	161

Spicy Chicken Wings	161	Mediterranean Cod	165
Rich Chicken Salad	162	Pork Tenderloin and Pomegranate Sauce	166
Salmon Casserole	162	Lemon Lamb Chops	166
Salmon and Chili Sauce	163	Chicken and Salsa	167
Calamari Stew	163	Green Beans Stew	168
Lamb Ribs and Sauce	163	Fish and Orange Sauce	168
Salmon and Veggies	164	Shrimp	168
Pasta with Salmon and Pesto	164	Spinach Pasta	169
Spicy Salmon	165	Chickpeas Cakes	169

SIDE DISH RECIPES 171

Baked Sweet Potatoes	171	Beans and Avocado Salsa	182
Broccoli Pasta	171	Spicy Zucchini	183
Refried Beans	172	Mexican Zucchini Side Dish	183
Sweet Brussels Sprouts	172	Zucchini and Mushrooms	184
Roasted Potatoes	173	Yellow Squash and Zucchini	184
Squash Risotto	173	Bell Peppers Stir Fry	185
Cabbage Side Dish	174	Bell Peppers and Sausages	185
Beans and Chorizo	174	Mixed Veggies Side Dish	186
Spanish Rice	175	Braised Endives	186
Spaghetti Squash Delight	175	Bok Choy Side Dish	187
Artichokes Side Dish	176	Bok Choy and Rice	187
Cabbage and Cream	176	Collard Greens and Bacon	188
Carrots and Kale	176	Collard Greens Side Dish	188
Beets Side Dish	177	Spicy Collard Greens	189
Sweet Potato Puree	177	Rice and Edamame	189
Broccoli and Garlic	178	Poached Fennel	189
Creamy Corn	179	Fennel and Shallots	190
Rice and Quinoa	179	Pea Rice	190
Mushrooms Side Dish	180	Rice with Fennel	191
Mashed Potatoes	180	Coconut Cabbage	191
Mushrooms and Asparagus	180	Corn on the Cob	192
Onion, Celery and Bread Side Dish	181	Steamed Leeks	193
Cranberry Side Dish	181	Sautéed Escarole	193
Green Beans and Bacon	182	Stir Fried Okra	193

SNACK AND APPETIZER RECIPES 195

Flavored Parmesan Mushrooms	195	Crispy Chicken	202
Buttery Potatoes	195	Boiled Peanuts	203
Beef Dip	195	Sweet Pearl Onion Mix	203
Potato Wedges	196	Arborio Rice Side Salad	204
Green Beans Fries	197	Roasted Hummus	204
Mixed Veggies	197	Brussels Sprouts and Chestnuts	204
BBQ Chicken Wings	197	Spinach Side Dish	205
Beef Meatballs	198	Brown Rice Salad	205
Corn Side Dish	198	Brussels Sprouts Side Salad	206
Tomatoes Side Salad	199	Pasta Appetizer Salad	206
Stuffed Chicken Breasts	199	Kidney Beans and Corn Side Dish	207
Vidalia Onions Mix	200	Eggplant and Cashews Mix	207
Parmesan Zucchini Fries	200	Honey Chicken Appetizer	207
Baby Back Ribs Appetizer	201	Shiitake Mushrooms Mix	208
Tomatoes and Corn Side Salad	201	Green Cabbage and Tomatoes Side Dish	209
Tomatoes and Burrata Side Salad	202	Radishes Side Salad	209

Turnip Mash 209	Sweet Potatoes Mash 213
Garlic Beets Salad 210	Squash and Apple Mash 213
Cauliflower and Grapes 210	Italian Dip 213
Hot Wings 211	Mussels Appetizer 214
Mango Side Salad 211	Turnips and Chili Pepper Side Dish 215
Sweet Potato Side Salad 211	Spinach and Squash Mix 215

DESSERT RECIPES 216

Pumpkin and Yogurt Cake 216	Peach Compote 237
Apple Bread 216	Carrot Cake 237
Cranberries Dessert Bowl 216	Ginger and Peach Marmalade 238
Sweet Soufflé 217	Peach and Cinnamon Compote 238
Blackberry Pie 217	Cheesecake 239
Banana Cake 218	Chocolate Pudding 239
Apple Cobbler 218	Ginger Cookies Cheesecake 240
Peanut Butter Cups 219	Winter Cherry Mix 241
Cake Bars 219	Carrot Pudding and Rum Sauce 241
Pumpkin Granola 220	Lemon Pudding 242
Rice Pudding 220	Strawberry and Chia Marmalade 243
White Chocolate Mousse 221	Lemon and Maple Syrup Pudding 243
Black Rice Pudding 221	Sweet Corn Pudding 243
Millet Pudding 222	Apricot Jam 244
Chocolate Cookies 222	Banana Cake 244
Berry Cobbler 223	Pineapple Pudding 245
Sweet Chia Pudding 223	Blueberry Jam 245
Lemon Marmalade 223	Bread Pudding 245
Ricotta Mousse 225	Coconut Cream and Cinnamon Pudding ... 246
Baked Custard 225	Plum Jam 246
Pumpkin Cake 226	Cranberry Bread Pudding 247
Apple Cake 226	Apples and Pears Salad 247
Rhubarb and Strawberries Mix 227	Blueberry and Coconut Sweet Bowls 248
Cherry Pie 227	Coconut Pancake 248
Chocolate Cake 227	Apples and Red Grape Juice 248
Apples and Wine 229	Strawberry Shortcakes 249
Stuffed Strawberries 229	Coconut and Avocado Pudding 249
Glazed Fruits 229	Cocoa and Milk Pudding 250
Apricots and Cranberries Pudding 230	Caramel Pudding 250
Beans Cake 230	Black Tea Cake 251
Lemon Cookies 231	Cocoa and Walnuts Sweet Cream 253
Chocolate Cake 231	Cream Cheese Pudding 253
Orange Cream 232	Green Tea Pudding 253
Pears with Garlic and Jelly 232	Lemon Curd 254
Apples and Wine Sauce 233	Egg and Coconut Cream 254
Cream and Cinnamon Puddings 233	Blueberries and Strawberries Compote 255
Classic Ricotta Cake 233	Apples and Honey 255
Spicy Tomato Jam 234	Strawberries Dessert 255
Poached Pears 234	Sweet Zucchini Bread 256
Flavored Pears 235	Poached Figs 256
Peach Jam 235	Peaches and Cream 257
Lime Pie 235	Pumpkin and Coconut Sweet Mix 257
Dates and Ricotta Cake 236	Apricot Marmalade 258
Lemon and Orange Jam 236	Stuffed Peaches 258

Milk and Cream Pudding	258
Fall Pear Cake	259
Cranberry and Pear Cake	259
Chocolate Fondue	260
Pear and Maple Dessert	260
Cherry Bowls	260
Cold Pineapple and Cherries Mix	261
Fall Plums Mix	261
Sweet Blueberry Butter	262
Sweet Quinoa Dessert	262
Sweet Baked Plums	**Error! Bookmark not defined.**

Ninja Foodi Pressure Cooker Guide

Introduction

Becoming a successful cook is a combination of passion and resources (such as cutlery, utensils, and appliances.) Pressure cookers are the best innovation that has happened to cooks both in commercial and domestic setups. These appliances have made cooking enjoyable by reducing electricity use and cook time.

Ninja Foodi pressure cooker is the latest design that may cook almost everything in a modern kitchen. This is because; it comprises of a pressure cooker, air fryer, and dehydrator. You can also prepare main and side meals in one pot. However, using it appropriately requires excellent mastery of its components, and that's why I have compiled this guide. It comprises of model types, description of components and their functionalities, cleaning guide, maintenance, safety precautions, and examples of ninja recipes. By reading through it, answers to disturbing questions will be provided.

What is a Ninja Foodi pressure cooker?

The advancing technology has introduced great innovations that have simplified our daily activities. The food industry is among the growing sectors with new designs of kitchenware, enabling exploration of recipes. Ninja Foodi pressure cooker is among the appliances that cooks are talking about. The multi-purpose pot can air fry, grill, slow cook, pressure cook, steam, sauté, and roast.

It was difficult to switch from my adorable instant pot to a Ninja Foodi. In this, I researched a lot from the internet, inquired from other cooks, and even contacted the company for further details. The truth is; before finding out about the Ninja Foodi, I had never thought of replacing my 3 year-old instant pot. However, I purchased the Ninja Foodi and explored my instant pot recipes using it. The table below compares its specifications, cooking capabilities, and accessories to that of my instant pot.

Comparison between Ninja Foodi and instant pot

Element	Ninja Foodi	Instant pot
Cooking capabilities	Air fry, grill, slow cook, pressure cook, steam, sauté, bake, dehydrate, sear, and roast. It keeps food warm up to 12 hours after cooking.	Low temperature cooking (sous vide,) pressure cook, simmer, sear, boil, ferment, and sauté. It's also a yogurt maker, food warmer, and rice cooker.
Controls	You can customize cooking temperature, pressure levels, and time.	You can set cooking duration, pressure level, temperature, delay start, and warm your food.
Cleaning	Easy since the accessories are ceramic coated.	Easy since its parts can be cleaned by a dishwasher.
sizes	6.5 quart available. 8.5 quart for special orders.	3 quarts, 6, and 8 available.
accessories	Pressure cooker lid, air frying/ crisping lid, reversible rack, and an air fryer basket.	Pressure cooker lid and a trivet.
Power consumption	1400W Plus	1100W and below
Start procedure	Switch it on, push start, and set the cooking temperature followed by time.	Set the cooking temperature and time.

Note: Once you become a Ninja Foodi pro, you can prepare all your instant pot recipes using it.

Models of Ninja Foodi pressure cooker

You may be wondering why your appliance lacks some of the specifications explained in this guide. Similar to other devices, Some Ninja Foodi cookers have different features that distinguish them from others. Acquiring it depends on your preferences and cost. Below is a list of the Ninja series alongside their specifications.

1. Model OP300

The 1400-watt unit lacks dehydration functions. Its other features include;
- A reversible rack
- Pressure and crisping lids
- 4-quart cook and crisp basket
- 6.5-quart ceramic pot
- 15 recipe guides

2. Model OP301
- A reversible rack
- 1400W unit
- Pressure and crisping lids
- 4-quart cook and crisp basket
- 6.5-quart ceramic pot
- 45 recipe guides

3. Model OP301C

The 1400-Watt unit appliance conducts the dehydration functions appropriately. Its other specifications include;
- A reversible broil/steam rack
- Pressure and crisping lids
- 4-quart cook and crisp basket
- Cook and crisp layered insert
- 6.5-quart ceramic pot
- 20 recipe guides

4. Model OP302
- A reversible broil/steam rack
- Pressure and crisping lids
- 4-quart cook and crisp basket
- 6.5-quart ceramic pot
- 45-plus recipe guides

5. Model OP305
- A reversible broil/steam rack
- Pressure and crisping lids
- 4-quart cook and crisp basket

- Cook and crisp layered insert
- 6.5-quart ceramic pot
- 45-plus recipe guides

6. Model OP401

Besides the 1700-watt unit containing a larger quart, it also executes the dehydration functions. Its other features include;
- A reversible broil/steam rack
- Pressure and crisping lids
- XL 5-quart cook and crisp basket
- Cook and crisp layered insert
- XL 8-quart ceramic pot
- 45-plus recipe guides

Descriptions of the Ninja Foodi accessories
Here, I will name the cooker's accessories and their functions. This will not only guide the potential users but also simplify their purpose to continuing users. It's unfortunate that even after some individuals acquiring the appliance; they continue preparing repetitive recipes due to the complexity of parts functions.

1. **The pressure lid**

It is a removable part of the ninja Foodi utilized when the device is used as a pressure cooker. It consists of a valve cap found on the lid's underside and a black valve on the Foodi top. These parts should be detached, cleaned, and inspected after using the lid following the manufacturer's directions. When using the lid, the valve should be loose and floating to allow the release of accumulated steam. However, it tightens after pressurizing. When setting the valve to "vent" position, it should be raised. The red button at the lid's top stays depressed when the Foodi is pressurizing before popping up. You should not open the pot when the button has popped up to prevent burns.

2. **Air-crisp lid**

The lid is screwed on the pot and remains intact even when pressure cooking. However, it remains open except when preparing crisped diets. It contains a fan for hot-air circulation and a heater. It can be flipped up anytime you need to check the cooking progress contrary to the pressure lid, which requires you first to release the built-in pressure.

3. **User's guide**

Although I will analyze critical details of the cooker, it's essential to study the comprehensive guide packaged alongside the appliance before using it. It consists of a; maintenance guide, troubleshooting guide, and the Foodi functions.

4. **Ninja cookbook**

This is a guide containing more than 45 ninja Foodi recipes. It also comprises of cooking charts that illustrate food timing and settings. However, when following the guidelines, you should consider your seasoning preferences since reviews indicate that the dishes are salty. Also, consider adding your favorite spices and eliminating/replacing the ones you dislike. Similarly, you can follow the quick start guide to understand the package contents and the pressure test. A cooking cheat sheet is also availed containing a roasted chicken recipe.

How to perform the Ninja Foodi functions

As seen from the cooker series, different models consist of varying features. These enable the cooker to execute its design functionalities. For instance; some recipes are cooked with a sealed crisping lid, others tightened pressure lids, and the rest opened pots. Additionally, while cooking different dishes opening the cooker lid is necessary on initial stages. Below is a description of the ninja Foodi functions.

1. **Pressure cooker functions**

This is attained with the pressure lid sealed. Its settings are either "High" or "Low." The user can also customize the cooking time up to four hours depending on your recipe. To achieve this, seal the black valve found at the top of the Foodi by turning it. Examples of pressure-cooked meals include; steak, desserts, and one-pot chili among others.
- When selecting the cooking time, you should consider the ingredient's temperature. For example; a frozen chicken takes longer cooking duration than thawed ones.
- Also, your cooking version matters a lot. For example; PIP style preferred when preparing meals by putting a pot inside your Ninja Foodi consumes more time than placing food in the cooker directly.
- When pressure cooking, the cooking time may depend on your food type. This includes food size and density. For instance; larger and denser foods consume more cooking time than smaller and lighter ones. This can be proven by cooking whole potatoes and sliced ones.

What amount of liquid is recommendable when using the pressure cooker? This is a controversial question that has stopped Ninja Foodi owners from using the appliance. The truth is; different recipes demands special treatment. For instance; when preparing a beef stew, I expect to serve it with gravy while plain rice should be dry. Also, depending on what you are cooking, some water will be absorbed while cooking and the rest released as steam. For instance; boiling meat requires more water than boiling pumpkins inconsiderate on what you will be preparing with the boiled ingredient. Similarly, large quantity of meals requires more fluid than smaller portions. In short, the amount of liquid to be added in the pressure cooker depends on what you are cooking and the expected results.

Hint: Thinner may be added to milky-recipes since milk does not generate steam. In doing this, remember some of the fluids will be absorbed by your meal and some released. For a tasty meal, you should also consider using broth in place of water.

2. **Steam functions**

This is attained by setting the black valve to "vent' instead of "seal." In this, no requirement for temperature adjustment, although the cooking duration can be customized up to half-hour depending on the dish prepared. Examples of steamed dishes include; vegetables, grains, and delicate fish, among others.

3. **Slow cook function**

The function is a replica of the slow cooker. This is attained with the lid on and black valve set to vent. Also, you can set temperatures high or low, depending on the meal. The feature also allows customization of the cooking duration to 12 hours maximally. Examples of slow-cooked recipes include; risotto and slow-pulled pork, among others.

4. **Sear/sauté**

When sautéing the meal, you can either seal the pressure lid or open it depending on your familiarity with the cooker. However, if you are new to the appliance, it's advisable to sauté with an open lid to enable regular checking of your meal. The feature allows temperature adjustments from high, medium-high, medium, medium-low, and low. In this, the user is supposed to switch off the cooker manually when the dish is ready since there are no settings for the cooking duration. Examples of sautéed dishes include; caramelized onion and steak, among others.

5. Air crisp

This functionality is attained with a crisping lid "on." The cooker has a setting to adjust the temperature from 300 to 400° F. The cooking duration can also be customized up to an hour. Examples of air frying recipes include; golden chips, crispy chicken, and crispy vegetables, among others.

6. Roast/Bake

It is also attained with a sealed crisping lid. When executing the function, the temperature can be adjusted from 250 to 400° F. The baking or roasting duration can be adjusted to four hours maximally. Examples of baked recipes include; Mediterranean vegetables and roasted potatoes.

7. Broil

The broiling feature also accomplishes its functions when a crisping lid is on. Although it does not have temperature adjustment settings, the cooking duration can be customized to half-hour. Examples of broiling recipes are; Broiled fish, garlic broiled chicken, and broiled beef among others.

8. Dehydration

The dehydration feature is found on some models, and it's executed using a crisping lid. It allows temperature adjustment from 105 to 195° F and cooking time customization from quarter-hour to 12hours. Examples of dehydrated recipes include; beef jerky, vegetable crisps, apples, and fruit leather, among others.

9. One-pot meal

The reversible rack allows the Ninja Cooker to prepare mains and side meals simultaneously. These include; layered grains, vegetables with meat, and fish, among others.

How to release the Ninja Foodi Pressure
The rotating lights demonstrate the pressure-building activity. Its accumulation duration varies depending on the size of the dish and the liquid contents on the pot. When the cooker is pressurizing, its lid locks until the pressure gets released. Here, full pressure is illustrated by the glow of the lid icon light. After that, the pressure cooking begins, and the timer countdown starts. Below are ways to release built-in pressure from your Ninja Foodi;

- NPR

After elapsing the cooking duration, the accumulated steam will start releasing naturally to allow lid opening. The process may take up to 30 minutes, depending on the amount of food cooked and the fluid remaining. During NPR, the cooker turns to "keep warm" mode which can be changed by pressing the keep warm button. After all pressure exits the pot, the red valve drops down, allowing lid opening.

- QPR

This option is distinguished for recipes that do not require steam softening. Immediately the cooking time elapses, the "keep warm" light switches on. Here, the cook is needed to turn the pressure valve to vent. This activity may consume at least 30 seconds, depending on your dish size and fluid.
Note: After releasing the built-in pressure either in NPR or QPR, the lid should be opened to allow the escape of the remaining pressure. Here, care should be taken to prevent dripping of the pot's vapor on its base. Also, when the pressure is releasing naturally, you can shift to quick-release by turning the pressure valve to vent.

How to use the Ninja Foodi pressure cooker
Before getting into cooking details, I would like to explain the Ninja Foodi abbreviations. This is because; when following a recipe, translating the required function may be confusing due to its shortened language. Besides that, you may find it hard to engage in related discussions. The following list contains the translation of such functions.

1. PIP: pot in pot

2. AC: air crisp
3. NPR: natural pressure release
4. SC: slow cook
5. IR: immediate release
6. TC: tender-crisp
7. AF: air fry
8. PC: pressure cook
9. NR: natural release
10. QR: quick release
11. QPR: quick pressure release

Now that you have understood the Ninja Foodi language, I will explain the recommendable stages you should follow after acquiring the new appliance. This involves cleaning the washable components after unpacking it. For instance; the inner pot, silicone ring, rack, and basket can be cleaned on a dishwasher. The cooker's lid can be washed by hand while its anti-clog cap can be scrapped using a fine toothbrush. However, the cap should be detached and inspected regularly to prevent spattering of food debris when releasing the accumulated pressure.

A condensation tray should be fitted on the Ninja cooker to collect moisture that may arise when steaming. The tray should also be removed and cleaned after cooking to prevent building-up of moulds due to accumulated vapor.

How to perform a pressure test
If you are not familiar with the Ninja Cooker, it's advisable to conduct a pressure test to understand how it works. This test may also verify the functionality of your cooker. The procedural steps involve;
1. Switch on your Ninja Foodi device, plug it power cable in the wall socket, and turn on the power button.
2. Pour around 3 cups of water in your Ninja pot.
3. Seal the pressure lid tightly by turning the black valve.
4. Press the "pressure" button. In this, use the arrows on the left to select "high."
5. Select the boiling duration (around 8 minutes) using the arrows on the right.
6. Press start. Rotation of lights implies that your cooker is heating.
7. Let the water boil until you see steam escaping from all-round the lid. Stop it.
8. Twist the black vent to a vent position for the steam to exit.
9. When all the in-built pressure has exited, remove the cooker's lid and allow your boiled water to cool.

Note: it's normal for steam to escape through the black valve, red button, or both. However, if you see it exiting all-round the lid surface, you should open the cooker's lid. The above procedure is a template of the Ninja Foodi cooking instructions.

How to use the Ninja Air-fryer
Lovers of crisped recipes, it's now your time to enjoy because Ninjashark has considered you in their innovation. You do not need an extra oven or other air fryers to prepare your favorite snack. Below is the procedure to follow when cooking air-fried meals using your Ninja Foodi;
1. As said earlier, the cooker has two lids. In this, only the crisping lid (already attached to the pot) is utilized.
2. Place the air-frying basket in the cooking pot.
3. You can either place your food on the basket or the grilling pan.
4. Flip down the lid and "switch on" the appliance.
5. Use the air-fryer chart to predict the cooking duration.
6. Press in the "air fry" button.
7. Customize the cooking temperature using +/- buttons.

8. Customize the cooking time using +/- buttons.
9. Hit start.

How to transform the Ninja cooker to an air fryer, pressure cooker, or slow cooker
Having said a lot about the cooker's accessories and functionality, I thought explaining its transformation concept was essential.
- A Ninja Foodi package consists of an attached air fryer lid to be flipped down when baking, broiling, or roasting. Also, a basket is inserted when preparing related recipes.
- In case you want to use your cooker as pressure or slow cooker, you will have to close the pressure lid. The lid resembles that of the instant pot. It comes along with a rack which is fitted inside the Ninja Foodi. It's also used when sautéing your meal using the "sauté" setting.

However, the new kitchenware has received mixed reactions from users and potential users. This depends on your love of exploration. Below are some of the benefits and limitations of the device according to its users.

Advantages of using the Ninja Foodi
- It reduces the cooking time.
- The multi-purpose cooker plays the role of four kitchen appliances.
- It's affordable compared to the total cost of individual devices.
- The gadget comes with a detailed user manual which it's easier to follow.
- Cleaning the Ninja cooker is easy since most parts are ceramic-coated.
- It has a digital screen that displays the pressure-building progress.
- It has a timer and temperature setting that mitigates cooking guesswork.

Disadvantages of using the Ninja Foodi
- Being a compact unit, its large size does not save the kitchen space.
- After air-frying, double cleaning is required (for the layered insert and the basket.)Who finds fun in cleaning?
- Sometimes the lid may leak when the pot is releasing pressure. This may happen when you start cooking without confirming its "seal" position.
- It's hard to predict cooking time for new recipes. This requires regular opening of the cooker which entails releasing the in-built pressure.
- The Ninja cooker sizes are limited (6-quarts and 8-quarts); therefore, buyers do not enjoy their freedom of choice.
- Their baskets are also small for larger meals. That means the user is forced to cook in batches.
- The attached air fryer lid inconveniences the user. This is because; it's usually open unless you are air crisping.

How to clean and maintain the Ninja Foodi
The appliance should be well cleaned after cooking to prevent the accumulation of food debris. Its cleaning instructions involve;
1. Unplugging the unit from the wall socket.
2. The cooker's base should not be immersed in water or put in the dishwasher. Its control panel and base should be wiped with a damp towel.
3. You can wash the basket, pot, diffuser, and silicone ring in a dishwasher.
4. The pressure valve and anti-clog cap can be cleaned using soapy water.
5. Do not disassemble the pressure valve when cleaning.
6. The crisping lid should be wiped using wet clothing.

7. Avoid using scouring pads to scrub food residue stuck on the rack, basket, or pot. If scrubbing is essential, a non-abrasive cleanser or a brush soaked in a liquid soap can be used. Also, soaking the pot in water for some time helps when removing stuck foods.
8. After cleaning the components, you can air-dry them for the next use.
9. The silicone ring should be taken off by pulling it outward part by part. Fixing it back involves placing it on the rack and pressing it down systematically.
10. Food debris should be removed from the anti-clog cap and ring immediately after use.
11. A damaged silicone ring should be replaced to allow pressure cooking and prevent its explosion.

Several elements may limit efficient use of your ninja Foodi cooker, and that's why I have compiled the below troubleshooting guide. They include;

1. **The cooker taking long to pressurize**
- Pressure-building up depends on the temperature of the cooking pot, ingredients, and the cooking temperature. Before making any judgments, you should confirm the status of the named elements.
- Check whether your silicone ring is in good condition and well-positioned.
- Confirm that your pressure lid is locked. The release valve should be in seal position when cooking.
2. **Slow cont-down timer**

Confirm whether you set the cooking duration in minutes or hours. This is because; when cooking, time should decrease in minutes.

3. **Lights displaying on the screen when steaming or pressure cooking**

This implies that your cooker is pressurizing. When the rotating lights stop, you can set your cook time to begin the countdown.

4. **The pressure lid is not getting off**

This is a safety feature. The lid opens after all pressure exits from your Ninja cooker. You can either use quick release or natural release depending on your recipe. Open the lid by turning it anticlockwise, lifting it, and placing it away. In this, the pressure valve should be loose to enable its transitioning from seal to vent.

5. **Cooker producing a hissing sound**

First, verify that you have positioned the pressure valve to a seal position. If it continues, check whether its silicone ring is well-installed by removing and inserting it.

6. **The timer counting upwards instead of downwards**

If you are experiencing this, do not worry. It implies that the cooking time has elapsed; therefore, your Ninja Foodi has reached the "keep warm" mode.

If you encounter more challenges, you can refer to the cooker's manual or inquire from its dealers.

Ninja Foodi safety precautions

After using the Ninja cooker, I identified a number of things that should be avoided by every user. This is to protect the gadget, its user, and the environment. They include;

- Spraying the inner pot with aerosol. This causes baking up of its base, making it hard to clean.
- Predicting the water portion well, especially when using the pressure cooking function. This may affect the final product. For instance; cooking a stew with low levels of water may dry it up. Similarly, cooking rice with large portions of water may leave it gravy.

- Similar to other home appliances, the Ninja cooker should be unplugged when not in use to prevent unexpected switching. This may cause burning off your home, damaging of the appliance, and even human accidents.
- The device should not be used on a stove. Turning on the stove's burner may melt the appliance ruining it.
- Avoid covering the pressure valve.
- Confirm that all parts are well-assembled before using your Ninja cooker.
- Avoid long power cords to reduce risks of getting entangled or being grabbed by children. Also, use pots recommended by the manufacturer to prevent electric shocks.
- Power cords, cooker base, plugs, and the crisping lid should not be immersed in liquids to prevent electric shock.
- Do not force opening the cooker's lid. The accumulated steam locks it. In this, you should either consider quick release or natural release to avoid scald issues.
- Avoid touching the appliance's hot surfaces when cooking to prevent burning accidents. If need be, use hot pads, knobs, handles, or oven mitts.
- Do not use a damaged silicone ring to prevent the pot from exploding, causing body burns.
- Care should be taken when preparing "expanding" meals using the cooker. In this, place the ingredients halfway or as instructed by the recipe.
- The unit should not be used when preparing instant rice.
- Allow the Ninja Foodi to cool before cleaning or tampering with it.

Tips for great cooking using Ninja Foodi
Now that you have learned all essential details about the Ninja cooker usage,
I have compiled some mouth-watering recipes for your trial.

Air fried chicken wings
Prep time: 4 MINUTES | Cooking time: 20 minutes | Servings: 4 people

Ingredients
- A pound of chicken wings
- A tablespoon of olive oil
- ½ teaspoon of salt
- A pinch of pepper
- 4 teaspoons of barbeque sauce

Cooking procedure
1. Spread the air fryer basket with half of the olive oil.
2. Align the chicken wings on the oiled basket.
3. Spray the wings with the remaining oil followed by salt and pepper depending on your seasoning preferences.
4. Flip-down the lid and cook the wings at 390° for around 10 minutes. Ensure the wings temperature is around 165°.
5. Flip their other side and cook with the same settings for time and temperature.
6. Transfer the golden-brown wings on a large bowl and spread them with the barbeque sauce.
7. Serve warm alongside rice, chips, or any other preferred meal.

Nutrition: calories 168kcal, fat 13g, sodium 52g, protein 11g

Air-fried seasoned asparagus
Prep time: 8 MINUTES | Cooking time: 10 minutes | Servings: 4 people

Ingredients
- 200g of trimmed asparagus
- A teaspoon of olive oil
- ½ teaspoon of garlic salt
- 50g of sliced mushrooms

Cooking procedure
1. Put the trimmed asparagus on the air fryer basket.
2. Spread it with olive oil.
3. Add your sliced mushrooms and season with garlic salt to attain your preferred taste.
4. Close the crisping lid and cook your asparagus at 390° for around 5 minutes.
5. Flip-up the cooker's lid and check whether your meal is ready. Turn it.
6. Cook its other side using the same cooker settings.
7. Transfer your seasoned asparagus to serving plates and enjoy.

Nutrition: calories 63kcal, fat 6g, carbohydrates 1g, protein 1g

Air fried plate nachos
Prep time: 10 MINUTES | Cooking time: 5 minutes | Servings: 4 people

Ingredients
- An ouch of tortilla chips
- An ouch of grilled chicken
- Drained and rinsed black beans
- A cup of white queso
- Halved grape tomatoes
- 2 Diced green onions

Cooking procedure
1. Line the air fryer basket with an aluminum foil and spread it with non-stick spray.
2. Mix the grilled chicken with beans and chips to form nachos.
3. Pour the queso over the nacho.
4. Cover the mixture with tomatoes and onions.
5. Close the air frying lid having set the fryer to 355°-Cook for around 5 minutes.
6. Open the lid and check whether your nacho attained your desired texture.
7. Serve your crispy nacho while warm.

Nutrition: calories 271kcal, fat 13g, carbohydrates 18g, protein 13g

Air fryer tacos
Prep time: 15 MINUTES | Cooking time: 8 minutes | Servings: 12 people

Ingredients
- 10 taco shells
- Rinsed and drained black beans
- A package of gluten-free taco seasoning
- Shredded lettuce

- A pound of ground turkey
- Mexican cheese (shredded)
- 2 sliced tomatoes
- A teaspoon of olive oil.
- A diced onion
- Salsa and other toppings

Cooking procedure
1. Put your turkey on a medium-sized skillet and fry until it turns brown.
2. Drain excess oil from your turkey and add the taco seasoning until it attains your desired taste.
3. Combine taco shells with lettuce, beans, cheese, and browned turkey to form tacos.
4. Line the air fryer basket with foil and spread it with olive oil.
5. Add your tacos to the fryer and close its lid.
6. Cook your turkey tacos for 4 minutes having set it to around 355° depending on your cooker settings.
7. Add salsa alongside other toppings and continue cooking at 355° for 4 minutes.
8. Serve your tacos warm.

Nutrition: calories 237kcal, fat 9g, carbohydrates 28g, protein 15g

Air fried sausage casserole
Prep time: 10 MINUTES | Cooking time: 20 minutes | Servings: 4 people

Ingredients
- A pound of hash browns
- A pound of ground sausage
- A diced bell pepper (green)
- A diced bell pepper (red)
- A diced bell pepper (yellow)
- ¼ cup of diced sweet onions
- 4 eggs
- A pound of shredded cheese

Cooking procedure
1. Line your air fryer basket with foil and place hash browns on it.
2. Add the ground sausage.
3. Top the mixture with the diced onions, shredded cheese, and peppers.
4. Close the crisping lid and cook the ingredients at 355° for around 10 minutes.
5. Open the lid and stir your casserole.
6. Crack the eggs and whisk them in separate bowls.
7. Pour them over your cooked casserole and continue cooking at 355° for 10 minutes.
8. Season your casserole with salt and pepper to attain your desired taste. Serve hot.

Nutrition: calories 573kcal, fat 45.3g, carbohydrates 23.4g, protein 31.3g

Pressure-cooked lasagna soup
Prep time: 10 MINUTES | Cooking time: 10 minutes | Servings: 6 people

Ingredients
- A pound of ground beef
- 20 OZ of meat sauce
- A cup of mozzarella cheese(shredded)
- A crushed garlic clove
- A cup of spinach leaves(fresh)
- 1 teaspoon of dried basil
- 12 oz of lasagna noodles
- 6 cups of water

Cooking procedure
1. Set your cooker to sauté mode and put the ground beef in it.
2. Cook the beef until it tenderizes and its fluid drains.
3. Turn the cooker off and add meat sauce followed by spinach, garlic, water, and basil. Stir the mixture.
4. Break your noodles into reasonable pieces and add it to the meat mixture.
5. Close the pressure lid and cook the mixture for 4 minutes.
6. Quick-release the accumulated steam and open the lid.
7. Transfer your cooked lasagna soup into a dish and serve with cheese toppings. Enjoy.

Nutrition: calories 339kcal, fat 25g, carbohydrates 13g, protein 34g

Pressure-cooked pork chops with cabbage
Prep time: 15 MINUTES | Cooking time: 10 minutes | Servings: 6 people

Ingredients
- 2 pounds of boneless pork chops
- A small-sized cabbage (roughly chopped)
- 2 cups of chicken broth
- ½ cup of butter
- ½ cup of steak seasoning
- A chopped pepper
- A teaspoon of salt

Cooking procedure
1. Pour the steak seasonings over the pork chops in a bowl.
2. Transfer the seasoned chops to the pressure pot.
3. Add cabbage chunks and chicken broth to the pork mixture. Add pepper and salt to your preferred taste.
4. Spread butter over the mixture and cook it on high-pressure mode for around 10 minutes.
5. Let the built-in steam release naturally for quarter-hour. Hit the quick-release button for any remaining pressure to exit.
6. Transfer your pork chops with cabbage to serving plates and enjoy.

Nutrition: calories 424kcal, fat 23g, carbohydrates 13g, protein 40g

Pressure-cooked-chicken Masala
Prep time: 10 MINUTES | Cooking time: 13 minutes | Servings: 4 people

Ingredients
- A cup of chicken broth
- A cup of Marsala wine
- 2 pounds of chicken breast
- A cup of flour
- 3 garlic cloves
- 2 teaspoons of butter
- 16 oz of mushrooms
- 2 teaspoons of olive oil

Cooking procedure
1. Subdivide your chicken breast into halves and season each with pepper and salt.
2. Dip the halves into a bowl containing flour for coating.
3. Set your Ninja Foodi to sauté mode and add butter followed by crushed garlic.
4. Add the coated chicken to the sautéed contents and cook each side for around 3 minutes or until it turns golden brown.
5. Add mushrooms, chicken broth, and Marsala wine into the chicken mixture.
6. Set the cooker to high-pressure mode and cook the added contents for around 10 minutes.
7. Select quick-release pressure.
8. Transfer your chicken Masala to a large bowl and serve hot alongside white rice.

Nutrition: calories 364kcal, fat 22g, carbohydrates 14g, protein 27g

Ninja Foodi yoghurt
Prep time: 5 MINUTES | Cooking time: 14 hours | Servings: 8 people

Ingredients
- 8 cups of milk
- ¼ cup of plain yoghurt

Cooking directions
1. Pour the milk into the Ninja inner pot.
2. Set the cooker to sauté mode and boil the milk until it reaches 181° while stirring it frequently to prevent scorching.
3. Stop the cooker and remove the pot. Place it on a cool surface and leave it until the milk reaches around 110°.
4. Add plain yoghurt to the milk and stir.
5. Seal the pot with an aluminum foil and return it to the Ninja cooker.
6. Flip down the crisping lid and cook the contents on dehydration mode for around 8 hours. Here, the cooking temperature should be set to around 180°.
7. Incubate your yoghurt by continuing cooking it with the same settings for around 6 hours.
8. Switch off your cooker and remove the inner pot.
9. Place it in the refrigerator and allow it to cool for around 12 hours.
10. Strain it until you attain your preferred texture.
11. You can add your favorite sweeteners and other mix-ins to obtain your desired flavor.

Nutrition: calories 153kcal, fat 8g, carbohydrates 12g, protein 7g

Beginner meals using the Ninja Foodi

Although there are hundreds of recipes experts can prepare using the cooker, I have compiled easy dishes to familiarize beginner users with the appliance. Everyone starts from somewhere!

- Crispy bacon
- Tasty popcorns
- Roasted chicken
- Fluffy rice
- Creamy yogurt
- Roasted yam

You can also try other Ninja Foodi recipes following its packaged manual. As time goes, you will get used to preparing a variety of meals using the appliance. In this, you should consider water portions to attain your preferred output. Also, study the listed safety precautions to avoid scald injuries.

Conclusion

Ninja Foodi cooker is a significant transformation to a modern kitchen. This is because; it can cook mains meals and sides simultaneously. With the multi-cooker, you can cook almost every recipe without using other appliances. If you use its buttons and settings appropriately, you can air fry, grill, slow cook, pressure cook, steam, sauté, and roast. However, proper mastery of the machine is required since handling it inappropriately may expose you to scald injuries. This is the reason why I have compiled this guide to ensure that you understand the appliance comprehensively. If you are new to the gadget, ensure you have understood all its instructions to avoid damaging it. Start using it by preparing easy recipes and within no time, you will become a pro. If you have not yet decided on buying the machine, I assure you, it's great. Your dining table will never be boring again. Good luck!

5 Ingredients Snack and Appetizer Recipes

Fish Balls

Preparation time: 10 minutes
Cooking time: 20 minutes
Servings: 16

Ingredients:
- 1 and ½ cups fish stock
- 1 and ½ pound pike fillets, skinless, boneless and ground
- 3 egg whites
- ¼ cup potato starch
- 1 carrot, grated

Directions:
1. In a bowl, mix fish meat with egg whites, potato starch and carrot and whisk well.
2. Put the stock in your pressure cooker, add fish balls, cover and cook on Low for 10 minutes.
3. Drain fish balls, arrange them on a platter and serve as an appetizer.

Nutrition: calories 162, fat 3, fiber 4, carbs 8, protein 4

Baby Carrots Snack

Preparation time: 10 minutes
Cooking time: 2 minutes
Servings: 6

Ingredients:
- 1 pound baby carrots
- ¼ cup soy sauce
- ¼ cup Chinese wine
- ¼ cup veggie stock
- 1 tablespoon liquid smoke

Directions:
1. In your pressure cooker, mix baby carrots with soy sauce, Chinese wine, stock and liquid smoke, toss, cover and cook on High for 2 minutes.
2. Drain carrots, arrange them on a platter and serve them as a snack with a dip on the side.

Nutrition: calories 176, fat 3, fiber 6, carbs 4, protein 4

Italian Mussels

Preparation time: 10 minutes
Cooking time: 6 minutes
Servings: 2

Ingredients:
- 20 ounces canned tomatoes, chopped

- 3 tablespoons onion, chopped
- 1 jalapeno peppers, chopped
- 2 tablespoons white wine
- 2 tablespoons olive oil
- 2 tablespoons balsamic vinegar
- 1 and ½ pounds mussels, scrubbed
- 1 tablespoon red pepper flakes
- 1 garlic cloves, minced
- A pinch of salt
- 2 tablespoons basil, chopped

Directions:
1. Set your pressure cooker on sauté mode, add the oil, heat it up, add onion and garlic, stir and cook for 2 minutes.
2. Add tomatoes, jalapeno, wine, vinegar, pepper flakes and salt, stir and simmer for 2 minutes more.
3. Add mussels, stir, cover and cook on High for 2 minutes.
4. Discard unopened mussels, divide them between 2 bowls and serve with basil sprinkled on top.

Nutrition: calories 94, fat 1, fiber 2, carbs 2, protein 2

Clams Appetizer

Preparation time: 10 minutes
Cooking time: 5 minutes
Servings: 4

Ingredients:
- 12 clams
- 1 garlic clove, minced
- 2 tablespoons butter
- 2 tablespoons parsley, chopped
- 2 tablespoons parmesan cheese, grated
- ½ teaspoon oregano, chopped
- ½ cup breadcrumbs
- 1 cup water

Directions:
1. In a bowl, mix breadcrumbs with parmesan, oregano, parsley, butter and garlic, stir, open clams and divide this into them.
2. Add the water into your pressure cooker, add the steamer basket, add clams inside, cover and cook on High for 5 minutes.
3. Divide clams on a platter and serve as an appetizer with lemon wedges on the side.

Nutrition: calories 100, fat 3, fiber 1, carbs 2, protein 5

Greek Meatballs

Preparation time: 10 minutes
Cooking time: 4 minutes
Servings: 20

Ingredients:
- 1 pound beef, ground
- ¼ cup white vinegar
- 3 tablespoons olive oil
- ¼ cup mint, chopped
- 1 egg, whisked

Directions:
1. In a bowl, mix beef with mint and egg, whisk well and shape 20 meatballs out of this mix.
2. Set your pressure cooker on sauté mode, add oil, heat it up, add meatballs and brown them for a few minutes on each side.
3. Add vinegar, toss, cover and cook on High for 4 minutes.
4. Arrange meatballs on a platter and serve them with a yogurt dip on the side.

Nutrition: calories 200, fat 4, fiber 4, carbs 8, protein 10

Cocktail Boiled Peanuts

Preparation time: 10 minutes
Cooking time: 1 hour and 10 minutes
Servings: 4

Ingredients:
- 1 pound peanuts
- ½ cup sugar
- 2 tablespoons lime juice
- ½ cup sea salt
- A pinch of chili powder
- Water, for the pressure cooker

Directions:
1. In your pressure cooker, mix peanuts with sugar, lime juice, sea salt and chili powder and toss.
2. Add water to cover peanuts and cook them on High for 1 hour and 10 minutes.
3. Drain peanuts, divide them into bowls and serve as a snack.

Nutrition: calories 100, fat 4, fiber 4, carbs 5, protein 2

Chinese Style Peanuts

Preparation time: 10 minutes
Cooking time: 1 hour and 20 minutes
Servings: 4

Ingredients:
- 1 pound raw peanuts
- 3 garlic cloves
- 3 cinnamon sticks
- 4 red chilies, dried and crushed
- 3-star anise

- Water, for the pressure cooker

Directions:
1. In your pressure cooker mix peanuts with garlic, cinnamon, chilies and star anise.
2. Add water to cover them and cook on High for 1 hour and 20 minutes.
3. Drain peanuts, divide them into bowls and serve as a snack.

Nutrition: calories 89, fat 3, fiber 3, carbs 6, protein 2

Southern Peanuts

Preparation time: 10 minutes
Cooking time: 1 hour and 15 minutes
Servings: 4

Ingredients:
- 1 pound peanuts
- 1 tablespoon Cajun seasoning
- 2 garlic cloves
- 1 jalapeno pepper, chopped
- ¼ cup sea salt
- Water, for the pressure cooker

Directions:
1. In your pressure cooker mix peanuts with sea salt, Cajun seasoning, garlic and jalapeno.
2. Add water to cover, cook on High for 1 hour and 15 minutes, drain, transfer to bowls and serve as a snack.

Nutrition: calories 100, fat 4, fiber 3, carbs 7, protein 2

Red Pepper Hummus

Preparation time: 10 minutes
Cooking time: 1 hour and 30 minutes
Servings: 4

Ingredients:
- 7 cups water, for the pressure cooker
- 1 pound chickpeas
- 3 red peppers, roasted
- 2 tablespoons sesame oil
- ½ cup lemon juice
- 1 tablespoon tahini paste

Directions:
1. In your pressure cooker, mix chickpeas with water, cover and cook on High for 1 hour and 30 minutes.
2. Drain chickpeas, transfer to a food processor, add roasted peppers, sesame oil, lemon juice and tahini paste, pulse well, divide into bowls and serve as an appetizer.

Nutrition: calories 162, fat 4, fiber 4, carbs 7, protein 8

Asian Wings

Preparation time: 10 minutes
Cooking time: 7 minutes
Servings: 4

Ingredients:
- 4 pounds chicken wings
- 2 tablespoon black soy sauce
- ¼ cup honey
- ¼ cup brown sugar
- ¼ cup water

Directions:
1. In your pressure cooker, mix chicken wings with black soy sauce, honey, sugar and water, stir, cover and cook on High for 5 minutes.
2. Transfer chicken wings to a baking sheet, broil for a few minutes, divide into bowls and serve as a snack and appetizer.

Nutrition: calories 221, fat 3, fiber 7, carbs 10, protein 6

Beet Appetizer Salad

Preparation time: 30 minutes
Cooking time: 30 minutes
Servings: 2

Ingredients:
- 2 cups water
- 2 small beets
- 1 small red onion, sliced
- 1 ounce goat cheese
- 2 tablespoons apple cider vinegar
- Salt and black pepper to the taste
- ½ tablespoons sugar
- 1 cup mixed cherry tomatoes, halved
- 2 tablespoons pecans
- ½ tablespoon olive oil

Directions:
1. Add 1 cup water to your pressure cooker, add the steamer basket, add beets inside, cover and cook on High for 20 minutes.
2. Transfer beets to a cutting board, cool them down, peel, roughly chop them, put them into a bowl, add tomatoes and leave aside for now.
3. Clean your pressure cooker, add the rest of the water, vinegar and sugar, stir, set the cooker on sauté mode and simmer for 2 minutes.
4. Strain this into a bowl, add onion and leave aside for 20 minutes.
5. Drain onions, add them to your salad and toss.

6. In a bowl, mix 1 tablespoon liquid from the onions with oil and whisk.
7. Add this to salad, also add, salt, pepper, goat cheese and pecans, toss, divide between 2 appetizer plates and serve.

Nutrition: calories 183, fat 2, fiber 3, carbs 8, protein 5

Onion Dip

Preparation time: 10 minutes
Cooking time: 30 minutes
Servings: 2

Ingredients:
- 2 tablespoons butter
- 1 pound yellow onion, chopped
- Salt and black pepper to the taste
- A pinch of baking soda

Directions:
1. Set your pressure cooker on Sauté mode, add butter, melt it, add onion and soda, stir, sauté for 3 minutes, cover the cooker and cook on High for 20 minutes.
2. Set the cooker on sauté mode again, add salt and pepper, stir and cook the dip for a few minutes more until it thickens.
3. Transfer to bowls and serve as a snack.

Nutrition: calories 142, fat 1, fiber 1, carbs 4, protein 3

Mexican Corn on the Cob

Preparation time: 10 minutes
Cooking time: 15 minutes
Servings: 4

Ingredients:
- 1 cup water, for the pressure cooker
- 4 ears of corn, husks removed
- ¼ cup mayonnaise
- 1 tablespoon butter
- A pinch of cayenne pepper
- ¾ cup feta cheese, crumbled

Directions:
1. Brush corn with mayo and butter and season with cayenne pepper.
2. Add the water to your pressure cooker, add steamer basket, add corn inside, cover and cook on High for 15 minutes.
3. Arrange corn on a platter, sprinkle cheese all over and serve as a snack.

Nutrition: calories 172, fat 4, fiber 6, carbs 5, protein 3

BBQ Square Ribs

Preparation time: 10 minutes
Cooking time: 20 minutes
Servings: 3

Ingredients:
- 1 rack pork spare ribs
- 1 onion, chopped
- 1 cup apple juice
- 1 cup bbq sauce
- 1 teaspoon liquid smoke

Directions:
1. In your pressure cooker, mix spare ribs with onion, apple juice, bbq sauce and liquid smoke, toss, cover and cook on High for 20 minutes.
2. Arrange ribs on a platter, drizzle bbq sauce all over and serve as an appetizer or snack.

Nutrition: calories 300, fat 8, fiber 5, carbs 12, protein 4

Grated Carrot Appetizer Salad

Preparation time: 10 minutes
Cooking time: 3 minutes
Servings: 4

Ingredients:
- 1 pound carrots
- ¼ cup water, for the pressure cooker
- 1 tablespoon lemon juice
- 1 teaspoon red pepper flakes
- 1 tablespoon parsley, chopped
- Salt to the taste

Directions:
1. In your pressure cooker, mix carrots with water and salt, cover and cook on High for 3 minutes.
2. Drain carrots, cool them down, grated and transfer them to a bowl.
3. Add lemon juice, pepper flakes and parsley, toss, divide into smaller bowls and serve as an appetizer

Nutrition: calories 152, fat 3, fiber 3, carbs 4, protein 3

Green Beans Appetizer Salad

Preparation time: 10 minutes
Cooking time: 2 minutes
Servings: 4

Ingredients:
- 1 pound green beans, trimmed
- ½ cup water, for the pressure cooker

- 2 red onions, sliced
- 1 tablespoon Creole mustard
- 1 tablespoon red wine vinegar
- A drizzle of olive oil

Directions:
1. In your pressure cooker, mix green beans with water, cover and cook on High for 2 minutes.
2. Drain green beans, transfer to a bowl, add onion slices, mustard, vinegar and oil, toss, divide on appetizer plates and serve as an appetizer.

Nutrition: calories 121, fat 4, fiber 4, carbs 6, protein 4

Mushrooms and Rosemary

Preparation time: 10 minutes
Cooking time: 10 minutes
Servings: 6

Ingredients:
- 3 pounds mixed mushroom caps
- ¾ cup olive oil
- 4 garlic cloves, minced
- 3 rosemary sprigs, chopped
- ½ cup white wine

Directions:
1. Set your pressure cooker on sauté mode, add oil, heat up, add garlic and rosemary, stir and cook for 2-3 minutes.
2. Add mushroom caps and wine, stir, cover and cook on High for 7-8 minutes.
3. Stir mushroom mix again, divide between plates and serve as a side dish.

Nutrition: calories 172, fat 3, fiber 4, carbs 17, protein 3

Chestnut Mushrooms

Preparation time: 10 minutes
Cooking time: 10 minutes
Servings: 4

Ingredients:
- 1 cup jarred chestnuts, halved
- 6 bacon slices, chopped
- 2 pounds mushrooms, halved
- 1 teaspoon Worcestershire sauce
- ½ cup veggie stock

Directions:
1. Set your pressure cooker on sauté mode, add bacon, stir and cook for a couple of minutes.
2. Add chestnuts, stir and cook for 1 minute more.
3. Add mushrooms, Worcestershire sauce and stock, stir, cover and cook on High for 8 minutes.
4. Divide everything between plates and serve as a side dish.

Nutrition: calories 180, fat 2, fiber 4, carbs 10, protein 2

Watercress Appetizer Salad

Preparation time: 10 minutes
Cooking time: 2 minutes
Servings: 4

Ingredients:
- 1 big bunch watercress, roughly torn
- 2 peaches, stones removed and cut into medium wedges
- 1 watermelon, cubed
- A drizzle of olive oil
- 1 tablespoon lemon juice
- ½ cup water, for the pressure cooker

Directions:
1. In your pressure cooker, mix watercress with water, cover and cook on High for 2 minutes.
2. Drain, transfer to a bowl, add peaches, watermelon, oil and lemon juice, toss, divide on appetizer plates and serve as an appetizer.

Nutrition: calories 111, fat 3, fiber 4, carbs 5, protein 3

Ham and Cheese Dip

Preparation time: 10 minutes
Cooking time: 12 minutes
Servings: four

Ingredients:
- 8 ounces cream cheese
- 1 cup Swiss cheese
- 1 cup cheddar cheese, grated
- 2 tablespoons parsley, chopped
- 8 ham slices, chopped

Directions:
1. Set your pressure cooker on sauté mode, add ham, stir and brown for 3-4 minutes.
2. Add Swiss, cheddar and cream cheese, stir, cover and cook on High for 6 minutes.
3. Add parsley, divide into bowls and serve as an appetizer.

Nutrition: calories 243, fat 4, fiber 7, carbs 7, protein 4

Scallion Spread

Preparation time: 10 minutes
Cooking time: 3 minutes
Servings: 6

Ingredients:
- ½ cup scallions, chopped
- 1 cup sour cream
- ¼ cup mayonnaise
- 3 tablespoons dill, chopped
- 1 tablespoon lemon zest, grated

Directions:
1. Set your pressure cooker on sauté mode, add scallions, stir and brown for 1 minute.
2. Add sour cream, stir, cover and cook on High for 2 minutes.

3. Leave this mix to cool down, add mayo, dill and lemon zest, stir well, divide into bowls and serve with tortilla chips on the side.

Nutrition: calories 222, fat 4, fiber 5, carbs 8, protein 4

Crab Spread

Preparation time: 10 minutes
Cooking time: 15 minutes
Servings: 4

Ingredients:
- 8 ounces crab meat
- ½ cup sour cream
- ¼ cup half and half
- ½ bunch scallions, chopped
- 1 teaspoon Worcestershire sauce

Directions:
1. In your pressure cooker, mix crab meat with sour cream, half-and-half, scallions and Worcestershire sauce, stir, cover and cook on High for 15 minutes.
2. Leave spread to cool down, divide into bowls and serve as an appetizer.

Nutrition: calories 241, fat 4, fiber 6, carbs 8, protein 3

Chili Dip

Preparation time: 10 minutes
Cooking time: 17 minutes
Servings: 2

Ingredients:
- 2 ounces red chilies, chopped
- 1 and ½ tablespoons sugar
- 1.5 ounces bird's eye chilies, chopped
- 5 garlic cloves, minced
- 2 ounces white vinegar
- 2 ounces water

Directions:
1. In your pressure cooker, mix water with sugar, red chilies, bird's eye chilies and garlic, stir, cover and cook on High for 7 minutes.
2. Add vinegar, blend everything using an immersion blender, set the cooker on sauté mode and simmer for 10 minutes.
3. Divide into bowls and serve as a snack with tortilla chips.

Nutrition: calories 100, fat 1, fiber 0, carbs 2, protein 4

Corn Dip

Preparation time: 10 minutes
Cooking time: 6 minutes
Servings: 2

Ingredients:
- ½ yellow onion, chopped
- ½ tablespoon olive oil
- ½ teaspoon white flour
- 1 cup chicken stock
- 2 tablespoons white wine
- 1 teaspoon thyme, dried
- 2 cups corn kernels
- Salt and black pepper to the taste
- 1 teaspoons butter

Directions:
1. Set your pressure cooker on Sauté mode, add oil, heat it up, add onion, stir and cook for 3 minutes.
2. Add flour and wine, stir and cook for 2 minutes more.
3. Add thyme, stock and corn, stir, cover and cook at High for 2 minutes.
4. Transfer everything to your blender, add salt, pepper and butter and pulse really well.
5. Return corn mix to your pressure cooker, set it on sauté mode again and simmer for a couple of minutes until it thickens.
6. Serve as a snack.

Nutrition: calories 121, fat 3, fiber 2, carbs 5, protein 5

Creamy Endives Appetizer Salad

Preparation time: 10 minutes
Cooking time: 18 minutes
Servings: 3

Ingredients:
- 3 big endives, roughly chopped
- ½ yellow onion, chopped
- 2 tablespoons extra virgin olive oil
- 1 cup veggie stock
- 3 tablespoons heavy cream

Directions:
1. Set your pressure cooker on Sauté mode, add oil, heat it up, add onion, stir and cook for 4 minutes.
2. Add endives, stir and cook for 4 minutes more.
3. Add stock, stir, cover and cook on High for 10 minutes.
4. Add heavy cream, stir, cook for 1 minute, divide into appetizer bowls and serve.

Nutrition: calories 253, fat 4, fiber 7, carbs 12, protein 15

Zucchini Spread

Preparation time: 10 minutes
Cooking time: 9 minutes
Servings: 6

Ingredients:
- 1 and ½ pounds zucchinis, chopped
- 1 tablespoon olive oil
- 2 garlic cloves, minced
- ½ cup water
- 1 bunch basil, chopped

Directions:
1. Set your pressure cooker on Sauté mode, add oil, heat it up, add garlic, stir and cook for 3 minutes.
2. Add zucchini and water, stir, cover and cook on High for 3 minutes.
3. Add basil, blend everything using an immersion blender, set the cooker on simmer mode and cook everything for a couple of minutes more.
4. Transfer to a bowl and serve as an appetizer.

Nutrition: calories 120, fat 2, fiber 4, carbs 7, protein 2

Cabbage Rolls

Preparation time: 15 minutes
Cooking time: 35 minutes
Servings: 2

Ingredients:
- ½ tablespoon olive oil
- ½ cup brown rice
- 4 cups water
- 1 and ½ cups mushrooms, chopped
- ½ yellow onion, chopped
- 1 garlic clove, minced
- Salt and black pepper to the taste
- 6 green cabbage leaves
- ½ teaspoon walnuts, chopped
- ½ teaspoon caraway seeds
- A pinch of cayenne pepper

Directions:
1. Put 2 cups water and rice in your pressure cooker, cover, cook on High for 15 minutes, drain rice and transfer to a bowl.
2. Heat up a pan with the oil over medium high heat, add onion, mushrooms, garlic, walnuts, caraway seeds, salt, pepper and cayenne, stir, cook for 5 minutes, add to rice and stir well.
3. Meanwhile, put the rest of the water into a pot, bring to a boil over medium high heat, add cabbage leaves, blanch them for 1 minute, drain them well, arrange on a working surface, divide rice mix in the middle, roll and seal edges.

4. Transfer cabbage rolls to your pressure cooker, add water to cover them, cover and cook on High for 10 minutes more.
5. Arrange cabbage rolls on a platter and serve as an appetizer.

Nutrition: calories 193, fat 2, fiber 6, carbs 8, protein 5

Tofu Appetizer

Preparation time: 10 minutes
Cooking time: 8 minutes
Servings: 2

Ingredients:
- ½ yellow onion, sliced
- 3 mushrooms, sliced
- 1 and ½ teaspoons tamari
- 4 ounces tofu, cubed
- 3 tablespoons red bell pepper, chopped
- 3 tablespoons green beans
- 2 tablespoons veggie stock
- Salt and white pepper to the taste

Directions:
1. Set your pressure cooker on sauté mode, add onion and mushroom, stir and brown for 2 minutes.
2. Add tofu and tamari, stir and cook for 2 minutes more.
3. Add stock, stir a bit, cover and cook on High for 3 minutes.
4. Add bell pepper and green beans, salt and pepper, cover and cook on High for 1 minute.
5. Divide into 2 small bowls and serve as an appetizer.

Nutrition: calories 143, fat 3, fiber 2, carbs 9, protein 6

Lemony Endives Appetizer

Preparation time: 10 minutes
Cooking time: 13 minutes
Servings: 4

Ingredients:
- 8 endives, trimmed
- 3 tablespoons olive oil
- Juice of ½ lemon
- ½ cup chicken stock
- 2 tablespoons parsley, chopped

Directions:
1. Set your pressure cooker on sauté mode, add oil, heat it up, add endives and cook them for 3 minutes.
2. Add lemon juice and stock, stir, cover and cook on High for 10 minutes.
3. Arrange endives on a platter, drizzle some of the cooking juices all over, sprinkle parsley and serve as an appetizer.

Nutrition: calories 120, fat 2, fiber 7, carbs 12, protein 4

Endives Platter

Preparation time: 10 minutes
Cooking time: 7 minutes
Servings: 4

Ingredients:
- 4 endives, trimmed and halved
- Salt to the taste
- A pinch of chili powder
- 1 tablespoon lemon juice
- 1 tablespoon butter

Directions:
1. Set your pressure cooker on Sauté mode, add butter, melt it, add endives, salt, chili powder and lemon juice, cover and cook on High for 7 minutes.
2. Arrange endives on a platter, drizzle cooking juice over them and serve as an appetizer.

Nutrition: calories 90, fat 4, fiber 7, carbs 12, protein 3

Maple Acorn Squash Dish

Preparation time: 10 minutes
Cooking time: 10 minutes
Servings: 4

Ingredients:
- 2 acorn squash, halved and cut into medium wedges
- 3 tablespoons butter
- ¼ cup maple syrup
- 2 teaspoons sriracha sauce
- 4 thyme sprigs, chopped

Directions:
1. Set your pressure cooker on sauté mode add butter, melt it, add acorn squash wedges, stir and cook for 1-2 minutes.
2. Add maple syrup, sriracha sauce and thyme, stir, cover and cook on Manual for 8 minutes.
3. Toss squash wedges gently, divide between plates and serve as a side dish.

Nutrition: calories 200, fat 2, fiber 4, carbs 5, protein 4

Red Onions and Apples Mix

Preparation time: 10 minutes
Cooking time: 6 minutes
Servings: 4

Ingredients:
- 2 red onions, cut into wedges
- ½ cup chicken stock
- 3 apples, cored and cut into medium wedges
- 3 tablespoons vegetable oil
- 3 tablespoons maple syrup

Directions:
1. Set your pressure cooker on sauté mode, add oil, heat it up, add onion and apple wedges, stir and cook for 2-3 minutes.
2. Add maple syrup and stock, stir a bit, cover and cook on High for 4 minutes.
3. Toss well, divide between plates and serve as a side dish.

Nutrition: calories 110, fat 3, fiber 6, carbs 4, protein 2

Cashew Spread

Preparation time: 10 minutes
Cooking time: 6 minutes
Servings: 8

Ingredients:
- ½ cup water
- ½ cup cashews, soaked overnight and drained
- 10 ounces chickpeas hummus

- ¼ cup nutritional yeast
- ¼ teaspoon garlic powder

Directions:
1. In your pressure cooker, mix cashews and water, stir, cover and cook on High for 6 minutes.
2. Transfer to your blender, add hummus, yeast and garlic powder, pulse really well, divide into bowls and serve as an appetizer spread.

Nutrition: calories 180, fat 2, fiber 2, carbs 4, protein 5

Mushroom Appetizer Salad

Preparation time: 10 minutes
Cooking time: 13 minutes
Servings: 4

Ingredients:
- 7 garlic cloves, minced
- 1 teaspoon olive oil
- 1 cup veggie stock
- 8 ounces mushrooms, halved
- 2 chipotle chilies in adobo sauce

Directions:
1. Set your pressure cooker on sauté mode, add oil, heat it up, garlic, stir and cook for 5 minutes.
2. Add chipotle chili peppers, stock and mushroom halves, toss, cover and cook on High for 8 minutes.
3. Divide mushroom salad into small bowls and serve as an appetizer.

Nutrition: calories 201, fat 5, fiber 8, carbs 13, protein 5

Lentils Patties

Preparation time: 15 minutes
Cooking time: 40 minutes
Servings: 2

Ingredients:
- ½ teaspoon ginger, grated
- 2 tablespoons mushrooms, chopped
- 1 small yellow onion, chopped
- ½ cup red lentils
- 1 cup veggie stock
- 1 small sweet potato, chopped
- Cooking spray
- ½ tablespoon parsley, finely chopped
- ½ tablespoon hemp seeds
- ½ tablespoon cilantro, finely chopped
- 2 teaspoons curry powder
- 2 tablespoons quick oats
- 1 tablespoon rice flour
- Salt and pepper to the taste

Directions:
1. Set your pressure cooker on Sauté more, add onion, mushroom and ginger, stir and cook for 3 minutes.
2. Add stock, sweet potatoes and lentils, stir, cover, cook on High for 6 minutes, transfer everything to a bowl and leave aside to cool down.
3. Add parsley, curry powder, salt, pepper, hemp seeds and cilantro, stir well and mash everything using a potato masher.
4. Add oats and rice flour and stir.
5. Shape 4 patties out of this mix, arrange them on a baking sheet after you've sprayed it with cooking spray, introduce in the oven, bake at 375 degrees F for 10 minutes, flip and cook for 10 minutes more.
6. Arrange patties on a platter and serve as an appetizer.

Nutrition: calories 140, fat 4, fiber 4, carbs 7, protein 11

Black Beans Patties

Preparation time: 15 minutes
Cooking time: 35 minutes
Servings: 2

Ingredients:
- ½ cup black beans, soaked for a few hours and drained
- ½ tablespoon flaxseed mixed with ½ tablespoon water
- ½ red onion, chopped
- 1 and ½ tablespoons olive oil
- 3 tablespoons quick oats
- A pinch of cumin, ground
- 1 teaspoon chipotle powder

- Salt to the taste
- 1 garlic clove, minced
- 1 teaspoon lemon zest, grated

Directions:
1. Put beans in your pressure cooker, add water to cover, cook on High for 20 minutes, drain beans, transfer them to a bowl, mash using a potato masher and leave aside for now.
2. Heat up a pan with half of the oil, over medium high heat, add onion and garlic, stir and cook for 5 minutes.
3. Cool this mix down, add to the bowl with the beans, also add flaxseed, oats, cumin, chipotle powder, salt to the taste and lemon zest, stir well and shape small patties out of this mix.
4. Heat up a pan with the rest of the oil over medium high heat, add patties, cook for 3 minutes on each side, transfer them to paper towels, drain grease, arrange on a platter and serve as an appetizer.

Nutrition: calories 271, fat 3, fiber 4, carbs 8, protein 10

Veggie Dumplings

Preparation time: 10 minutes
Cooking time: 15 minutes
Servings: 6

Ingredients:
- 12 dumpling wrappers
- 1 tablespoon olive oil
- 1 cup shiitake mushrooms, sliced
- ½ cup carrot, chopped
- 2 tablespoons soy sauce
- 1 and ½ cups water, for the pressure cooker

Directions:
1. Set your pressure cooker on sauté mode, add olive oil, heat it up, add mushrooms, stir and cook them for 2 minutes.
2. Add carrots and soy sauce, stir and cook for 2 minutes more.
3. Place wrappers on a working surface, divide mushroom mix on each and seal dumplings using your wet hands.
4. Add the water to your pressure cooker, add steamer basket, add dumplings inside, cover and cook on Low for 7 minutes.
5. Arrange dumplings on a platter and serve them as an appetizer.

Nutrition: calories 300, fat 4, fiber 7, carbs 18, protein 6

Tomatoes and Garlic Dip

Preparation time: 10 minutes
Cooking time: 15 minutes
Servings: 6

Ingredients:
- ½ cup water
- 32 ounces canned tomatoes, roughly chopped
- A pinch of salt
- 4 garlic cloves, minced

- ¼ teaspoon red pepper flakes, crushed

Directions:
1. In your pressure cooker, mix water with tomatoes, salt, pepper flakes and garlic, stir, cover and cook on High for 15 minutes.
2. Divide dip into small bowls and serve as a party dip

Nutrition: calories 110, fat 1, fiber 1, carbs 4, protein 2

Chickpeas Appetizer

Preparation time: 10 minutes
Cooking time: 20 minutes
Servings: 2

Ingredients:
- ½ cup chickpeas, soaked for a couple of hours and drained
- ½ teaspoon thyme, dried
- ½ teaspoon cumin, ground
- 1 bay leaf
- A pinch of salt and black pepper
- ½ teaspoon garlic powder
- 1 and ½ tablespoons tomato paste
- 3 tablespoons whole wheat flour

Directions:
5. Put chickpeas in your pressure cooker, add water to cover, cumin powder, bay leaf, garlic powder, thyme, onion, salt and pepper, stir, cover, cook on High for 15 minutes, discard bay leaf, drain chickpeas, transfer them to your blender and pulse really well.
6. Add tomato paste and flour, blend again and shape small patties out of this mix.
7. Place them on preheated grill over medium high heat, cook them for a couple of minutes on each side, arrange on a platter and serve them as an appetizer.

Nutrition: calories 122, fat 1, fiber 4, carbs 8, protein 4

Mushroom Cakes

Preparation time: 10 minutes
Cooking time: 15 minutes
Servings: 2

Ingredients:
- ½ tablespoon canola oil
- 1 small garlic clove, minced
- 2 green onions, chopped
- ½ yellow onion, chopped
- A pinch of cumin, ground
- 7 ounces canned pinto beans, drained
- ½ cup mushrooms, chopped
- ½ teaspoon parsley, chopped
- Salt and black pepper to the taste
- 2 tablespoons olive oil

Directions:
1. Set your pressure cooker on Sauté mode, add canola oil, heat it up, add garlic, yellow onion, green onions, mushrooms, salt, pepper and cumin, stir, sauté for 5 minutes, cover pot, cook on Low for 5 minutes, transfer to a bowl and cool down.
2. Put the beans in your food processor, pulse them, add them and parsley to mushrooms mix, stir well and shape small cakes out of this mixture.
3. Heat up a pan with the olive oil over medium high heat, add cakes, cook for 3 minutes on each side, arrange them on a platter and serve as an appetizer.

Nutrition: calories 170, fat 2, fiber 3, carbs 8, protein 10

Appetizer Egg Spread

Preparation time: 10 minutes
Cooking time: 5 minutes
Servings: 4

Ingredients:
- 12 eggs
- ½ cup mayonnaise
- Salt to the taste
- A drizzle of olive oil
- 2 green onions, chopped
- 1 cup water, for the pressure cooker

Directions:
1. Grease a baking dish with a drizzle of oil and crack eggs in it.
2. Add the water to your pressure cooker, add trivet inside, add baking dish, cover and cook on High for 5 minutes.
3. Cool eggs down, mash using a potato masher, mix with mayo, green onions and salt and whisk well.
4. Divide into small bowls and serve as an appetizer.

Nutrition: calories 222, fat 3, fiber 7, carbs 10, protein 4

Potatoes and Shrimp Appetizer Salad

Preparation time: 10 minutes
Cooking time: 13 minutes
Servings: 4

Ingredients:
- 2 cups water, for the pressure cooker
- 2 pounds shrimp, peeled and deveined
- 8 potatoes, cut into quarters
- 4 tablespoons olive oil
- Juice of 1 lemon
- 1 tablespoon watercress

Directions:
1. Add the water to the pot, add steamer basket, add potatoes inside, cover, cook on High for 10 minutes, transfer them to a bowl and clean the pot.

2. Set the cooker in Sauté mode, add oil, heat it up, add shrimp, lemon juice and return potatoes as well, stir, cover and cook on High for 3 minutes
3. Divide watercress into appetizer bowls, top with shrimp and potato mix, drizzle some of the lemony cooking juice all over and serve as an appetizer.

Nutrition: calories 167, fat 4, fiber 4, carbs 7, protein 20

Stuffed Bell Peppers Appetizer

Preparation time: 10 minutes
Cooking time: 12 minutes
Servings: 4

Ingredients:
- 4 mixed colored bell peppers, blanched, tops and seeds removed
- 16 ounces beef, ground
- 2 eggs
- 2 yellow onions, chopped
- 20 ounces canned tomato soup

Directions:
1. In a bowl, mix beef with eggs and onions and stir very well.
2. Stuff bell peppers with this mix and place them in your pressure cooker.
3. Add tomato soup, cover pot, cook on High for 12 minutes, arrange them on a platter and serve as a delicious appetizer.

Nutrition: calories 185, fat 10, fiber 4, carbs 14, protein 8

Brussels Sprouts and Potatoes Appetizer Salad

Preparation time: 10 minutes
Cooking time: 5 minutes
Servings: 4

Ingredients:
- 1 and ½ pounds Brussels sprouts, washed and trimmed
- 1 cup new potatoes, chopped
- 1 and ½ tablespoons breadcrumbs
- ½ cup chicken stock
- 1 and ½ tablespoons butter

Directions:
1. Put sprouts and potatoes in your pressure cooker, add stock, cover and cook on High for 5 minutes.
2. Set the cooker in Sauté mode, add butter and breadcrumbs, toss to coat well, divide between plates and serve as an appetizer.

Nutrition: calories 121, fat 3, fiber 6, carbs 16, protein 2

Chinese Mustard Greens

Preparation time: 10 minutes
Cooking time: 7 minutes
Servings: 4

Ingredients:
- 2 Chinese sausages, chopped
- 2 teaspoons ginger, grated
- 2 tablespoons vegetable oil
- 2 pounds mustard greens, chopped
- ½ cup veggie stock

Directions:
1. Set your pressure cooker on sauté mode, add oil, heat it up, add ginger, stir and cook for 30 seconds.
2. Add Chinese sausages, stir and cook for 1 minute more.
3. Add mustard greens and stock, stir, cover and cook on High for 4 minutes.
4. Divide everything between plates and serve as a side dish.

Nutrition: calories 178, fat 5, fiber 3, carbs 8, protein 9

Acorn Squash Side Dish

Preparation time: 10 minutes
Cooking time: 15 minutes
Servings: 4

Ingredients:
- 2 acorn squash, halved and cut into medium wedges
- 1 cup water, for the pressure cooker
- 4 tablespoons butter
- 1 tablespoon brown sugar
- 1 teaspoon smoked paprika
- 3 tablespoons pepitas, roasted

Directions:
1. Put the water in your pressure cooker, add steamer basket, add acorn wedges inside, cover, cook on High for 5 minutes and transfer to a bowl.
2. Clean the pot, set it on sauté mode, add butter, melt it, add acorn wedges, sugar, paprika and pepitas, stir and cook for 10 minutes.
3. Divide between plates and serve as a side dish.

Nutrition: calories 128, fat 4, fiber 3, carbs 6, protein 8

Brussels Sprouts and Broccoli Appetizer Salad

Preparation time: 10 minutes
Cooking time: 5 minutes
Servings: 6

Ingredients:
- 1 pound Brussels sprouts, halved
- 1 broccoli head, florets separated
- ½ cup walnut oil
- ¼ cup balsamic vinegar
- 2 teaspoons mustard
- 1 and ½ cups water, for the pressure cooker

Directions:
1. Put the water in your pressure cooker, add steamer basket, add broccoli and Brussels sprouts, cover, cook on High for 4 minutes, drain and transfer to a bowl.
2. Clean the pot, set on sauté mode, add oil, heat it up, add broccoli and Brussels sprouts, stir and cook for 1 minute.
3. Add vinegar, toss, cook for a couple of seconds more and transfer to a bowl.
4. Add mustard, toss well, divide on appetizer plates and serve.

Nutrition: calories 200, fat 6, fiber 7, carbs 8, protein 5

Crunchy Brussels Sprouts Salad

Preparation time: 10 minutes
Cooking time: 6 minutes
Servings: 4

Ingredients:
- 1 tablespoon brown sugar
- 1 pound Brussels sprouts, halved
- ½ cup pecans, chopped
- 1 tablespoon olive oil
- 2 tablespoons apple cider vinegar
- 1 and ½ cups water, for the pressure cooker

Directions:
1. Put the water in your pressure cooker, add steamer basket, add Brussels sprouts, cover, cook on High for 4 minutes, drain and transfer to a bowl.
2. Clean the pot, set on sauté mode, add oil, heat it up, add Brussels sprouts and vinegar, toss and cook for 1 minute.
3. Add sugar and pecans, stir, cook for 30 seconds more, divide into appetizer plates and serve.

Nutrition: calories 186, fat 4, fiber 5, carbs 9, protein 3

Brussels Sprouts and Apples Appetizer

Preparation time: 10 minutes
Cooking time: 6 minutes
Servings: 4

Ingredients:
- 1 green apple, cored and roughly chopped
- 1 pound Brussels sprouts, halved

- 1 cup cranberries, dried
- 2 tablespoons lemon juice
- 2 tablespoons canola oil
- 1 and ½ cups water, for the pressure cooker

Directions:
1. Put the water in your pressure cooker, add steamer basket, add Brussels sprouts, cover, cook on High for 4 minutes, drain and transfer to a bowl.
2. Clean the pot, set it on sauté mode, add oil, heat it up, add Brussels sprouts, stir and cook for 1 minute.
3. Add apple, cranberries and lemon juice, toss, cook for 1 minutes, divide into appetizer plates and serve.

Nutrition: calories 163, fat 3, fiber 4, carbs 6, protein 3

Sweet Brussels Sprouts Appetizer

Preparation time: 10 minutes
Cooking time: 6 minutes
Servings: 4

Ingredients:
- 2 pounds Brussels sprouts, halved
- ¼ cup orange juice
- 1 teaspoon orange zest, grated
- 1 tablespoon butter
- 2 tablespoons maple syrup

Directions:
1. Set your pressure cooker on sauté mode, add butter, melt it, add orange juice, orange zest and maple syrup, stir and cook for 1-2 minutes.
2. Add Brussels sprouts, toss, cover and cook on High for 4 minutes.
3. Divide into appetizer plates and serve.

Nutrition: calories 90, fat 2, fiber 3, carbs 12, protein 3

Beets Cakes

Preparation time: 15 minutes
Cooking time: 20 minutes
Servings: 2

Ingredients:
- 1 beet
- 1 potato
- A pinch of turmeric powder
- ½ teaspoon fennel powder
- A pinch of red chili powder
- Salt and black pepper to the taste
- A pinch of coriander powder
- A pinch of garam masala powder

- A pinch of chaat masala
- 1 small green chili, chopped
- 1 teaspoon lemon juice
- 1 teaspoon ginger, grated
- 1 tablespoon semolina
- ½ slice of whole wheat bread, soaked and squeezed
- Vegetable oil

Directions:
1. Put beetroot and potato in your pressure cooker, add water to cover, cook on High for 10 minutes, drain, cool them down, peel, grated them and put in a bowl
2. Add turmeric, fennel powder, red chili powder, coriander powder, garam masala, chaat masala, green chili, lemon juice, ginger, salt, pepper and bread, stir well, shape small cakes out of this mix and coat them in semolina.
3. Heat up a pan with vegetable oil over medium high heat, add cakes, cook for a few minutes on each side, transfer to a platter and serve as an appetizer.

Nutrition: calories 180, fat 3, fiber 4, carbs 7, protein 9

Mango Salsa

Preparation time: 10 minutes
Cooking time: 22 minutes
Servings: 2

Ingredients:
- ½ shallot, chopped
- 2 teaspoons olive oil
- A pinch of cinnamon powder
- 2 teaspoons ginger, grated
- A pinch of cardamom
- 1 small red hot chili pepper, minced
- 1 small apple, peeled, cored and chopped
- 1 mango, peeled and chopped
- A pinch of salt
- 1 tablespoon raisins
- 2 tablespoons white vinegar
- 2 tablespoons white wine

Directions:
1. Set your pressure cooker on Sauté mode, add the oil, heat it up, add shallot, ginger, cinnamon, chili peppers and cardamom, stir and cook for 3 minutes.
2. Add mango, apple, salt, raisins, sugar and vinegar, stir, cover pot, cook on High for 15 minutes, transfer to a bowl and serve with crackers on the side.

Nutrition: calories 80, fat 1, fiber 2, carbs 7, protein 1

Broccoli Appetizer Salad

Preparation time: 10 minutes
Cooking time: 10 minutes

Servings: 4

Ingredients:
- 1 broccoli head, florets separated
- ½ cup almonds, chopped
- 2 tablespoons olive oil
- ¼ cup apple juice
- 2 tablespoons tamari sauce
- 1 and ½ cups water, for the pressure cooker

Directions:
1. Put the water in your pressure cooker, add steamer basket, add broccoli florets, cover, cook on High for 4 minutes, drain and transfer to a bowl.
2. Clean the pot, set it on sauté mode, add oil, heat it up, add kale, stir and cook for 2 minutes.
3. Return broccoli, also add, apple juice and tamari, stir, cover and cook on High for 2 minutes more.
4. Add almonds, toss, divide into bowls and serve as an appetizer.

Nutrition: calories 192, fat 2, fiber 4, carbs 7, protein 4

Creamy Broccoli Appetizer

Preparation time: 10 minutes
Cooking time: 3 minutes
Servings: 4

Ingredients:
- 1 broccoli head, florets separated
- 1 apple, cored and cut into medium wedges
- ½ cup Greek yogurt
- 2 tablespoons mayonnaise
- 1 tablespoon honey
- 1 cup water, for the pressure cooker

Directions:
1. Put the water in your pressure cooker, add steamer basket, add broccoli inside, cover and cook on High for 3 minutes.
2. Drain broccoli florets, transfer to a bowl, add apple, mayo, yogurt and honey, toss well, divide on appetizer plates and serve.

Nutrition: calories 200, fat 3, fiber 4, carbs 7, protein 3

Broccoli and Bacon Appetizer Salad

Preparation time: 10 minutes
Cooking time: 4 minutes
Servings: 4

Ingredients:
- 1 broccoli head, florets separated
- ¼ cup cilantro, chopped
- 4 bacon slices, chopped

- 2 tablespoons olive oil
- ½ tablespoon apple cider vinegar
- 1 and ½ cups water, for the pressure cooker

Directions:
1. Put the water in your pressure cooker, add steamer basket, add broccoli, cover, cook on High for 3 minutes, drain and transfer to a bowl.
2. Clean the pot, set on sauté mode, add bacon, stir and cook until it's crispy.
3. Roughly chop broccoli, add to pressure cooker, stir and cook for 1 minute more.
4. Add oil, cilantro and vinegar, toss well, divide into bowls and serve as an appetizer.

Nutrition: calories 200, fat 4, fiber 5, carbs 6, protein 4

Cheesy Broccoli Appetizer Salad

Preparation time: 10 minutes
Cooking time: 4 minutes
Servings: 4

Ingredients:
- 1 broccoli head, florets separated
- 4 ounces cheddar cheese, cubed
- 1/8 cup pumpkin seeds
- 1 cup mayonnaise
- 2 tablespoons balsamic vinegar
- 1 and ½ cups water, for the pressure cooker

Directions:
1. Put the water in your pressure cooker, add steamer basket, add broccoli, cover, cook on High for 3 minutes, drain, chop and transfer to a bowl.
2. Add cheese, pumpkin seeds, mayo and vinegar, toss well, divide on appetizer plates and serve.

Nutrition: calories 182, fat 4, fiber 5, carbs 7, protein 4

Mushroom Dip

Preparation time: 10 minutes
Cooking time: 20 minutes
Servings: 2

Ingredients:
- 5 mushrooms, chopped
- ½ yellow onion, chopped
- 1 garlic clove, minced
- ½ teaspoon thyme, dried
- ½ cup veggie stock
- A pinch of rosemary, dried
- ¼ teaspoon sage, dried
- ½ teaspoon sherry

- ½ tablespoon water
- ½ tablespoon nutritional yeast
- ½ tablespoon soy sauce
- Salt and black pepper to the taste
- 2 tablespoons milk
- 1 tablespoon white flour

Directions:
1. Set your pressure cooker on Sauté mode, add onion, brown for 5 minutes, add mushrooms, garlic and the water, stir and cook for 4 minutes more.
2. Add water, stock, yeast, sherry, soy sauce, salt, pepper, sage, thyme and rosemary, stir, cover and cook on High for 4 minutes.
3. Add milk mixed with flour, stir, cover, cook on High for 6 minutes, transfer to a bowl and serve as a dip

Nutrition: calories 90, fat 4, fiber 3, carbs 6, protein 2

Cauliflower Dip

Preparation time: 10 minutes
Cooking time: 10 minutes
Servings: 2

Ingredients:
- ½ cup cauliflower florets
- ¼ teaspoon onion powder
- ½ cup water
- 1 garlic clove, minced
- ¼ teaspoon mustard powder
- ¼ teaspoon smoked paprika
- A pinch of turmeric
- 1 tablespoon nutritional yeast
- 2 teaspoons chickpea miso
- 2 teaspoons cornstarch
- Salt to the taste
- 2 teaspoons lemon juice

Directions:
1. Put the water, cauliflower, garlic, paprika, powder, turmeric and mustard in your pressure cooker, stir, cover and cook on High for 10 minutes.
2. Transfer everything to your blender, add yeast, chickpea miso, cornstarch, lemon juice and salt to the taste, blend well, transfer to a bowl and serve with veggie sticks on the side.

Nutrition: calories 80, fat 1, fiber 2, carbs 4, protein 2

Tomatoes Appetizer Salad

Preparation time: 10 minutes
Cooking time: 30 minutes
Servings: 6

Ingredients:
- 1 and ½ cups water, for the pressure cooker
- 8 beets, trimmed
- 1 pint mixed cherry tomatoes, halved
- 1 cup apple cider vinegar
- 1 red onion, chopped
- 2 teaspoons sugar

Directions:
1. Put the water in your pressure cooker, add steamer basket, add beets inside, cover and cook on High for 20 minutes.
2. Drain beets, cool them down, peel, grate them and transfer to a bowl.
3. Clean the pot, set on sauté mode, add mixed cherries and sugar, toss them and cook for a couple of minutes.
4. Add onion and vinegar, stir and cook for 2 minutes more.
5. Add beets, stir, sauté everything for another 2 minutes, divide everything on appetizer plates and serve.

Nutrition: calories 118, fat 3, fiber 2, carbs 5, protein 3

Kale and Carrots Salad

Preparation time: 10 minutes
Cooking time: 7 minutes
Servings: 4

Ingredients:
- 10 ounces kale, roughly chopped
- 3 carrots, sliced
- ½ cup chicken stock
- 1 tablespoon olive oil
- 1 red onion, chopped

Directions:
1. Set your pressure cooker on sauté mode, add oil, heat it up, add onion and carrots, stir and cook for 1-2 minutes.
2. Add kale and stock, stir a bit, cover and cook on High for 5 minutes.
3. Divide into small bowls and serve as an appetizer.

Nutrition: calories 128, fat 2, fiber 4, carbs 8, protein 4

Kale and Wild Rice Appetizer Salad

Preparation time: 10 minutes
Cooking time: 4 minutes
Servings: 4

Ingredients:
- 1 cup wild rice, already cooked
- 1 avocado, peeled, pitted and chopped
- 1 kale bunch, roughly chopped
- 1 teaspoon olive oil

- 3 ounces goat cheese, crumbled

Directions:
1. Set your pressure cooker on sauté mode, add oil, heat it up, add rice and toast it for 2-3 minutes stirring often.
2. Add kale, stir, cover and cook on Manual for 2 minutes.
3. Add avocado, toss, divide on appetizer plates, sprinkle cheese on top and serve.

Nutrition: calories 182, fat 3, fiber 2, carbs 4, protein 3

Minty Kale Salad

Preparation time: 10 minutes
Cooking time: 3 minutes
Servings: 4

Ingredients:
- 1 bunch kale, roughly chopped
- 1 teaspoon sesame oil
- 2 tablespoons lemon juice
- 1 cup pineapple, chopped
- 2 tablespoons mint, chopped

Directions:
1. Set your pressure cooker on sauté mode, add oil, heat it up, add kale, stir and cook for 1 minute.
2. Add pineapple, lemon juice and mint, toss, divide on appetizer plates and serve.

Nutrition: calories 121, fat 1, fiber 2, carbs 4, protein 2

Braised Collard Greens

Preparation time: 10 minutes
Cooking time: 20 minutes
Servings: 4

Ingredients:
- 1 bunch collard greens, trimmed
- 2 tablespoons olive oil
- ½ cup chicken stock
- 2 tablespoons tomatoes, chopped
- 1 tablespoon balsamic vinegar

Directions:
1. In your pressure cooker, mix collard greens with stock, oil, tomatoes and vinegar, stir, cover and cook on Manual for 20 minutes.
2. Divide kale mix on plates and serve as a side dish.

Nutrition: calories 122, fat 7, fiber 4, carbs 10, protein 4

Collard Greens and Peas

Preparation time: 10 minutes
Cooking time: 40 minutes
Servings: 5

Ingredients:
- 1 pound collard greens, trimmed and roughly chopped
- 1 pound black-eyed peas, dried
- 1-quart chicken stock
- 1 onion, chopped
- 1 smoked ham hock

Directions:
1. In your pressure cooker, mix peas with stock, onion and ham hock, stir, cover and cook on manual for 38 minutes.
2. Add collard greens, stir, cover the cooker again and cook on High for 2 minutes more.
3. Divide collard greens and peas between plates and serve as a side dish.

Nutrition: calories 271, fat 4, fiber 7, carbs 12, protein 4

Pinto Bean Dip

Preparation time: 10 minutes
Cooking time: 8 minutes
Servings: 4

Ingredients:
- 8 ounces canned pinto beans, drained
- 4 rosemary sprigs, chopped
- 1 and ¼ cup parsley, chopped
- 3 tablespoons lemon juice
- 2 tablespoons tomatoes, chopped

Directions:
1. In your pressure cooker, mix pinto beans with rosemary and tomatoes, stir, cover and cook on High for 8 minutes.
2. Blend using an immersion blender, add parsley and lemon juice, stir again, divide into bowls and serve as an appetizer.

Nutrition: calories 272, fat 3, fiber 8, carbs 9, protein 8

Light Lemon Dip

Preparation time: 10 minutes
Cooking time: 10 minutes
Servings: 6

Ingredients:

- 2 lemons, roasted in the oven and pulp separated
- 1 tablespoon olive oil
- 1 cup sour cream
- ½ cup chives, chopped
- 1 cup mayonnaise

Directions:
1. In your pressure cooker, mix lemon pulp with sour cream and oil, whisk well, cover and cook on High for 5 minutes.
2. Leave aside dip to cool down, add chives and mayo, whisk well, divide into bowls and serve as an appetizer.

Nutrition: calories 200, fat 3, fiber 4, carbs 6, protein 8

Green Olive Pate

Preparation time: 10 minutes
Cooking time: 2 minutes
Servings: 4

Ingredients:
- 2 cups green olives, pitted
- 2 anchovy fillets
- 2 garlic cloves, minced
- 1 tablespoon capers, chopped
- ½ cup olive oil

Directions:
1. In a food processor, mix olives with anchovy fillets, garlic, capers and olive oil, pulse well, transfer to your pressure cooker, cover and cook on High for 2 minutes.
2. Divide into bowls and serve cold as an appetizer.

Nutrition: calories 118, fat 2, fiber 2, carbs 5, protein 4

Shrimp and Tomatoes Appetizer Mix

Preparation time: 10 minutes
Cooking time: 4 minutes
Servings: 6

Ingredients:
- 1 and ½ cups onion, chopped
- 2 tablespoons butter
- 15 ounces canned tomatoes, chopped
- 1 pound shrimp, shelled
- 1 cup feta cheese, crumbled

Directions:
1. Set your pressure cooker on sauté mode, add butter, melt it, add onion, stir and cook for 2 minutes.
2. Add shrimp and tomatoes, toss a bit, cover and cook on Low for 2 minutes.

3. Divide shrimp and tomatoes mix into small bowls and serve as an appetizer with feta cheese on top.

Nutrition: calories 201, fat 3, fiber 4, carbs 7, protein 4

Red Pepper Dip

Preparation time: 10 minutes
Cooking time: 2 hours
Servings: 2

Ingredients:
- 3 cups water
- 2 red bell peppers
- Salt to the taste
- ½ tablespoon sesame oil
- 1/3 pound garbanzo beans
- A pinch of cumin
- 2 tablespoons lemon juice
- 2 teaspoons olive oil
- 1 garlic clove, roasted
- 2 tablespoons sesame seeds, toasted

Directions:
1. Put beans in your pressure cooker, add water and salt, cover and cook on High for 1 hour and 30 minutes.
2. Transfer beans to a bowl and reserve cooking liquid.
3. Add some water to the pot, add the steamer basket, add bell peppers inside, cover and cook on High for 15 minutes.
4. Peel peppers, chop them and put them in another bowl.
5. Heat up a pan with half of the sesame oil over medium high heat, add sesame seeds and garlic, stir and cook for 6 minutes.
6. In your blender, mix beans with toasted sesame seeds and garlic, peppers, lemon juice, olive oil, the rest of the sesame oil, some of the cooking liquid from the beans, salt and cumin, pulse well and serve as a dip with pita bread.

Nutritional value: calories 80, fat 6, carbs 6, fiber 2, protein 2

Artichokes Spread

Preparation time: 15 minutes
Cooking time: 15 minutes
Servings: 2

Ingredients:
- ½ cup cannellini beans, soaked overnight and drained
- ½ pound artichokes, cut lengthwise
- ½ cup water
- 2 tablespoons lemon juice
- 1 garlic clove, minced

- 2 tablespoons Greek yogurt
- Salt and pepper to the taste

Directions:
1. Put artichokes in a bowl, add the lemon juice, leave aside for 15 minutes, add them to pressure cooker, also add beans, cover and cook on High for 15 minutes.
2. Discard excess water, transfer artichokes and beans to your blender, add garlic, salt, pepper and yogurt, pulse well and serve as a snack.

Nutrition: calories 100, fat 3, fiber 4, carbs 7, protein 3

Chicken Dip

Preparation time: 10 minutes
Cooking time: 15 minutes
Servings: 6

Ingredients:
- 3 cups chicken, cooked and shredded
- 4 ounces cream cheese
- 1 cup mozzarella cheese, shredded
- ½ cup hot sauce
- 1 cup Greek yogurt

Directions:
1. In your pressure cooker, mix chicken with cream cheese and hot sauce, stir, cover and cook on High for 15 minutes.
2. Add yogurt and mozzarella, stir, leave aside for a few minutes, divide into bowls and serve as an appetizer.

Nutrition: calories 188, fat 4, fiber 7, carbs 8, protein 4

Blue Cheese Dip

Preparation time: 10 minutes
Cooking time: 4 minutes
Servings: 6

Ingredients:
- 4 tablespoons blue cheese, crumbled
- 1 cup sour cream
- 2 tablespoons chives, chopped
- 1 and ½ teaspoons rosemary, chopped
- Black pepper to the taste

Directions:
1. In your pressure cooker, mix blue cheese with sour cream, rosemary and black pepper, stir, cover and cook on Manual for 4 minutes.
2. Add chives, whisk dip, divide into bowls and serve as an appetizer.

Nutrition: calories 200, fat 7, fiber 5, carbs 7, protein 4

Chunky Warm Salsa

Preparation time: 10 minutes
Cooking time: 4 minutes
Servings: 5

Ingredients:
- 1 red bell pepper, cut into medium pieces
- 2 peaches, roughly chopped
- 1 red onion, roughly chopped
- A drizzle of olive oil
- 2 tablespoons lime juice

Directions:
1. Set your pressure cooker on sauté mode, add oil, heat it up, add onion, stir and cook for 1 minute.
2. Add red pepper, peaches and lime juice, toss, cover and cook on High for 3 minutes.
3. Leave this appetizer to cool down, divide into small bowls and serve.

Nutrition: calories 152, fat 2, fiber 3, carbs 4, protein 4

Cumin Dip

Preparation time: 10 minutes
Cooking time: 2 minutes
Servings: 4

Ingredients:
- 1 cup sour cream
- 1/3 cup mayonnaise
- 1 and ¼ teaspoon cumin, ground
- 1 tablespoon hot sauce
- 1 tablespoon lime juice

Directions:
1. In your pressure cooker, mix sour cream with cumin and hot sauce, stir, cover and cook on High for 2 minutes.
2. Leave dip to cool down, add mayo and lime juice, stir, divide into bowls and serve.

Nutrition: calories 209, fat 6, fiber 3, carbs 7, protein 7

Tortillas

Preparation time: 10 minutes
Cooking time: 14 minutes
Servings: 2

Ingredients:

- ½ yellow onion, finely chopped
- ½ tablespoon olive oil
- 1 garlic clove, minced
- ½ green bell pepper, sliced
- 1 and ½ cups canned pinto beans, drained
- 1 hot chili peppers, minced
- 2 tablespoon cilantro, chopped
- Salt to the taste
- ½ cup water
- ½ teaspoon cumin powder
- 4 whole wheat tortillas
- Salsa for serving
- 1 cup cheddar cheese, shredded
- Black olives, for serving

Directions:
1. Set your pressure cooker on Sauté mode, add the oil, heat it up, add onion and garlic, stir and cook for 4 minutes
2. Add green pepper, pinto beans, chili peppers, salt, water, cumin and cilantro, stir, cover cooker and cook on High for 10 minutes.
3. Transfer mix to a bowl, mash everything, divide this on each tortilla, also divide cheese, salsa and olives, roll them up and serve as a snack.

Nutrition: calories 170, fat 3, fiber 8, carbs 10, protein 12

White Beans Dip

Preparation time: 10 minutes
Cooking time: 13 minutes
Servings: 2

Ingredients:
- ½ cup white beans, soaked overnight and drained
- 1 and ½ tablespoons lemon juice
- 1 garlic clove, minced
- 2 tablespoons olive oil
- 1 teaspoon cumin, ground
- 1 teaspoon chili powder
- A pinch of red pepper flakes
- Salt and black pepper to the taste
- 1 and ½ tablespoons cilantro, chopped

Directions:
1. Put beans in your pressure cooker, add water to cover and cook on High for 13 minutes.
2. Drain beans, transfer them to your food processor, add garlic, lemon juice, oil, cumin, chili powder, pepper flakes, salt and pepper and pulse really well.
3. Add cilantro, stir a bit, transfer to a bowl and serve as a snack.

Nutrition: calories 211, fat 4, fiber 5, carbs 12, protein 14

Black Bean Salsa

Preparation time: 10 minutes
Cooking time: 8 minutes
Servings: 4

Ingredients:
- 1 small white onion, chopped
- 8 ounces canned black beans, drained
- 2 tablespoons lime juice
- 1 tablespoon olive oil
- 2 red jalapenos, chopped

Directions:
1. Set your pressure cooker on sauté mode, add oil, heat it up, add onion, stir and cook for 2-3 minutes.
2. Add black beans, lime juice and jalapenos, stir, cover and cook on High for 3 minutes.
3. Divide into bowls and serve warm.

Nutrition: calories 172, fat 3, fiber 4, carbs 6, protein 3

Ranch Spread

Preparation time: 10 minutes
Cooking time: 10 minutes
Servings: 12

Ingredients:
- 1 cup sour cream
- 1 pound bacon, chopped
- 1 cup mayonnaise
- 1 cup Monterey jack cheese, shredded
- 4 green onions, chopped

Directions:
1. Set your pressure cooker on sauté mode, add bacon, stir and cook until it is crispy.
2. Add sour cream and green onions, stir, cover and cook on High for 6 minutes.
3. Add cheese and mayo, stir well, leave aside for a few minutes, divide into bowls and serve as an appetizer.

Nutrition: calories 261, fat 4, fiber 6, carbs 7, protein 4

Spinach and Salami

Preparation time: 10 minutes
Cooking time: 6 minutes
Servings: 4

Ingredients:
- 3 salami slices, chopped
- 3 garlic cloves, minced
- 3 tablespoons olive oil
- 10 ounces baby spinach

- ½ cup chicken stock

Directions:
1. Set your pressure cooker on sauté mode, add oil, heat it up, add garlic, stir and cook for 1 minute.
2. Add salami, stir and cook for 2 minutes more.
3. Add spinach and stock, stir a bit, cover and cook on high for 3 minutes.
4. Divide between plates and serve as a side dish.

Nutrition: calories 172, fat 3, fiber 6, carbs 12, protein 3

Creamy Spinach

Preparation time: 10 minutes
Cooking time: 6 minutes
Servings: 4

Ingredients:
- 10 ounces spinach, roughly chopped
- 2 tablespoons butter
- 2 shallots, chopped
- 2 cups heavy cream
- A pinch of nutmeg, ground

Directions:
1. Set your pressure cooker on sauté mode, add butter, melt it, add shallots, stir and cook for 2 minutes.
2. Add spinach, stir and cook for 30 seconds more.
3. Add cream and nutmeg, stir, cover and cook on High for 3 minutes.
4. Divide everything between plates and serve as a side dish.

Nutrition: calories 200, fat 3, fiber 5, carbs 15, protein 3

Chicken Appetizer Salad

Preparation time: 1 hour
Cooking time: 5 minutes
Servings: 2

Ingredients:
- 1 chicken breast, skinless and boneless
- 3 cups water
- 2 garlic cloves, minced
- 1 tablespoon honey
- Salt and black pepper to the taste
- 1 tablespoon mustard
- 2 tablespoons olive oil
- 1 tablespoon balsamic vinegar
- Mixed salad greens
- A handful cherry tomatoes, halved

Directions:

1. In a bowl, mix 2 cups water with salt to the taste and chicken, toss a bit and keep in a cold place for 1 hour
2. Add the rest of the water to your pressure cooker, add the steamer basket, drain chicken and add to the pot, cover, cook on High for 5 minutes, transfer to a cutting board, cool down, cut into thin strips, add to a bowl and mix with tomatoes and salad greens,
3. In a bowl, mix garlic with salt, pepper, mustard, honey, vinegar and olive oil and whisk very well.
4. Drizzle this vinaigrette over chicken salad, toss, divide between appetizer plates and serve.

Nutrition: calories 173, fat 2, fiber 4, carbs 10, protein 6

Octopus Appetizer

Preparation time: 10 minutes
Cooking time: 35 minutes
Servings: 2

Ingredients:
- 1 pound octopus, cleaned, head removed and tentacles separated
- 1/2 pound potatoes
- 1 garlic clove, minced
- A pinch of peppercorns
- 1 bay leaf
- 1 tablespoon parsley, chopped
- 2 tablespoons vinegar
- Salt and black pepper salad
- 1 tablespoon olive oil

Directions:
1. Put potatoes in your pressure cooker, add water to cover, cook at High for 15 minutes, transfer them to a cutting board, cool them down, peel, chop and leave them aside in a bowl for now.
2. Put octopus in your pressure cooker, add water to cover, bay leaf, peppercorns, salt and pepper, stir, cover, cook on High for 20 minutes, drain, chop and add to the bowl with the potatoes.
3. In a bowl, mix olive oil with vinegar, garlic, salt and pepper, whisk well, drizzle over salad, toss, divide it on appetizer plates and serve with parsley sprinkled on top.

Nutrition: calories 261, fat 5, fiber 2, carbs 8, protein 12

Orange and Beet Appetizer

Preparation time: 10 minutes
Cooking time: 10 minutes
Servings: 2

Ingredients:
- 1 pound beets, halved
- 1 teaspoon orange zest, grated
- 1 orange peel strip
- 1 tablespoons cider vinegar
- 3 tablespoons orange juice
- 1 tablespoon brown sugar

- 1 scallion, chopped
- 1 teaspoon Dijon mustard
- 1 cup arugula

Directions:
1. In your pressure cooker, mix orange peel strips with vinegar, orange juice and beets, cover, cook them on High for 7 minutes, transfer to a cutting board, cool them down, peel, chop and put them into a bowl.
2. Discard peel strip from the pot, add mustard and sugar whisk well.
3. Add scallion and orange zest to beets and toss them.
4. Add liquid from the cooker and arugula over beets, toss to coat, divide everything on appetizer plates and serve.

Nutrition: calories 173, fat 2, fiber 4, carbs 7, protein 5

Hulled Barley Appetizer

Preparation time: 10 minutes
Cooking time: 20 minutes
Servings: 2

Ingredients:
- ½ cup hulled barley
- 1 cup water
- ½ cup spinach pesto
- 1 green apple, peeled, cored and chopped
- 2 tablespoons celery, chopped
- Salt and white pepper to the taste

Directions:
1. Put barley, water, salt and pepper in your pressure cooker, stir, cover, cook at High for 20 minutes, strain and transfer to a bowl,
2. Add celery, apple, spinach pesto, salt and pepper, toss to coat, divide between appetizer plates and serve.

Nutrition: calories 162, fat 1, fiber 3, carbs 6, protein 8

Garlic Green Beans

Preparation time: 10 minutes
Cooking time: 7 minutes
Servings: 4

Ingredients:
- 1 cup water, for the pressure cooker
- 4 garlic cloves, minced
- ½ teaspoon red pepper flakes
- 1 and ½ pounds green beans
- 3 tablespoons olive oil
- 1 tablespoon parmesan, shaved

Directions:
1. Put the water in your pressure cooker, add steamer basket, add green beans inside, cover, cook on High for 2 minutes, drain and transfer to a bowl.

2. Clean the pot, set it on sauté mode, add oil, heat it up, add garlic, stir and cook for 30 seconds.
3. Return green beans, also add pepper flakes, stir and sauté everything or 4 minutes more.
4. Divide green beans on plates, sprinkle shaved parmesan on top and serve as a side dish.

Nutrition: calories 172, fat 3, fiber 3, carbs 6, protein 4

Kale Sauté

Preparation time: 10 minutes
Cooking time: 7 minutes
Servings: 4

Ingredients:
- 1 pound kale, trimmed
- 1 tablespoon olive oil
- 3 garlic cloves
- ½ cup veggie stock
- Juice of ½ lemon

Directions:
1. Set your pressure cooker on sauté mode, add oil, heat it up, add garlic, stir and cook for 2 minutes.
2. Add kale, stock and lemon juice, stir a bit, cover and cook on High for 5 minutes.
3. Stir kale mix one more time, divide between plates and serve as a side dish.

Nutrition: calories 132, fat 3, fiber 6, carbs 8, protein 2

Wheat Berries Appetizer

Preparation time: 10 minutes
Cooking time: 35 minutes
Servings: 2

Ingredients:
- 1 cup wheat berries
- 1 and ½ tablespoons olive oil
- Salt and black pepper to the taste
- 2 cups water
- ½ tablespoon balsamic vinegar
- ½ cup cherry tomatoes, halved
- 1 green onion, chopped
- 1 ounce feta cheese, crumbled
- 3 tablespoons kalamata olives, pitted and sliced
- 1 tablespoon basil leaves, chopped
- 1 tablespoon parsley leaves, chopped

Directions:
1. Set your pressure cooker on Sauté mode, add ½ tablespoon oil, heat it up, add wheat berries, stir, cook for 5 minutes, add water, salt and pepper, cover cooker and cook on High for 30 minutes.
2. Drain wheat berries, transfer to a bowl and mix with the rest of the oil, balsamic vinegar, tomatoes, green onion, olives, cheese, basil and parsley.
3. Toss to coat, divide between appetizer plates and serve.

Nutrition: calories 200, fat 4, fiber 5, carbs 8, protein 6

Veggies and Wheat Appetizer Salad

Preparation time: 10 minutes
Cooking time: 15 minutes
Servings: 2

Ingredients:

- 4 tablespoons whole wheat, cracked
- 1 cup water
- 1 tomato, chopped
- 1 potato, cubed
- 3 cauliflower florets, chopped
- A pinch of salt and black pepper
- ¼ teaspoon mustard seeds
- ¼ teaspoon cumin seeds
- ½ teaspoon ginger, grated
- ½ tablespoon chana dal
- 1 garlic clove, minced
- ½ yellow onion, chopped
- 1 curry leaf
- 1 and ½ teaspoon olive oil
- A pinch of garam masala
- 2 teaspoons cilantro, chopped

Directions:

1. Set your pressure cooker on Sauté mode, add the oil, heat it up, add cumin, mustard seeds, onion, garlic, chana dal, ginger, garam masala and curry leaf, stir and cook for 3 minutes.
2. Add cauliflower, potatoes and tomatoes, stir and cook for 4 minutes.
3. Add wheat, salt, pepper and water, stir, cover, cook on High for 5 minutes, divide into small bowls, sprinkle cilantro and serve as an appetizer.

Nutrition: calories 173, fat 3, fiber 4, carbs 10, protein 7

Bulgur Appetizer

Preparation time: 15 minutes
Cooking time: 12 minutes
Servings: 2

Ingredients:

- Zest from ½ orange, grated
- Juice from 1 orange
- 1 garlic clove, minced
- 1 teaspoons olive oil
- 1 tablespoon ginger, grated
- ½ cup bulgur, rinsed
- ½ tablespoon soy sauce
- 2 tablespoons scallions, chopped
- 2 tablespoons almonds, chopped
- Salt to the taste
- 1 teaspoon brown sugar

- 4 tablespoons water

Directions:
1. Set your pressure cooker on Sauté mode, add oil, heat it up, add ginger, garlic, sugar, bulgur, water and orange juice, stir and cook for 1 minutes.
2. Cover pot, cook on High for 5 minutes, transfer to a bowl and leave aside to cool down a bit.
3. Heat up a pan over medium heat, add almonds, stir and toast them for 3 minutes.
4. Add orange zest, salt, soy sauce, scallions and bulgur, stir, cook for 1 minute more, divide into 2 bowls and serve as an appetizer.

Nutrition: calories 128, fat 4, fiber 4, carbs 8, protein 8

Summer Lentils Appetizer

Preparation time: 10 minutes
Cooking time: 8 minutes
Servings: 2

Ingredients:
- 1 cup chicken stock
- ½ cup lentils
- 1 bay leaf
- ¼ teaspoon thyme, dried
- 2 tablespoons red onion, chopped
- 3 tablespoons celery, chopped
- 2 tablespoons red bell pepper, chopped
- 1 tablespoon olive oil
- ½ tablespoon garlic, minced
- ¼ teaspoon oregano, dried
- Juice of ½ lemon
- 1 tablespoon parsley, chopped
- Salt and black pepper to the taste

Directions:
1. Put lentils in your pressure cooker, add bay leaf, thyme and stock, cover, cook on High for 8 minutes, drain and transfer lentils to a bowl.
2. Add celery, onion, bell pepper, garlic, parsley, oregano, lemon juice, olive oil, salt and pepper, toss to coat, divide between 2 appetizer plates and serve.

Nutrition: calories 187, fat 3, fiber 4, carbs 7, protein 10

Green Beans and Cranberries Side Dish

Preparation time: 10 minutes
Cooking time: 6 minutes
Servings: 6

Ingredients:
- ½ cup water, for the pressure cooker
- 2 pounds green beans
- 3 tablespoons oil
- ¼ cup cranberries, dried
- ¼ cup almonds, chopped
- A pinch of salt

Directions:
1. Put the water in your pressure cooker, add steamer basket, add green beans and cranberries, cover, cook on High for 2 minutes and transfer to a bowl.
2. Clean the pot, set on sauté mode, add oil, heat it up, add green beans and cranberries, almonds and a pinch of salt, toss and cook for 4 minutes more.
3. Divide everything between plates and serve as a side dish.

Nutrition: calories 130, fat 3, fiber 3, carbs 7, protein 4

Green Beans and Blue Cheese

Preparation time: 10 minutes
Cooking time: 7 minutes
Servings: 4

Ingredients:
- ½ cup water, for the pressure cooker
- 1 and ½ pounds green beans
- ½ cup almonds, chopped
- ¼ cup olive oil
- 2 tablespoons blue cheese, crumbled
- 2 tablespoons lemon juice

Directions:
1. Put the water in your pressure cooker, add steamer basket, add green beans inside, cover, cook on High for 2 minutes, drain and transfer them to a bowl.
2. Clean the pot, set on sauté mode, add oil, heat it up, add green beans, stir and cook for 3 minutes.
3. Add lemon juice and almonds, stir and cook for 2 minutes more.
4. Divide on plates, sprinkle blue cheese all over and serve as a side dish.

Nutrition: calories 200, fat 4, fiber 4, carbs 7, protein 4

Pork Burritos

Preparation time: 15 minutes
Cooking time: 15 minutes
Servings: 2

Ingredients:
- 4 ounces pork meat, ground
- Salt and black pepper
- ½ teaspoon thyme, dried
- ½ teaspoon sage, dried
- ½ teaspoon fennel seeds
- ½ teaspoon brown sugar
- A pinch of nutmeg, ground
- A pinch of red pepper flakes, crushed
- 1 cup water + ½ tablespoon
- 4 tortilla shells
- 4 eggs

- 2 teaspoons olive oil
- 2 tablespoons milk
- Cheddar cheese, shredded
- Salsa for serving

Directions:
1. In a bowl, mix pork with salt, pepper, thyme, sage, fennel, pepper flakes, nutmeg, sugar and ½ tablespoon water and stir well.
2. Brush tortilla shells with the olive oil, arrange them on a baking sheet, cover them with tin foil and seal edges.
3. In a heat proof dish, mix eggs with salt, pepper, milk and meat, stir and cover with some tin foil
4. Add 1 cup water to your pressure cooker, add the steamer basket, place heatproof dish inside, add wrapped tortilla shells on top, cover and cook on High for 15 minutes.
5. Unwrap tortilla shells, stuff them with meat mix, top with salsa and cheddar cheese, arrange on a platter and serve as an appetizer.

Nutrition: calories 264, fat 5, fiber 8, carbs 12, protein 8

Beef Sandwiches

Preparation time: 10 minutes
Cooking time: 40 minutes
Servings: 2

Ingredients:
- ½ tablespoon brown sugar
- 1 pound beef roast, cut into small chunks
- Salt and black pepper to the taste
- ½ teaspoon smoked paprika
- 1 teaspoon garlic powder
- ½ teaspoons mustard powder
- ½ teaspoons onion flakes
- 1 cup beef stock
- 2 teaspoons balsamic vinegar
- ½ tablespoon Worcestershire sauce
- 1 tablespoon butter, melted
- 2 hoagie rolls
- 2 cheddar cheese slices

Directions:
1. Put the meat in your pressure cooker, add salt, pepper, paprika, garlic powder, mustard powder, onion flakes, stock, vinegar and Worcestershire sauce, stir well, cover the cooker and cook at High for 40 minutes.
2. Transfer meat to a cutting board, shred it using 2 forks and divide between the 2 rolls after you've greased them with the butter.
3. Divide cheese on top of the meat, introduce sandwiches in preheated broiler, broil them for a couple of minutes and serve them as a snack with some of the cooking liquid from the pressure cooker on the side.

Nutrition: calories 284, fat 6, fiber 2, carbs 8, protein 20

Carrots Mix

Preparation time: 10 minutes
Cooking time: 10 minutes
Servings: 6

Ingredients:
- 2 and ½ pounds baby carrots
- 2 tablespoons olive oil
- 3 shallots, chopped
- 1 teaspoon thyme
- ¼ cup Greek yogurt
- 1 cup water, for the pressure cooker

Directions:
1. In a bowl, mix baby carrots with thyme and oil and toss.
2. Add the water to your pressure cooker, add steamer basket, add carrots inside, cover, cook on High for 5 minutes and transfer them to a bowl.
3. Clean the pot, set on sauté mode, add shallots and brown them for a couple of minutes.
4. Add carrots, toss and heat them up.
5. Add yogurt, toss, divide between plates and serve as a side dish.

Nutrition: calories 162, fat 4, fiber 5, carbs 12, protein 5

Minty Carrots

Preparation time: 10 minutes
Cooking time: 5 minutes
Servings: 4

Ingredients:
- 16 ounces baby carrots
- 1 tablespoon butter
- 1 tablespoon mint, chopped
- 1 teaspoon sweet paprika
- Salt to the taste
- 1 cup water, for the pressure cooker

Directions:
1. In your pressure cooker, mix carrots with water, cover, cook on High for 3 minutes, drain and transfer to a bowl.
2. Clean the pot, set on sauté mode, add butter and heat it up.
3. Add mint, stir and cook for 1 minute.
4. Add carrots, salt and paprika, toss, divide between plates and serve as a side dish.

Nutrition: calories 172, fat 3, fiber 7, carbs 8, protein 4

Turnips Spread

Preparation time: 10 minutes
Cooking time: 5 minutes
Servings: 2

Ingredients:

- 2 turnips, peeled and chopped
- Salt and black pepper
- ½ yellow onion, chopped
- 2 tablespoons sour cream
- 1/3 cup chicken stock

Directions:
1. In your pressure cooker, mix turnips with stock and onion, stir, cover, cook on High for 5 minutes, drain and transfer turnips to your blender.
2. Add sour cream, salt and pepper, pulse really well and serve as a party spread.

Nutrition: calories 100, fat 3, fiber 2, carbs 6, protein 2

Calamari Salad

Preparation time: 10 minutes
Cooking time: 32 minutes
Servings: 2

Ingredients:
- 1 pound calamari, tentacles separated and cut into strips
- Salt and black pepper
- 7 ounces canned tomatoes, chopped
- ½ bunch parsley, chopped
- 1 garlic clove, minced
- 3 tablespoons white wine
- ½ cup water
- 1 anchovy
- 1 tablespoon olive oil
- Juice of ½ lemon
- A pinch of red pepper flakes

Directions:
1. Set your pressure cooker on Sauté mode, add oil, pepper flakes, garlic, anchovies and calamari, stir and cook for 9 minutes.
2. Add wine, tomatoes, water, half of the parsley, salt and pepper, stir, cover and cook on High for 25 minutes.
3. Add the rest of the parsley, the lemon juice, salt and pepper, stir, divide into bowls and serve as an appetizer.

Nutrition: calories 200, fat 4, fiber 2, carbs 7, protein 12

Carrots and Walnuts Salad

Preparation time: 10 minutes
Cooking time: 5 minutes
Servings: 4

Ingredients:
- 2 pounds baby carrots
- 1 cup water, for the pressure cooker
- 2 tablespoons butter
- 3 ounces canned walnuts in syrup
- Salt to the taste

- A splash of vinegar

Directions:
1. Put the water in your pressure cooker, add carrots, stir, cover, cook on High for 3 minutes, drain and transfer to a bowl.
2. Clean the pot, set it on sauté mode, add butter, heat it up, add carrots, stir and cook for 1 minute.
3. Add walnuts and syrup, salt and vinegar, toss, cook for 1 minute more, divide between plates and serve as a side dish.

Nutrition: calories 172, fat 3, fiber 6, carbs 10, protein 4

Sweet and Sour Side Salad

Preparation time: 10 minutes
Cooking time: 7 minutes
Servings: 8

Ingredients:
- 1 cup water, for the pressure cooker
- 3 pounds rainbow carrots, chopped
- 1 onion, chopped
- 3 tablespoons butter
- 3 tablespoons vinegar
- 3 tablespoons honey

Directions:
1. Add the water to your pressure cooker, add carrots, cover, cook on High for 3 minutes, drain and transfer to a bowl.
2. Clean the pot, set on sauté mode, add butter, melt it, add onion, stir and cook for 2 minutes.
3. Add vinegar, honey and return carrots, stir, cover and cook on High for 2 minutes more.
4. Divide between plates and serve as a side dish.

Nutrition: calories 192, fat 3, fiber 4, carbs 10, protein 3

Cauliflower Salad

Preparation time: 10 minutes
Cooking time: 6 minutes
Servings: 2

Ingredients:
- ½ cauliflower head, florets separated
- ½ pound broccoli head, florets separated
- ½ romanesco cauliflower head, florets separated
- 1 orange, peeled and sliced
- Zest from ½ orange, grated
- Juice from ½ orange
- A pinch of hot pepper flakes
- 2 anchovies
- ½ cup water
- ½ tablespoon capers, chopped
- Salt and black pepper to the taste
- 2 tablespoons olive oil

Directions:
1. In a bowl, mix orange zest with orange juice, pepper flakes, anchovies, capers salt, pepper and olive oil and whisk well.
2. Add the water to your pressure cooker, add the steamer basket, add cauliflower and broccoli inside, cover and cook on Low for 6 minutes.
3. Transfer cauliflower and broccoli to a bowl, add orange slices and the vinaigrette you've made earlier, toss to coat, divide between 2 appetizer plates and serve.

Nutrition: calories 200, fat 3, fiber 4, carbs 7, protein 4

Chicken Sandwiches

Preparation time: 10 minutes
Cooking time: 15 minutes
Servings: 2

Ingredients:
- 2 chicken breasts, skinless and boneless
- 3 ounces canned orange juice
- 1 tablespoons lemon juice
- 4 ounces canned peaches and their juice
- ½ teaspoon soy sauce
- 7 ounces canned pineapple, chopped
- 2 teaspoons cornstarch
- 1 tablespoon brown sugar
- 2 hamburger buns
- 2 pineapple slices, grilled

Directions:
1. In a bowl, mix orange juice with soy sauce, lemon juice, canned pineapples pieces, peaches and sugar, stir well, pour half of this mix into your pressure cooker, add chicken, then pour the rest of the orange mix, cover and cook on High for 20 minutes
2. Transfer chicken to a cutting board, cool it down, shred and transfer to a bowl.
3. In a bowl, mix cornstarch with 1 tablespoon cooking juice, pour into the pot, return chicken meat as well, set the cooker on sauté mode and cook for a couple of minutes.
4. Divide this chicken mix on hamburger buns, top with grilled pineapple pieces and serve as a snack.

Nutrition: calories 200, fat 4, fiber 4, carbs 7, protein 10

Pearl Onions Side Dish
Preparation time: 10 minutes
Cooking time: 10 minutes
Servings: 6

Ingredients:
- 1 pound rainbow carrots, cut into quarters
- 2 cups pearl onions
- ½ cup water, for the pressure cooker
- 3 tablespoons butter
- 2 tablespoons balsamic vinegar
- 2 tablespoons parsley, chopped

Directions:
1. In your pressure cooker, mix carrots with onions and water, cover, cook on High for 4 minutes, drain and transfer to a bowl.
2. Clean the pot, set on sauté mode, add butter, melt it, add onions and carrots, vinegar and parsley, stir and sauté for 5 minutes.
3. Toss again, divide between plates and serve as a side dish.

Nutrition: calories 162, fat 4, fiber 8, carbs 12, protein 4

Haricots Verts Side Salad

Preparation time: 10 minutes
Cooking time: 8 minutes
Servings: 4

Ingredients:
- 4 ounces pancetta, chopped
- 2 pounds haricots verts
- ½ cup dates, sliced
- ½ cup chicken stock
- Black pepper to the taste

Directions:
1. Set your pressure cooker on sauté mode, add pancetta, stir and cook for 3 minutes.
2. Add haricot verts, dates and black pepper, stir and cook for 2 minutes more.
3. Add stock, stir a bit more, cover and cook on High for 3 minutes.
4. Divide everything between plates and serve as a side dish.

Nutrition: calories 128, fat 3, fiber 6, carbs 16, protein 4

Lamb Ribs

Preparation time: 15 minutes
Cooking time: 26 minutes
Servings: 2

Ingredients:
- 4 lamb ribs
- 1 garlic clove, minced
- 1 carrot, chopped
- 6 ounces veggie stock
- 2 rosemary sprigs
- 1 tablespoon olive oil
- Salt and black pepper
- 1 tablespoon white flour

Directions:
1. Set your pressure cooker on Sauté mode, add the oil, heat it up, add lamb, garlic, salt and pepper and brown it on all sides.
2. Add flour, stock, rosemary and carrots, stir, cover the pot, cook on High for 20 minutes, arrange ribs on a platter and serve with cooking juices on the side.

Nutrition: calories 213, fat 4, fiber 6, carbs 7, protein 20

Pork Cakes

Preparation time: 10 minutes
Cooking time: 10 minutes
Servings: 2

Ingredients:
- ½ pound ground pork meat
- ½ tablespoon parsley, chopped
- 1 egg
- ½ bread slice, soaked and squeezed
- 1 garlic clove, minced
- Salt and black pepper
- ½ cup beef stock
- A pinch of nutmeg, ground
- 1 and ½ tablespoon flour
- ¼ teaspoon Worcestershire sauce
- ¼ teaspoon sweet paprika
- 1 tablespoon olive oil
- 1 bay leaf
- 2 tablespoons white wine

Directions:
1. In a bowl, combine meat with bread, egg, salt, pepper, parsley, paprika, garlic and nutmeg and stir well.
2. Add a splash of stock and Worcestershire sauce, stir, shape small cakes out of this mix and dredge them in flour
3. Set your pressure cooker on Sauté mode, add oil, heat it up, add cakes and brown them on all sides.
4. Add bay leaf, stock and wine, cover the cooker and cook at High for 6 minutes.
5. Discard bay leaf, arrange cakes on a platter and serve them as an appetizer.

Nutrition: calories 283, fat 4, fiber 7, carbs 10, protein 14

Breakfast Recipes

Espresso Steel Cut Oats

Preparation time: 10 minutes
Cooking time: 10 minutes
Servings: 4

Ingredients:
- 2 and ½ cups water
- 1 cup milk
- 1 cup steel cut oats
- 2 tablespoons sugar
- 1 teaspoon espresso powder

Directions:
1. In your pressure cooker, mix water with milk, oats, sugar and espresso powder, stir a bit, cover and cook on High for 10 minutes.
2. Stir your oatmeal again, divide into bowls and serve for breakfast.

Nutrition: calories 120, fat 2, fiber 4, carbs 10, protein 5

Chocolate Oatmeal

Preparation time: 10 minutes
Cooking time: 10 minutes
Servings: 6

Ingredients:
- 1 cup milk
- 2 cups oatmeal
- 6 cups water
- 2 and ½ tablespoons cocoa powder
- 1 teaspoon cinnamon powder

Directions:
1. In your pressure cooker, mix water with milk, oatmeal, cocoa powder and cinnamon, stir, cover and cook on High for 10 minutes.
2. Stir oatmeal again, divide into bowls and serve.

Nutrition: calories 110, fat 4, fiber 5, carbs 8, protein 5

Ham And Egg Casserole

Preparation time: 10 minutes
Cooking time: 25 minutes
Servings: 2

Ingredients:
- 6 eggs
- ½ yellow onion, chopped
- 1 cup ham, chopped
- 1 cup cheddar cheese, shredded

- 4 red potatoes, cubed
- 1 cup milk
- Cooking spray
- 2 cups water
- A pinch of salt and black pepper

Directions:
1. In a bowl, mix eggs with milk, salt, pepper, potatoes, ham, onion and cheese, whisk and pour into a cooking pan sprayed with cooking oil.
2. Put the water in your pressure cooker, add the steamer basket inside, add the pan with the eggs mix, cover and cook on Manual for 25 minutes.
3. Leave your casserole to cool down a bit, slice, divide between 2 plates and serve for breakfast.

Nutrition: calories 210, fat 2, fiber 3, carbs 5, protein 7

Egg Bake

Preparation time: 10 minutes
Cooking time: 20 minutes
Servings: 2

Ingredients:
- 3 bacon slices, chopped
- 2 tablespoons milk
- 1 cup hash browns
- ¼ cup cheddar cheese, shredded
- A pinch of salt and black pepper
- 3 eggs
- 1 and ½ cups water
- 1 small red bell pepper, chopped
- 2 mushrooms, chopped

Directions:
1. Set your pressure cooker on Sauté mode, add bacon, stir and cook for a couple of minutes.
2. Add mushrooms and bell pepper, stir and cook for 3 minutes more.
3. Add hash browns, stir, cook for 2 minutes more, transfer everything to a bowl and clean your pressure cooker.
4. Add eggs, milk, salt, pepper and cheese to the bowl with the veggies and the ham, whisk everything and transfer to a greased heatproof dish.
5. Add the water to your pressure cooker, add the steamer basket, place the heatproof dish inside, cover and cook on High for 10 minutes.
6. Leave casserole to cool down a bit, slice and serve for breakfast.

Nutrition: calories 231, fat 4, fiber 1, carbs 4, protein 7

Peaches Oatmeal

Preparation time: 10 minutes
Cooking time: 10 minutes
Servings: 8

Ingredients:

- 4 cups rolled oats
- 3 and ½ cups milk
- 3 and ½ cups water
- 1/3 cup sugar
- 4 peaches, stones removed and chopped

Directions:
1. In your pressure cooker, mix water with milk, oats, sugar and peaches, stir, cover and cook on High for 10 minutes.
2. Stir oatmeal a bit more, divide into bowls and serve.

Nutrition: calories 152, fat 4, fiber 7, carbs 8, protein 4

Apple Steel Cut Oats

Preparation time: 10 minutes
Cooking time: 4 minutes
Servings: 4

Ingredients:
- 1 and ½ cups water
- 2 apples, peeled, cored and chopped
- ½ cup Greek yogurt
- 1 cup steel cut oats
- ¼ cup maple syrup

Directions:
1. In your pressure cooker, mix water with apples, oats and maple syrup, stir, cover and cook on Manual for 4 minutes.
2. Stir oatmeal again, divide into bowls, top with yogurt and serve.

Nutrition: calories 142, fat 4, fiber 6, carbs 6, protein 4

Breakfast Meat Soufflé

Preparation time: 10 minutes
Cooking time: 30 minutes
Servings: 2

Ingredients:
- 3 eggs, whisked
- A pinch of salt and black pepper
- ¼ cup milk
- 2 bacon slices, cooked and crumbled
- ½ cup sausage, cooked and ground
- ¼ cup ham, chopped
- ½ cup cheddar cheese, shredded
- 1 green onion, chopped
- 1 cup water

Directions:
1. In a bowl, mix eggs with milk, salt, pepper, sausage, bacon, green onion, ham and cheese, stir and pour into a soufflé dish.

2. Put the water in your pressure cooker, add the steamer basket, add the soufflé dish, cover the dish with some tin foil, cover cooker and cook on High for 30 minutes.
3. Serve hot for breakfast.

Nutrition: calories 212, fat 2, fiber 4, carbs 6, protein 10

Cheddar Quiche

Preparation time: 10 minutes
Cooking time: 30 minutes
Servings: 2

Ingredients:
- 1 cup water
- 3 eggs
- ¼ cup milk
- A pinch of salt and black pepper
- 1 tablespoon chives, chopped
- ½ cup cheddar cheese, shredded
- Cooking spray

Directions:
1. IN a bowl, mix eggs with salt, pepper, chives and milk and whisk well.
2. Wrap a cake pan with tin foil, grease with cooking spray and add the cheese into the pan.
3. Pour eggs mixture over cheese and spread evenly.
4. Add the water to your pressure cooker, add the steamer basket inside, add the cake pan, cover and cook on High for 30 minutes.
5. Divide between 2 plates and serve for breakfast.

Nutrition: calories 214, fat 4, fiber 2, carbs 7, protein 8

Western Omelet

Preparation time: 10 minutes
Cooking time: 30 minutes
Servings: 4

Ingredients:
- 6 eggs, whisked
- 8 ounces bacon, chopped
- ½ cup half and half
- A pinch of salt
- 4 spring onions, chopped
- 1 and ½ cups water, for the pressure cooker

Directions:
1. In a bowl, mix eggs with half-and-half, bacon, spring onions and salt, whisk well and pour into a soufflé dish.
2. Add water to your pressure cooker, add steamer basket, add soufflé dish inside, cover and cook on High for 30 minutes.
3. Leave omelet to cool down a bit, slice, divide between plates and serve for breakfast.

Nutrition: calories 200, fat 6, fiber 5, carbs 12, protein 6

Pepper Frittata

Preparation time: 10 minutes
Cooking time: 5 minutes
Servings: 6

Ingredients:
- 1 tablespoon almond milk
- 5 eggs, whisked
- A pinch of salt
- 2 tablespoons cheddar cheese, grated
- 1 red bell pepper, chopped
- 1 and ½ cups water, for the pressure cooker

Directions:
1. In a bowl, mix eggs with almond milk, salt, cheese and red bell pepper, whisk well and pour into 6 baking molds.
2. Add water to your pressure cooker, add steamer basket, add baking molds inside, cover and cook on High for 5 minutes.
3. Serve your frittatas hot.

Nutrition: calories 200, fat 4, fiber 5, carbs 7, protein 6

Mexican Breakfast

Preparation time: 10 minutes
Cooking time: 26 minutes
Servings: 2

Ingredients:
- 2 eggs, whisked
- 1 small red onion, chopped
- ¼ pound sausage, ground
- 1 small red bell pepper, chopped
- 2 ounces black beans
- 2 green onions, chopped
- 2 tablespoons flour
- ¼ cup cotija cheese, shredded
- ¼ cup mozzarella cheese, shredded
- 1 tablespoon cilantro, chopped

Directions:
1. Set your pressure cooker on sauté mode, add red onion and sausage, stir and cook for 6 minutes.
2. In a bowl, mix eggs with flour and whisk well.
3. Add eggs to the cooker and stir.
4. Also, add beans, red bell pepper, green onion, cotija and mozzarella cheese, stir a bit, cover and cook on High for 20 minutes.
5. Divide your Mexican breakfast between 2 plates, sprinkle cilantro on top and serve for breakfast.

Nutrition: calories 254, fat 5, fiber 3, carbs 7, protein 10

French Toast

Preparation time: 10 minutes
Cooking time: 25 minutes
Servings: 2

Ingredients:
- 3 French bread slices, cubed
- 1 tablespoon brown sugar
- 2 bananas, sliced
- 2 eggs
- 1 tablespoon cream cheese
- ¼ cup milk
- ½ tablespoon white sugar
- 1 tablespoon butter
- A pinch of cinnamon powder
- ½ teaspoon vanilla extract
- 2 tablespoons pecans, chopped
- Cooking spray
- ¾ cup water

Directions:
1. Grease a heatproof dish with cooking spray and add a layer of bread cubes on the bottom.
2. Add a layer of banana slices and sprinkle the brown sugar all over.
3. Add melted cream cheese and spread evenly.
4. Add the rest of the bread cubes and banana slices, butter and sprinkle half of the pecans all over.
5. In a bowl, mix eggs with white sugar, milk, cinnamon and vanilla, whisk well and pour this over bread and banana mix.
6. Add the water to your pressure cooker, add the trivet inside, add the heatproof dish, cover and cook on High for 25 minutes.
7. Divide this mix into 2 plates, sprinkle the rest of the pecans on top and serve.

Nutrition: calories 200, fat 3, fiber 3, carbs 5, protein 8

French Eggs

Preparation time: 10 minutes
Cooking time: 8 minutes
Servings: 4

Ingredients:
- 4 slices bacon
- 4 eggs
- 4 tablespoons chives, chopped
- A drizzle of olive oil
- A pinch of salt
- 1 cup water, for the pressure cooker

Directions:
1. Grease 4 ramekins with a drizzle of oil, crack an egg in each, add a bacon slice on top, season with a pinch of salt and top each with chives.

2. Add water to your pressure cooker, add steamer basket, add ramekins inside, cover and cook on High for 8 minutes.
3. Serve your baked eggs right away.

Nutrition: calories 182, fat 5, fiber 4, carbs 10, protein 5

Eggs and Bacon Breakfast Risotto

Preparation time: 10 minutes
Cooking time: 10 minutes
Servings: 2

Ingredients:
- ¾ cup Arborio rice
- 2 eggs, poached.
- 3 bacon slices, chopped
- 1 and ½ cups chicken stock
- 2 tablespoons parmesan, grated

Directions:
1. Set your pressure cooker on sauté mode, add bacon, stir and cook for 5 minutes.
2. Add rice, stir and cook for 1 minute.
3. Add stock, stir, cover and cook on Manual for 5 minutes.
4. Add parmesan, stir and divide risotto between plates.
5. Add eggs on the side and serve for breakfast.

Nutrition: calories 214, fat 5, fiber 6, carbs 12, protein 5

Burrito Casserole

Preparation time: 10 minutes
Cooking time: 13 minutes
Servings: 2

Ingredients:
- 2 eggs
- ½ pound red potatoes, cubed
- A pinch of salt and black pepper
- 1 small yellow onion, chopped
- 1 small jalapeno, chopped
- 2 ounces ham, cubed
- A pinch of mesquite seasoning
- A pinch of chili powder
- A pinch of taco seasoning
- 1 small avocado, pitted, peeled and chopped
- Salsa for serving
- 2 tortillas
- 1 cup water+ 1 tablespoon

Directions:
1. In a bowl, mix eggs with salt, pepper, mesquite seasoning, chili powder, 1 tablespoon water and taco seasoning and whisk well.
2. Add ham, potatoes, onion and jalapeno, stir and pour everything into a heatproof dish.

3. Add 1 cup water to your pressure cooker, add the trivet, and the heatproof dish inside, cover and cook on Manual for 13 minutes.
4. Divide this into 2 tortillas, divide avocado, spread salsa, roll burritos and serve them for breakfast.

Nutrition: calories 253, fat 4, fiber 4, carbs 6, protein 8

Spanish Frittata

Preparation time: 10 minutes
Cooking time: 18 minutes
Servings: 2

Ingredients:
- 3 eggs
- 2 ounces hash browns
- ½ tablespoon butter, melted
- 2 tablespoons scallions, chopped
- A pinch of salt and black pepper
- 1 small garlic clove, minced
- 1 tablespoon Bisquick
- 2 tablespoons milk
- ½ teaspoon tomato paste
- 1 and ½ cups water
- 2 ounces cheddar cheese, grated

Directions:
1. In a bowl, mix bisquick with milk and tomato paste and stir.
2. In another bowl, mix eggs with garlic, scallions, salt, pepper and milk mix and whisk everything.
3. Spread hash browns into a greased baking dish, add melted butter and pour eggs mix all over.
4. Spread eggs and top with cheese.
5. Put the water in your pressure cooker, add the trivet, add casserole inside, cover and cook on High for 20 minutes.
6. Divide frittata between 2 plates and serve.

Nutrition: calories 215, fat 4, fiber 3, carbs 6, protein 8

Blueberry Breakfast Bowl

Preparation time: 1 hour and 10 minutes
Cooking time: 1 minute
Servings: 4

Ingredients:
- 1 and ½ cups water
- 1 and ½ cups quinoa
- 1 tablespoon honey
- 3 tablespoons blueberries
- 1 cup apple juice

Directions:
1. In your pressure cooker, mix water with quinoa, stir, cover, cook on High for 1 minute, stir a bit and leave aside for 10 minutes.
2. Divide quinoa into bowls, add honey, apple juice and blueberries, toss a bit and serve for breakfast.

Nutrition: calories 172, fat 5, fiber 4, carbs 5, protein 6

Quinoa Bowls

Preparation time: 10 minutes
Cooking time: 1 minute
Servings: 4

Ingredients:
- 1 and ½ cups quinoa
- 2 tablespoons honey
- 2 and ¼ cups water
- ¼ teaspoon pumpkin pie spice
- 2 cups strawberries, chopped

Directions:
1. In your pressure cooker, mix quinoa with honey, water, spice and strawberries, stir, cover and cook on High for 1 minute.
2. Leave quinoa aside for 10 minutes, stir a bit, divide everything into bowls and serve.

Nutrition: calories 162, fat 3, fiber 3, carbs 6, protein 3

Breakfast Oatmeal

Preparation time: 10 minutes
Cooking time: 3 minutes
Servings: 2

Ingredients:
- ½ cup steel cut oats
- 1 and ½ cups water
- 1 teaspoon vanilla extract

Directions:
1. Put the water in your pressure cooker, add vanilla extract and oats, stir a bit, cover and cook on High for 3 minutes.
2. Divide into 2 bowls and serve for breakfast.

Nutrition: calories 142, fat 1, fiber 1, carbs 2, protein 2

Scotch Eggs

Preparation time: 10 minutes
Cooking time: 12 minutes
Servings: 2

Ingredients:
- 2 eggs
- ½ pound sausage, ground
- 1 tablespoon olive oil
- A pinch of chili powder
- Black pepper to the taste
- 2 cups water

Directions:
1. Put 1 cup water in your pressure cooker, add the steamer basket, place eggs inside, cover, cook on High for 6 minutes, transfer eggs to a bowl filled with ice water, cool them down and peel them quickly.
2. In a bowl, mix sausage meat with black pepper and chili powder and stir well.
3. Divide sausage meat into 2 pieces, flatten each on a working surface, add eggs in the middle, wrap them in meat and shape 2 meatballs.
4. Set your pressure cooker on Sauté mode, add the oil, heat it up, add scotch eggs, brown them on all sides and transfer to a plate.
5. Clean your pressure cooker, add the rest of the water, add the steamer basket, place eggs inside, cover and cook on High for 6 minutes more.
6. Divide eggs between 2 plates and serve them for breakfast with a tasty side salad.

Nutrition: calories 174, fat 4, fiber 1, carbs 6, protein 10

Quinoa Breakfast

Preparation time: 10 minutes
Cooking time: 1 minute
Servings: 2

Ingredients:
- 1 cup quinoa
- 2 cups water
- 1 tablespoon maple syrup
- ¼ teaspoon vanilla extract
- A pinch of cinnamon powder
- ¼ cup fresh berries

Directions:
1. Put quinoa in your pressure cooker, add cinnamon, vanilla, water and maple syrup, stir, cover and cook on High for 1 minute.
2. Leave quinoa aside for 10 minutes, fluff with a fork, divide into 2 bowls, top each with fresh berries and serve for breakfast.

Nutrition: calories 173, fat 1, fiber 2, carbs 2, protein 3

Breakfast Cake

Preparation time: 10 minutes
Cooking time: 25 minutes
Servings: 2

Ingredients:
- 1 cup water
- 3 eggs
- 2 tablespoons sugar
- 1 tablespoon butter, melted
- 5 tablespoons ricotta cheese
- 5 tablespoons yogurt
- 1 teaspoon vanilla extract
- ½ cup whole wheat flour
- 1 teaspoon baking powder
- ½ cup berry compote
- Cooking spray

Directions:
1. In a bowl, mix eggs with sugar and whisk until it dissolves.
2. Add ricotta cheese, butter, vanilla and yogurt and whisk well again.
3. In another bowl, mix baking powder with flour, stir and add this to eggs mix.
4. Stir well, pour this into a cake pan greased with cooking spray and spread evenly.
5. Drop spoonfuls of berry compote over cake mix and swirl with a knife.
6. Add the water to your pressure cooker, add the trivet inside, add cake pan, cover cooker and cook on High for 25 minutes.
7. Divide cake between 2 plates and serve for breakfast.

Nutrition: calories 251, fat 1, fiber 2, carbs 4, protein 7

Cornmeal Porridge

Preparation time: 10 minutes
Cooking time: 20 minutes
Servings: 4

Ingredients:

- 1 cup cornmeal
- 1 cup milk
- 4 cups water
- ½ teaspoon nutmeg, ground
- ½ cup sweetened condensed milk

Directions:
1. In a bowl, mix 1 cup water with cornmeal and stir well.
2. In your pressure cooker, mix the rest of the water with milk and cornmeal mix and stir.
3. Also add nutmeg, stir, cover and cook on High for 6 minutes.
4. Add condensed milk, stir, divide into bowls and serve.

Nutrition: calories 241, fat 4, fiber 6, carbs 12, protein 6

Breakfast Rice Pudding

Preparation time: 10 minutes
Cooking time: 20 minutes
Servings: 6

Ingredients:
- 2 cups nut milk
- 1 and ¼ cups water
- 1 cup basmati rice
- 1 cup coconut cream
- ¼ cup maple syrup

Directions:
1. In your pressure cooker, mix nut milk with water, rice, cream and maple syrup, stir well, cover and cook on High for 20 minutes.
2. Stir pudding again, divide into bowls and serve.

Nutrition: calories 251, fat 5, fiber 3, carbs 6, protein 5

Pumpkin Oatmeal

Preparation time: 10 minutes
Cooking time: 3 minutes
Servings: 2

Ingredients:
- 2 cups water
- ½ cup steel cut oats
- ½ cup pumpkin puree
- ½ teaspoon cinnamon powder
- ½ teaspoon allspice
- ½ teaspoon vanilla extract

For the topping:
- 2 tablespoons pecans, chopped
- 3 tablespoons brown sugar
- ½ tablespoon cinnamon powder

Directions:

1. In your pressure cooker, mix water with steel cut oats, pumpkin puree, ½ teaspoon cinnamon, allspice and vanilla, stir, cover and cook on High for 3 minutes.
2. Meanwhile, in a bowl, mix pecans with brown sugar and ½ tablespoon cinnamon powder and stir well.
3. Divide pumpkin oatmeal into 2 bowls, spread some of the pecans topping and serve.

Nutrition: calories 132, fat 1, fiber 2, carbs 2, protein 4

Buckwheat Porridge

Preparation time: 10 minutes
Cooking time: 6 minutes
Servings: 2

Ingredients:
- 1 cup buckwheat groats, rinsed
- ¼ cup raisins
- 3 cups rice milk
- 1 banana, peeled and sliced
- ½ teaspoon vanilla extract

Directions:
1. Put buckwheat in your pressure cooker, add raisins, milk, banana and vanilla, stir a bit, cover and cook on High for 6 minutes.
2. Divide buckwheat porridge into 2 bowls and serve for breakfast.

Nutrition: calories 162, fat 1, fiber 2, carbs 2, protein 5

Breakfast Tortillas

Preparation time: 10 minutes
Cooking time: 13 minutes
Servings: 6

Ingredients:
- 2 pound red potatoes, cubed
- 4 eggs, whisked
- 6 ounces ham, cubed
- 6 tortillas, for serving
- ¼ cup yellow onion, chopped
- 1 cup water, for the pressure cooker

Directions:
1. In a bowl, mix eggs with ham, onion and potatoes and whisk well.
2. Add this to a baking dish and spread.
3. Add water to your pressure cooker, add trivet, add baking dish inside, cover and cook on High for 13 minutes.
4. Arrange tortillas on a working surface, divide eggs mix on each, wrap and serve for breakfast.

Nutrition: calories 212, fat 3, fiber 7, carbs 9, protein 12

Pancake

Preparation time: 10 minutes
Cooking time: 45 minutes
Servings: 4

Ingredients:
- 2 cups white flour
- 2 eggs
- 1 and ½ cups milk
- 2 tablespoons sugar
- 2 and ½ teaspoons baking powder

Directions:
1. In a bowl, mix flour with eggs, milk, sugar and baking powder and whisk really well.
2. Add this to your pressure cooker, spread, cover and cook on Manual for 45 minutes.
3. Leave your pancake to cool down, slice, divide between plates and serve.

Nutrition: calories 251, fat 5, fiber 2, carbs 6, protein 3

Squash Porridge

Preparation time: 10 minutes
Cooking time: 8 minutes
Servings: 2

Ingredients:
- 3 small apples cored
- 1 small delicata squash
- 1 and ½ tablespoon gelatin
- 2 tablespoon slippery elm
- ½ cup water
- 1 and ½ tablespoons maple syrup
- A pinch of cinnamon powder
- A pinch of ginger powder
- A pinch of cloves, ground

Directions:
1. Put the squash and apples in your pressure cooker, add water, cinnamon, ginger and cloves, cover and cook on Manual for 8 minutes.
2. Leave squash to cool down, transfer to a cutting board, halve, deseed and transfer to your blender.
3. Add apples, water and spices as well and pulse really well.
4. Add slippery elm, maple syrup and gelatin, blend well, divide into 2 big bowls and serve for breakfast.

Nutrition: calories 174, fat 2, fiber 1, carbs 3, protein 4

Breakfast Banana Bread

Preparation time: 10 minutes
Cooking time: 50 minutes
Servings: 2

Ingredients:
- 2 bananas, peeled and mashed
- ½ tablespoon vanilla
- ½ stick butter, soft
- ¼ cup sugar

- 1 cup flour
- 1 egg
- ½ teaspoon baking powder
- 1 cup water
- Cooking spray

Directions:
1. In a bowl, mix banana puree with vanilla, butter, sugar, flour, egg and baking powder and stir well until you obtain a bread batter.
2. Grease a loaf pan with cooking spray and pour bread mixture into it.
3. Add the water to your pressure cooker, add the trivet, and loaf pan inside, cover and cook on High for 50 minutes.
4. Divide breakfast bread into 2 plates and serve for breakfast.

Nutrition: calories 261, fat 3, fiber 3, carbs 6, protein 7

Millet and Oats Porridge

Preparation time: 10 minutes
Cooking time: 13 minutes
Servings: 8

Ingredients:
- 1 cup millet
- ½ cup rolled oats
- 3 cups water
- ½ teaspoon ginger powder
- 2 apples, cored and chopped

Directions:
1. Set your pressure cooker on sauté mode, add millet, stir and toast for 3 minutes.
2. Add oats, water, ginger and apples, stir, cover and cook on High for 10 minutes.
3. Stir porridge again, divide into bowls and serve.

Nutrition: calories 200, fat 2, fiber 3, carbs 4, protein 5

Sweet Potato Hash

Preparation time: 10 minutes
Cooking time: 10 minutes
Servings: 4

Ingredients:
- 1 tablespoon Italian seasoning
- 6 eggs
- 1 sweet potato, cubed
- ½ pound pork sausage, ground
- 1 yellow onion, chopped
- 2 cups water, for the pressure cooker

Directions:
1. Set your pressure cooker on sauté mode, add onion, sausage meat and sweet potato, stir, cook for 5 minutes and transfer to a baking dish.
2. In a bowl, mix eggs with Italian seasoning, whisk well and pour over sausage mixture.

3. Add the water to your pressure cooker, add trivet, add baking dish inside, cover and cook on High for 5 minutes.
4. Leave hash to cool down a bit, divide between plates and serve.

Nutrition: calories 216, fat 6, fiber 3, carbs 12, protein 5

Blueberry Breakfast Delight

Preparation time: 5 minutes
Cooking time: 6 minutes
Servings: 2

Ingredients:
- 2/3 cup old fashioned oats
- 2/3 cup Greek yogurt
- 2/3 cup almond milk
- 2/3 cup blueberries
- 2 tablespoons chia seeds
- 1 teaspoon sugar
- A pinch of cinnamon powder
- ½ teaspoon vanilla
- 1 and ½ cups water

Directions:
1. In a heatproof bowl, mix oats with milk, yogurt, blueberries, chia seeds, sugar, cinnamon and vanilla and stir.
2. Put the water in your pressure cooker, add the trivet, add the bowl inside, cover and cook on High for 6 minutes.
3. Stir blueberries mix again, divide into 2 bowls and serve.

Nutrition: calories 154, fat 2, fiber 1, carbs 2, protein 3

Breakfast Bacon Potatoes

Preparation time: 10 minutes
Cooking time: 7 minutes
Servings: 2

Ingredients:
- ½ pound red potatoes, cubed
- 1 bacon strip, chopped
- 1 teaspoon parsley, dried
- A pinch of salt and black pepper
- ½ teaspoon garlic powder
- 1.5-ounce cheddar cheese, grated
- 1 ounce ranch dressing
- 1 tablespoon water

Directions:
1. In your pressure cooker with potatoes with bacon, parsley, salt, pepper, garlic powder and water, stir a bit, cover and cook on Manual for 7 minutes.
2. Add cheese and dressing, toss, divide between 2 plates and serve for breakfast.

Nutrition: calories 258, fat 2, fiber 6, carbs 9, protein 12

Potato and Spinach Hash

Preparation time: 10 minutes
Cooking time: 10 minutes
Servings: 4

Ingredients:
- 3 sweet potatoes, baked, peeled and cubed
- 12 ounces chorizo, chopped
- 11 ounces baby spinach
- A pinch of salt
- 1 small yellow onion, chopped

Directions:
1. Set your pressure cooker on sauté mode, add chorizo and onion, stir and cook for 2-3 minutes.
2. Add potato cubes, baby spinach and salt, toss a bit, cover and cook on High for 7 minutes.
3. Divide between plates and serve for breakfast.

Nutrition: calories 192, fat 4, fiber 7, carbs 6, protein 2

Breakfast Banana Bread

Preparation time: 10 minutes
Cooking time: 1 hour
Servings: 8

Ingredients:
- 1 and ½ cups water, for the pressure cooker
- 1 and ½ cups steel cut oats
- 2 bananas, peeled and chopped
- 4 eggs, whisked
- 1/3 cup honey
- ½ teaspoon baking soda

Directions:
1. In your blender, mix oats with bananas, eggs, honey and baking soda, pulse well and pour into a loaf pan.
2. Add water to your pressure cooker, add trivet, add pan inside, cover and cook on High for 1 hour.
3. Slice, divide between plates and serve for breakfast.

Nutrition: calories 192, fat 5, fiber 5, carbs 6, protein 2

Veggie Breakfast Casserole

Preparation time: 10 minutes
Cooking time: 30 minutes
Servings: 2

Ingredients:
- 3 eggs
- 3 tablespoons milk
- 3 tablespoons white flour

- A pinch of salt and black pepper
- 1 small red bell pepper, chopped
- ½ cup tomatoes, chopped
- 1 green onion, chopped
- ½ cup cheddar cheese, shredded
- 1 small zucchini, chopped
- 1 cup water

Directions:
1. In a bowl, mix eggs with flour, milk, salt, pepper, bell pepper, tomatoes, onion, zucchini and half of the cheese and stir well.
2. Pour this into a heatproof dish and cover with some tin foil.
3. Put the water in your pressure cooker, add the trivet, and the dish with the veggies mix, cover cooker and cook on High for 30 minutes.
4. Uncover dish, sprinkle the rest of the cheese all over, divide between 2 plates and serve.

Nutrition: calories 200, fat 1, fiber 2, carbs 3, protein 8

Peach Breakfast

Preparation time: 10 minutes
Cooking time: 3 minutes
Servings: 2

Ingredients:
- 1 cup rolled oats
- ½ peach, chopped
- 2 cups water
- ½ teaspoon vanilla extract
- 1 tablespoon flax meal
- 3 tablespoons almonds, chopped
- Maple syrup to the taste

Directions:
1. In your pressure cooker, mix oats with peach, water and vanilla extract, stir a bit, cover and cook on High for 3 minutes.
2. Stir you oatmeal again, divide into 2 bowls, top with flax meal, almonds and maple syrup and serve for breakfast.

Nutrition: calories 143, fat 3, fiber 1, carbs 4, protein 6

Bread Pudding

Preparation time: 10 minutes
Cooking time: 15 minutes
Servings: 10

Ingredients:
- 1 bread loaf, cubed
- 2 cups coconut milk
- 4 eggs
- ½ cup butter
- ½ cup maple syrup
- 2 cups water, for your pressure cooker

Directions:
1. In a blender, mix coconut milk with eggs, butter and maple syrup and pulse well.
2. Transfer this to a pudding pan, add bread cubes, toss well and cover pan with tin foil.
3. Add the water to your pressure cooker, add trivet, add pudding pan, cover and cook on High for 15 minutes.
4. Divide between plates and serve for breakfast.

Nutrition: calories 271, fat 4, fiber 6, carbs 12, protein 10

Egg Muffins

Preparation time: 10 minutes
Cooking time: 8 minutes
Servings: 4

Ingredients:
- 1 and ½ cups water, for the pressure cooker
- 4 eggs
- 4 tablespoons cheddar cheese, shredded
- 4 bacon slices, cooked and crumbled
- 1 green onion, chopped
- A pinch of salt

Directions:
1. In a bowl, mix eggs with cheese, bacon, onion and salt, whisk well and divide into muffin cups.
2. Add the water to your pressure cooker, add steamer basket, add muffin cups inside, cover and cook on High for 8 minutes.
3. Divide muffins between plates and serve them for breakfast.

Nutrition: calories 182, fat 7, fiber 4, carbs 8, protein 12

Chocolate Bread Pudding

Preparation time: 10 minutes
Cooking time: 11 minutes
Servings: 2

Ingredients:
- 1 egg
- ¼ cup milk
- 2 cups challah bread, cubed
- ½ teaspoon cinnamon powder
- ¼ cup condensed milk
- 1/3 cup chocolate, cut into medium chunks
- 1 cup water

Directions:
1. In a bowl, mix egg with milk, condensed milk and cinnamon and stir.
2. Add bread cubes and chocolate, stir gently and divide this into 2 ramekins.
3. Put the water in your pressure cooker, add the trivet, add ramekins inside, cover and cook on High for 11 minutes.
4. Serve your puddings hot.

Nutrition: calories 164, fat 3, fiber 1, carbs 3, protein 3

Fruit Cobbler

Preparation time: 10 minutes
Cooking time: 10 minutes
Servings: 2

Ingredients:
- 1 plum, stone removed and chopped
- 1 apple, cored and chopped
- 1 pear, cored and chopped
- 3 tablespoons coconut oil
- 2 tablespoons honey
- ½ teaspoon cinnamon powder
- ¼ cup coconut, shredded and unsweetened
- 2 tablespoons sunflower seeds, roasted
- ¼ cup pecans, chopped

Directions:
1. In the steel bowl of your pressure cooker, mix plum with apple, pear, oil, honey and cinnamon, stir, cover, steam for 10 minutes and transfer to a bowl.
2. Put pecans, sunflower seeds and coconut in your pressure cooker bowl, set on Sauté mode, cook for 5 minutes and sprinkle all over fruits mix.
3. Divide into 2 bowls and serve for breakfast.

Nutrition: calories 132, fat 2, fiber 3, carbs 4, protein 4

Buckwheat Porridge

Preparation time: 10 minutes
Cooking time: 6 minutes
Servings: 4

Ingredients:
- 1 cup buckwheat
- 1 banana, peeled and sliced
- 3 cups rice milk
- 1 teaspoon cinnamon powder
- ¼ cup raisins

Directions:
1. In your pressure cooker, mix buckwheat with banana, milk, cinnamon and raisins, stir, cover and cook on High for 6 minutes.
2. Stir porridge, divide into bowls and serve.

Nutrition: calories 182, fat 4, fiber 3, carbs 6, protein 7

Squash Porridge

Preparation time: 10 minutes
Cooking time: 8 minutes
Servings: 4

Ingredients:
- 4 small apples, cored and chopped
- 1 squash, peeled and chopped
- 2 tablespoons cinnamon powder
- 2 tablespoons maple syrup
- ½ cup water

Directions:
1. In your pressure cooker, mix apples with squash, cinnamon, maple syrup and water, stir, cover and cook on High for 8 minutes.
2. Stir porridge one more time, divide into bowls and serve.

Nutrition: calories 162, fat 5, fiber 6, carbs 8, protein 2

Espresso Oatmeal

Preparation time: 10 minutes
Cooking time: 10 minutes
Servings: 2

Ingredients:
- 1 and ¼ cups water
- 1 tablespoon white sugar
- ½ cup steel cut oats
- ½ cup milk
- ½ teaspoon espresso powder
- 1 teaspoon vanilla extract
- A pinch of salt
- Grated chocolate for serving
- Whipped cream for serving

Directions:
1. In your pressure cooker, mix water with oats, milk, sugar, salt and espresso powder, stir, cover and cook on High for 10 minutes.
2. Add vanilla extract, stir, cover pot, leave everything aside for 5 minutes and divide into bowls.
3. Top with grated chocolate and whipped cream and serve.

Nutrition: calories 200, fat 2, fiber 1, carbs 3, protein 4

Breakfast Rice Pudding

Preparation time: 10 minutes
Cooking time: 20 minutes
Servings: 2

Ingredients:
- 1 cup milk
- 1 cup water
- 1 cup basmati rice
- 4 tablespoons heavy cream
- 2 tablespoons maple syrup
- ½ teaspoon vanilla extract
- A pinch of salt

Directions:
1. In your pressure cooker, mix milk with water, rice, salt and maple syrup, stir, cover and cook on High for 20 minutes.
2. Add cream and vanilla extract, stir, divide into 2 bowls and serve for breakfast.

Nutrition: calories 193, fat 3, fiber 1, carbs 3, protein 4

Apple Butter

Preparation time: 10 minutes
Cooking time: 10 minutes
Servings: 6

Ingredients:
- 30 ounces pumpkin puree
- 4 apples, cored, peeled and cubed
- 12 ounces apple cider
- 1 cup sugar
- 1 tablespoon pumpkin pie spice

Directions:
1. In your pressure cooker, mix pumpkin puree with apples, cider, sugar and spice, stir, cover and cook on High for 10 minutes.
2. Stir butter again, divide into small jars and serve cold for breakfast.

Nutrition: calories 182, fat 6, fiber 7, carbs 8, protein 2

Veggie Quiche

Preparation time: 10 minutes
Cooking time: 30 minutes
Servings: 6

Ingredients:
- ½ cup milk
- 8 eggs, whisked
- 1 red bell pepper, chopped
- 2 green onions, chopped
- Salt to the taste
- 1 cup water, for the pressure cooker

Directions:
1. In a bowl, mix eggs with milk, bell pepper, onions and salt, whisk well and pour into a pan.
2. Add the water to your pressure cooker, add trivet inside, add pan, cover it with tin foil, cover cooker and cook on High for 30 minutes.
3. Slice quiche, divide between plates and serve for breakfast.

Nutrition: calories 200, fat 3, fiber 4, carbs 7, protein 6

Strawberry Quinoa Bowl

Preparation time: 10 minutes
Cooking time: 1 minute:
Servings: 2

Ingredients:
- 1 cup quinoa
- 1 tablespoon honey
- 1 and ½ cups water
- ½ teaspoon vanilla
- A pinch of pumpkin pie spice
- 1 cup strawberries, sliced
- ½ cup vanilla yogurt

Directions:
1. In your pressure cooker, mix quinoa with water, honey, vanilla, pumpkin pie spice, yogurt and strawberries, stir a bit, cover and cook on High for 1 minute.
2. Leave quinoa mix aside for 10 minutes, fluff with a fork, divide into 2 bowls and serve for breakfast.

Nutrition: calories 173, fat 2, fiber 2, carbs 3, protein 7

Cornmeal Porridge

Preparation time: 10 minutes
Cooking time: 20 minutes
Servings: 2

Ingredients:

- 2 cups water
- ½ cup milk
- ½ cup cornmeal
- 1 cinnamon stick
- 2 pimiento berries
- ½ teaspoon vanilla extract
- A pinch of nutmeg, ground
- 1/3 cup condensed milk

Directions:
1. In your pressure cooker, mix water with milk and cornmeal and stir really well.
2. Add cinnamon, berries, nutmeg, vanilla extract and condensed milk, stir, cover and cook on High for 6 minutes.
3. Divide into 2 bowls and serve for breakfast.

Nutrition: calories 200, fat 1, fiber 3, carbs 3, protein 8

Breakfast Cobbler

Preparation time: 10 minutes
Cooking time: 15 minutes
Servings: 2

Ingredients:
- 1 plum, stone removed and chopped
- 1 apple, cored and chopped
- 3 tablespoons coconut oil
- 2 tablespoons honey
- ¼ cup coconut, shredded

Directions:
1. In your pressure cooker, mix plum with apple, half of the oil and honey, stir, cover and cook on Manual for 10 minutes.
2. Transfer this to bowls and clean your pressure cooker.
3. Set the cooker on sauté mode, add the rest of the oil, heat it up, add coconut, stir and toast for 5 minutes.
4. Sprinkle this over fruit mixture and serve.

Nutrition: calories 172, fat 7, fiber 3, carbs 6, protein 2

Tofu and Sweet Potato Mix

Preparation time: 10 minutes
Cooking time: 10 minutes
Servings: 4

Ingredients:
- 1 pound extra firm tofu, cubed
- 1 cup sweet potato, chopped
- 2 teaspoons sesame seed oil
- 1/3 cup veggie stock
- 2 tablespoons red pepper sauce

Directions:

1. Set your pressure cooker on sauté mode, add oil, heat it up, add sweet potato, stir and cook for 2 minutes.
2. Add tofu and stock, stir, cook for 2 minutes more, cover cooker and cook on High for 3 minutes.
3. Add pepper sauce, toss, divide into bowls and serve for breakfast.

Nutrition: calories 172, fat 7, fiber 1, carbs 20, protein 6

Breakfast Apple Dish

Preparation time: 10 minutes
Cooking time: 8 minutes
Servings: 2

Ingredients:
- 1 teaspoon cinnamon powder
- 2 apples, cored, peeled and cut into medium chunks
- A pinch of nutmeg, ground
- ½ cup water
- ½ tablespoon maple syrup
- 2 tablespoons butter
- 2/3 cup old fashioned rolled oats
- 2 tablespoons flour
- 2 tablespoons brown sugar

Directions:
1. Put apples in your pressure cooker, sprinkle cinnamon and nutmeg and add water and maple syrup over them.
2. In a bowl, mix butter with oats, flour and sugar and stir.
3. Drop spoonfuls of this mix over apples, cover and cook on High for 8 minutes.
4. Divide between 2 plates and serve.

Nutrition: calories 183, fat 3, fiber 1, carbs 3, protein 6

Brown Rice Mix

Preparation time: 10 minutes
Cooking time: 40 minutes
Servings: 2

Ingredients:
- 1/3 cup brown rice
- 2 cups mushroom stock
- 1 cup bok choy, chopped
- 1 tablespoon ginger, grated
- 1 cup shiitake mushrooms, chopped
- 1 garlic clove, minced
- ½ cup water
- 1 tablespoon scallions, chopped
- A drizzle of soy sauce

Directions:
1. In your pressure cooker, mix rice with mushroom stock, bok choy, ginger, mushrooms, garlic and water, stir, cover and cook on Manual for 40 minutes.

2. Divide into bowls, sprinkle scallions on top, drizzle soy sauce all over and serve for breakfast.

Nutrition: calories 193, fat 3, fiber 1, carbs 2, protein 4

Quinoa and Tomatoes Breakfast Mix

Preparation time: 10 minutes
Cooking time: 12 minutes
Servings: 6

Ingredients:
- 1 small yellow onion, chopped
- 28 ounces canned tomatoes, chopped
- 14 ounces coconut milk
- ¼ cup quinoa
- 1 tablespoon ginger, grated

Directions:
1. In your pressure cooker, mix onion with quinoa, tomatoes, milk and ginger, stir, cover and cook on High for 12 minutes
2. Stir one more time, divide into bowls and serve for breakfast.

Nutrition: calories 260, fat 9, fiber 11, carbs 30, protein 7

Breakfast Rice and Chickpeas Medley

Preparation time: 10 minutes
Cooking time: 27 minutes
Servings: 4

Ingredients:
- 1 tablespoon olive oil
- 1 red onion, chopped
- 1 cup chickpeas
- 14 ounces tomatoes, chopped
- 1 and ½ cups brown rice

Directions:
1. Set your pressure cooker on sauté mode, add the oil, heat it up, add onion, stir and cook for 7 minutes.
2. Add tomatoes, chickpeas and rice, stir, cover and cook on High for 20 minutes.
3. Stir one more time, divide into bowls and serve for breakfast.

Nutrition: calories 253, fat 4, fiber 3, carbs 9, protein 7

Quinoa Salad

Preparation time: 10 minutes
Cooking time: 5 minutes
Servings: 2

Ingredients:
- ½ cup quinoa
- 1 cup strawberries, sliced
- 1 cup water

- 1 cup pecans, chopped
- 2 green onion, chopped
- ½ cup broccoli, chopped

For the dressing:
- A pinch of garlic powder
- A drizzle of olive oil
- 1 tablespoon balsamic vinegar
- ½ tablespoon basil, chopped

Directions:
1. Put water and quinoa in your pressure cooker, cover, cook on High for 5 minutes, leave aside for 10 more minutes, fluff with a fork and transfer to a bowl.
2. Add strawberries, pecans, onion and broccoli and toss.
3. In a separate bowl, mix garlic powder with oil, basil and vinegar and whisk really well.
4. Add this to quinoa salad, toss, divide between 2 plates and serve for breakfast.

Nutrition: calories 124, fat 2, fiber 1, carbs 3, protein 4

Breakfast Beans

Preparation time: 10 minutes
Cooking time: 15 minutes
Servings: 2

Ingredients:
- ½ cup anasazi beans, soaked overnight and drained
- 1 cup onion, sliced
- ½ tablespoon olive oil
- 1/3 cup mushrooms, sliced
- A pinch of sugar
- ¼ teaspoon liquid smoke
- 1 cup beef stock
- ½ teaspoon smoked paprika
- 1 teaspoon red miso
- 1/3 cup water
- ½ teaspoon tamari

Directions:
1. Put the oil in your pressure cooker, set on sauté mode, heat it up, add sugar and onion, stir and sauté for 10 minutes.
2. Add beans, mushrooms, smoke, beef stock, water, paprika, miso and tamari, stir, cover and cook on High for 5 minutes.
3. Divide between 2 plates and serve for breakfast.

Nutrition: calories 193, fat 4, fiber 4, carbs 6, protein 8

Breakfast Arugula Salad

Preparation time: 10 minutes
Cooking time: 15 minutes
Servings: 6

Ingredients:
- 2 cups water

- 1 cup kamut grains, soaked for 12 hours
- 1 teaspoon sunflower oil
- 4 ounces arugula
- 2 blood oranges, peeled and cut into medium segments

Directions:
1. In your pressure cooker, mix kamut grains with sunflower oil and the water, stir, cover and cook on High for 15 minutes.
2. Drain kamut, transfer to a bowl, add arugula and orange segments, toss well and serve for breakfast.

Nutrition: calories 163, fat 6, fiber 2, carbs 7, protein 3

Cranberry Beans Salad

Preparation time: 10 minutes
Cooking time: 15 minutes
Servings: 4

Ingredients:
- 1 cup cranberry beans, soaked and drained
- 1 and ½ cups green beans
- ½ red onion, chopped
- 5 tablespoons apple cider vinegar
- 4 tablespoons olive oil
- 1 cup water, for the pressure cooker

Directions:
1. Put the water in your pressure cooker, add steamer basket, add cranberry and green beans inside, cover and cook on High for 15 minutes.
2. Drain all beans, transfer them to a salad bowl, add onion, vinegar and oil, toss and serve for breakfast.

Nutrition: calories 170, fat 4, fiber 7, carbs 15, protein 6

Wild Rice Breakfast Salad

Preparation time: 10 minutes
Cooking time: 30 minutes
Servings: 2

Ingredients:
- 1 garlic clove, minced
- ½ shallot, chopped
- ½ teaspoon rosemary, dried
- 1 and ½ cups veggie stock
- ½ cup wild rice
- Juice from 1 orange
- 1/3 cup cranberries, dried
- 1 tablespoon maple syrup
- ½ tablespoon mustard
- ½ tablespoon tamari
- 1/3 cup pecans, chopped

Directions:
1. Set your pressure cooker on sauté mode, add half of the stock, shallot and garlic, stir and sauté for 5 minutes.
2. Add rosemary, rice, the rest of the stock, cranberries and orange juice, stir, cover and cook on Manual for 25 minutes.
3. Add maple syrup, tamari, mustard and pecans, stir, divide between 2 plates and serve for breakfast.

Nutrition: calories 254, fat 1, fiber 4, carbs 10, protein 5

Rice and Black Beans Breakfast Dish

Preparation time: 10 minutes
Cooking time: 28 minutes
Servings: 2

Ingredients:
- ½ cup onion, chopped
- 2 garlic cloves, minced
- 1 cup brown rice
- 1 cup black beans
- 4 and ½ cups water
- A pinch of salt
- 1 lime, cut into wedges
- 1 avocado, pitted, peeled and sliced

Directions:
1. In your pressure cooker, mix rice with beans, water, salt, garlic and onion, stir, cover and cook on Manual for 28 minutes.
2. Divide into 2 bowls, top with avocado pieces and serve for breakfast with lime wedges on the side.

Nutrition: calories 200, fat 4, fiber 5, carbs 10, protein 8

Pineapple and Peas Breakfast Curry

Preparation time: 10 minutes
Cooking time: 20 minutes
Servings: 4

Ingredients:
- 1 cup peas, soaked and drained
- 4 cups water
- 1 teaspoon curry powder
- 1 cup canned pineapple, cut into medium chunks
- ¼ cup cashew butter

Directions:
1. In your pressure cooker, mix peas with water, cover and cook on High for 16 minutes.
2. Drain peas, transfer to a bowl, clean the cooker and set it in sauté mode.
3. Add peas, curry powder, pineapple and cashew butter, toss well, cook for 1 minute, cover pot, cook on High for 2 minutes, divide into bowls and serve for breakfast.

Nutrition: calories 181, fat 6, fiber 6, carbs 15, protein 8

Brussels Sprouts and Potato Bowls

Preparation time: 10 minutes
Cooking time: 7 minutes
Servings: 4

Ingredients:
- 1 and ½ pounds Brussels sprouts, trimmed
- 1 cup small potatoes, roughly chopped
- 1 and ½ tablespoons olive oil
- ½ cup veggie stock
- Salt to the taste

Directions:
1. In your pressure cooker, mix sprouts with potatoes, stock and salt, stir a bit, cover and cook on High for 5 minutes.
2. Set the cooker on sauté mode, add oil, toss a bit, cook for 1-2 minutes, divide into bowls and serve right away for breakfast

Nutrition: calories 121, fat 4, fiber 7, carbs 14, protein 5

Parsnip and Quinoa Breakfast Mix

Preparation time: 10 minutes
Cooking time: 30 minutes
Servings: 2

Ingredients:
- 1 pound parsnips, peeled and roughly chopped
- 1 and ½ tablespoon balsamic vinegar
- 2 tablespoons veggie stock
- 1 tablespoon maple syrup
- A pinch of salt and black pepper
- ½ cup quinoa, already cooked
- 1 avocado, pitted, peeled and chopped
- 3 tablespoons cashews, roasted
- Juice from ½ lemon

Directions:
1. In your pressure cooker, mix parsnips with vinegar and stock, stir, cover, cook on High for 3 minutes, transfer to a bowl, mix with maple syrup, a pinch of salt and pepper and toss.
2. In a large bowl, mix quinoa with cashews and avocado and toss.
3. Add parsnips, toss again, divide into 2 bowls and serve with lemon juice on top.

Nutrition: calories 200, fat 4, fiber 1, carbs 3, protein 4

Potato Salad

Preparation time: 10 minutes
Cooking time: 4 minutes
Servings: 2

Ingredients:
- 2 potatoes, peeled and cubed

- 2 eggs
- 1 and ½ cups water
- 1 small yellow onion, chopped
- ¼ cup mayonnaise
- 1 tablespoon parsley, chopped
- 1 tablespoon mustard
- A pinch of salt and black pepper

Directions:
1. Put the water in your pressure cooker, add the steamer basket, add eggs and potatoes, cover and cook on High for 4 minutes.
2. Drain potatoes and eggs, peel everything, chop and transfer to a bowl.
3. Add onion, parsley, salt and pepper and toss.
4. Add mustard and mayo, toss again, divide into 2 bowls and serve for breakfast.

Nutrition: calories 194, fat 4, fiber 2, carbs 5, protein 8

Italian Eggplants Bowls

Preparation time: 10 minutes
Cooking time: 9 minutes
Servings: 3

Ingredients:
- 4 cups eggplant, cubed
- 1 tablespoon olive oil
- 1 tablespoon garlic powder
- 3 garlic cloves, minced
- 1 cup tomato sauce

Directions:
1. Set your pressure cooker on Sauté mode, add oil, heat it up, add garlic, stir and cook for a couple of minutes.
2. Add eggplant, garlic powder and tomato sauce, stir, cover and cook on High for 7 minutes.
3. Divide into bowls and serve for breakfast.

Nutrition: calories 172, fat 4, fiber 5, carbs 7, protein

Cauliflower and Barley Bowls

Preparation time: 10 minutes
Cooking time: 34 minutes
Servings: 4

Ingredients:
- 4 tablespoons extra virgin olive oil
- 1 cauliflower head, florets separated
- ½ cup parmesan, grated
- 1 cup pearl barley
- 3 cups chicken stock

Directions:
1. Set your pressure cooker on Sauté mode, add 3 tablespoons oil, heat it up, add cauliflower, some salt and pepper, stir and sauté for 10 minutes.

2. Add half of the parmesan, stir and cook for 3-4 minutes more.
3. Add the rest of the oil, barley and stock, stir, cover and cook on High for 20 minutes.
4. Add the rest of the parmesan, toss, divide into bowls and serve for breakfast.

Nutrition: calories 252, fat 4, fiber 6, carbs 20, protein 6

Breakfast Egg Salad

Preparation time: 10 minutes
Cooking time: 5 minutes
Servings: 2

Ingredients:
- 4 eggs
- 2 tablespoons mayonnaise
- A pinch of salt and black pepper
- A drizzle of olive oil
- 1 cup water

Directions:
1. Grease a baking dish with a drizzle of oil and crack eggs into the dish.
2. Put the water in your pressure cooker, add the trivet, add the baking dish inside, cover and cook on High for 5 minutes.
3. Leave eggs to cool down, mash them with a potato masher, transfer to a bowl, mix with salt, pepper and mayo, stir well and serve for breakfast.

Nutrition: calories 193, fat 2, fiber 1, carbs 2, protein 4

Strawberry Jam

Preparation time: 20 minutes
Cooking time: 4 minutes
Servings: 2

Ingredients:
- 2 pounds strawberries, halved
- ¼ cup sugar
- Juice from ½ orange

Directions:
1. In your pressure cooker, mix strawberries with orange juice and sugar, stir and leave them aside for 20 minutes.
2. Cover pot, cook your jam on Manual for 4 minutes, blend everything using an immersion blender and serve for breakfast.

Nutrition: calories 164, fat 4, fiber 2, carbs 5, protein 3

Celeriac Breakfast Mix

Preparation time: 10 minutes
Cooking time: 8 minutes
Servings: 6

Ingredients:

- 2 teaspoons parsley, dried
- 3 bacon strips
- 2 pounds celeriac, peeled and cubed
- 4 ounces cheddar cheese, shredded
- 2 tablespoons chicken stock

Directions:
1. Set your pressure cooker on sauté mode, add bacon, stir and cook for a couple of minutes.
2. Add parsley, celeriac and stock, stir, cover and cook on High for 6 minutes.
3. Add cheese, toss, divide between plates and serve for breakfast.

Nutrition: calories 164, fat 3, fiber 2, carbs 6, protein 7

Turkey Breast Breakfast Mix

Preparation time: 10 minutes
Cooking time: 7 minutes
Servings: 4

Ingredients:
- 4 avocado slices
- 4 turkey breast slices, already cooked
- 2 tablespoons olive oil
- 4 eggs, whisked
- 2 tablespoons veggie stock

Directions:
1. Set your pressure cooker on sauté mode, oil, heat it up, add turkey, brown for a couple of minutes and divide between plates.
2. Heat up the cooker again, add eggs and veggie stock, stir, cover and cook on High for 5 minutes.
3. Divide eggs and avocado slices next to turkey breast slices and serve for breakfast.

Nutrition: calories 185, fat 2, fiber 2, carbs 16, protein 6

Fresh Peach Jam

Preparation time: 10 minutes
Cooking time: 16 minutes
Servings: 2

Ingredients:
- 2 cups peaches, stones removed and roughly chopped
- Juice from 1/3 lemon
- ¼ cup honey
- ½ tablespoon vanilla extract

Directions:
1. In your pressure cooker, mix peaches with lemon juice, honey and vanilla, stir, cover and cook on High for 1 minute,
2. Turn pressure cooker to Sauté mode, cook your jam for 15 minutes more, blend using an immersion blender and serve for breakfast.

Nutrition: calories 164, fat 2, fiber 1, carbs 2, protein 3

Breakfast Orange Marmalade

Preparation time: 10 minutes
Cooking time: 10 minutes
Servings: 2

Ingredients:
- ½ pound oranges, thinly sliced
- ½ cup water
- 1 cup sugar

Directions:
1. In your pressure cooker, mix oranges with water and sugar, stir, cover and cook on High for 10 minutes.
2. Serve this for breakfast the next day!

Nutrition: calories 153, fat 3, fiber 2, carbs 3, protein 6

Pomegranate Oatmeal

Preparation time: 5 minutes
Cooking time: 3 minutes
Servings: 4

Ingredients:
- 2 cups coconut, shredded
- 2 cup water
- 1 cup pomegranate juice
- Seeds of 2 pomegranates
- 2 tablespoon sugar

Directions:
1. In your pressure cooker, mix coconut with water and pomegranate juice, stir, cover and cook on High for 3 minutes.
2. Add pomegranate seeds and sugar, stir, divide into bowls and serve for breakfast.

Nutrition: calories 153, fat 3, fiber 5, carbs 10, protein 4

Cheesy Cauliflower Bowls

Preparation time: 10 minutes
Cooking time: 4 minutes
Servings: 6

Ingredients:
- 1 cauliflower head, florets separated
- ½ cup veggie stock
- 1/3 cup parmesan, grated
- 1 tablespoon parsley, chopped
- 3 tablespoons olive oil

Directions:
1. In a bowl, mix oil with cauliflower florets, toss and transfer to your pressure cooker.
2. Add stock, cover cooker and cook on High for 4 minutes.

3. Add parsley and parmesan, toss, divide into bowls and serve for breakfast.

Nutrition: calories 120, fat 2, fiber 3, carbs 5, protein 3

Breakfast Potatoes

Preparation time: 10 minutes
Cooking time: 25 minutes
Servings: 2

Ingredients:
- 2 gold potatoes
- 4 cups water
- ½ red bell pepper, chopped
- ½ pound pork sausage
- 1 small yellow onion, chopped
- ½ yellow onion, chopped
- A pinch of potato seasoning
- A pinch of garlic powder
- A pinch of salt and black pepper
- 1 tablespoon green onions, chopped
- Hot sauce to the taste
- Cooking spray
- 2 eggs
- 2 tablespoons apple cider vinegar

Directions:
1. Put the water in your pressure cooker, add the steamer basket, add potatoes inside, cover and cook on High for 20 minutes.
2. Meanwhile, grease a pan with cooking spray, heat it up over medium heat, add yellow onion, stir and cook for 2 minutes.
3. Add seasoning, sausage, salt, pepper, garlic powder, orange and red pepper, stir and cook for 2 minutes.
4. Drain potatoes, split them a bit, scrape sides, leave skins aside and transfer potato pulp to a bowl.
5. Add onion and sausage mix, stir well and stuff potatoes with this mix.
6. Put some water in a pot, add the vinegar, bring to a boil over medium heat, crack eggs, poach them for 5 minutes and divide them on top of potatoes.
7. Sprinkle green onions, drizzle hot sauce all over and serve them for breakfast.

Nutrition: calories 214, fat 3, fiber 1, carbs 2, protein 4

Sweet Potatoes Casserole

Preparation time: 10 minutes
Cooking time: 30 minutes
Servings: 2

Ingredients:
- 1 and ½ cups water
- 1 tablespoon olive oil
- 1 teaspoon garlic, minced
- ½ cup leeks, chopped

- ½ cup kale, chopped
- 3 eggs
- 4 tablespoons sweet potato, grated
- ½ cup sausage, cooked

Directions:
1. Put the oil in your pressure cooker, set it on sauté mode, heat it up, add garlic, leeks and kale, stir, cook for 2 minutes, transfer them to a bowl and clean the pot.
2. Add sweet potato, sausage and eggs to the bowl with the veggies, whisk everything and pour into a greased heatproof dish.
3. Add the water to your pressure cooker, add the trivet, add the dish inside, cover with a tin foil, cover the cooker as well and cook on Manual for 25 minutes.
4. Divide between 2 plates and serve for breakfast.

Nutrition: calories 200, fat 1, fiber 3, carbs 6, protein 9

Swiss Chard Salad

Preparation time: 10 minutes
Cooking time: 5 minutes
Servings: 4

Ingredients:
- 1 bunch Swiss chard, cut into strips
- 2 tablespoons olive oil
- 1 tablespoon balsamic vinegar
- ¼ teaspoon red pepper flakes
- ¼ cup pine nuts, toasted

Directions:
1. Set your pressure cooker on sauté mode, add oil, heat it up, add chard, stir and cook for 2 minutes.
2. Add pepper flakes and vinegar, stir, cover and cook on High for 3 minutes.
3. Add pine nuts, toss, divide into bowls and serve for breakfast.

Nutrition: calories 110, fat 2, fiber 1, carbs 6, protein 4

Beets Spread

Preparation time: 10 minutes
Cooking time: 12 minutes
Servings: 6

Ingredients:
- 8 carrots, chopped
- 4 beets, peeled and chopped
- 1 cup veggie stock
- ¼ cup lemon juice
- 1 bunch basil, chopped

Directions:
1. In your pressure cooker, mix beets with stock and carrots, stir, cover and cook on High for 12 minutes.

2. Blend using an immersion blender, add lemon juice and basil, stir, divide into bowls and serve for breakfast.

Nutrition: calories 100, fat 1, fiber 6, carbs 10, protein 3

Millet Porridge

Preparation time: 10 minutes
Cooking time: 10 minutes
Servings: 2

Ingredients:
- 3 tablespoons millet
- 1 cup water
- 1 small apple, cored and chopped
- 2 tablespoons rolled oats
- ¼ teaspoon cinnamon powder
- ¼ teaspoon ginger powder
- A pinch of salt

Directions:
1. In your pressure cooker, mix millet with oats, water, apple, cinnamon, ginger and salt, stir, cover and cook on High for 10 minutes.
2. Divide into 2 bowls and serve.

Nutrition: calories 132, fat 1, fiber 2, carbs 2, protein 3

Quinoa with Sausages

Preparation time: 10 minutes
Cooking time: 6 minutes
Servings: 2

Ingredients:
- ½ pound sausage meat, casings removed
- 1 tablespoon olive oil
- 1 small yellow onion, chopped
- ½ teaspoon sweet paprika
- A pinch of turmeric powder
- 1 cup quinoa
- 1 cup chicken stock
- 1 red bell pepper, chopped
- ½ small broccoli head, florets separated
- 1 ounce Bella mushrooms, halved

Directions:
1. Put the oil in your pressure cooker, set on sauté mode, heat it up, add sausage and onion, stir and brown for a few minutes.
2. Add turmeric and paprika and stir.
3. Add stock, quinoa, bell pepper, mushrooms and bell pepper, stir, cover and cook on High for 1 minute.
4. Leave pressure cooker aside covered for 10 minutes, fluff quinoa with a fork, divide into 2 bowls and serve.

Nutrition: calories 174, fat 2, fiber 1, carbs 3, protein 4

Avocado Spread

Preparation time: 10 minutes
Cooking time: 2 minutes
Servings: 4

Ingredients:
- ½ cup cilantro, chopped
- 2 avocados, pitted, peeled and halved
- ¼ teaspoon stevia
- Juice of 2 limes
- 1 cup coconut milk
- 1 cup water, for the pressure cooker

Directions:
1. Add the water to your pressure cooker, add the steamer basket, add avocados, cover and cook on High for 2 minutes.
2. Transfer to your blender, add cilantro, stevia, lime juice and coconut milk, blend well, divide into small bowls and serve for breakfast.

Nutrition: calories 190, fat 6, fiber 4, carbs 10, protein 4

Pinto Beans Breakfast Salad

Preparation time: 10 minutes
Cooking time: 30 minutes
Servings: 2

Ingredients:
- ½ pound pinto beans, soaked and drained
- 1 tablespoon olive oil
- ½ yellow onion, chopped
- 1 and ½ cups veggie stock
- 1 red bell pepper, roughly chopped

Directions:
1. In your pressure cooker, mix beans with stock, stir, cover and cook on High for 30 minutes.
2. Drain beans, transfer them to a bowl, add onion, bell pepper and oil, toss, divide into bowls and serve for breakfast.

Nutrition: calories 201, fat 5, fiber 7, carbs 16, protein 5

Breakfast Chickpeas Spread

Preparation time: 10 minutes
Cooking time: 18 minutes
Servings: 2

Ingredients:
- 1/3 cup chickpeas
- 2 garlic cloves
- 1 bay leaf

- ½ tablespoon tahini
- Juice from 1/3 lemon
- A pinch of cumin, ground
- A pinch of sea salt and white pepper
- 1 tablespoon parsley
- A drizzle of olive oil
- A pinch of sweet paprika
- 2 cups water

Directions:
1. In your pressure cooker, mix chickpeas with bay leaf, salt, pepper and water, stir, cover and cook on High for 18 minutes.
2. Drain chickpeas, transfer them to your blender, add garlic, tahini, lemon juice, cumin and pulse really well.
3. Transfer to a bowl, sprinkle parsley and paprika, drizzle oil all over and serve for breakfast.

Nutrition: calories 194, fat 2, fiber 1, carbs 2, protein 4

Breakfast Cheese Spread

Preparation time: 10 minutes
Cooking time: 20 minutes
Servings: 2

Ingredients:
- 1/3 pound American cheese
- 1/3 tablespoon butter
- 1/3 cup queso, shredded
- 2 ounces cream cheese
- 1/3 tablespoon garlic, minced
- 1/3 tablespoon milk
- ¼ teaspoon oregano, dried
- 1 cup water

Directions:
1. In a heatproof bowl, mix American cheese with queso, cream cheese, butter, garlic, oregano and milk and whisk well.
2. Add the water to you pressure cooker, add the trivet on the bottom, cover the heatproof dish with tin foil, add it to the pot, cover and cook on High for 18 minutes.
3. Stir spread again and serve for breakfast.

Nutrition: calories 183, fat 2, fiber 3, carbs 2, protein 4

Creamy Squash Bowl

Preparation time: 10 minutes
Cooking time: 10 minutes
Servings: 3

Ingredients:
- ½ tablespoon olive oil
- 1 small yellow onion, chopped
- 1 big yellow squash, peeled and roughly chopped
- 3 tablespoons chicken stock

- ½ tablespoon sour cream

Directions:
1. Set your pressure cooker on sauté mode, add oil, heat it up, add onion, stir and cook for 3 minutes.
2. Add squash and stock, stir a bit, cover and cook on High for 7 minutes.
3. Add sour cream, toss, divide into bowls and serve for breakfast.

Nutrition: calories 200, fat 5, fiber 5, carbs 10, protein 2

Italian Eggplant Breakfast Mix

Preparation time: 10 minutes
Cooking time: 11 minutes
Servings: 4

Ingredients:
- 3 eggplants, cubed
- 3 garlic cloves, chopped
- 1 bunch oregano, chopped
- 2 tablespoons olive oil
- ½ cup chicken stock

Directions:
1. Set your pressure cooker on sauté mode, add oil, heat it up, add garlic, stir and cook for 1 minute.
2. Add eggplants and stock, stir, cover and cook on High for 10 minutes.
3. Stir eggplant mix again, add oregano, toss, divide between plates and serve for breakfast.

Nutrition: calories 142, fat 6, fiber 2, carbs 10, protein 4

Breakfast Butter

Preparation time: 10 minutes
Cooking time: 35 minutes
Servings: 2

Ingredients:
- ½ pound apples, cored and roughly chopped
- 1/3 cup apple juice
- A pinch of cinnamon powder
- A pinch of nutmeg, ground
- A pinch of cloves, ground

Directions:
1. In your pressure cooker, mix apples with apple juice, stir, cover and cook on High for 20 minutes.
2. Blend using an immersion blender, add cinnamon, nutmeg and cloves, stir, set the cooker on sauté mode and cook apple butter for 15 minutes.
3. Serve cold for breakfast.

Nutrition: calories 172, fat 2, fiber 2, carbs 5, protein 3

Breakfast Apple Dumplings

Preparation time: 10 minutes
Cooking time: 10 minutes
Servings: 2

Ingredients:
- 2 ounces crescent rolls
- 1 apple, cored, peeled and cut into 4 wedges
- ¼ cup brown sugar
- 1 tablespoon butter
- A pinch of cinnamon powder
- ½ teaspoon vanilla extract
- A pinch of nutmeg, ground
- 2 tablespoons apple cider

Directions:
1. Roll crescents rolls on a working surface.
2. Wrap each apple piece in crescent rolls dough.
3. Put the butter in your pressure cooker, set it on sauté mode and melt it.
4. Add vanilla, sugar, nutmeg and cinnamon and stir.
5. Add dumplings and apple cider, cover the cooker and cook on High for 10 minutes.
6. Divide between 2 plates and serve for breakfast.

Nutrition: calories 213, fat 2, fiber 2, carbs 3, protein 3

Carrot Breakfast Salad

Preparation time: 5 minutes
Cooking time: 4 minutes
Servings: 5

Ingredients:
- 2 pounds carrots, shredded
- 1 tablespoon maple syrup
- 1 tablespoon olive oil
- 1 cup water
- ¼ cup raisins

Directions:
1. In your pressure cooker mix carrots with maple syrup, water and raisins, stir, cover and cook on High for 4 minutes.
2. Stir again, divide into bowls, drizzle oil on top and serve for breakfast.

Nutrition: calories 80, fat 1, fiber 2, carbs 8, protein 2

Tapioca Pudding

Preparation time: 10 minutes
Cooking time: 8 minutes
Servings: 6

Ingredients:
- 1/3 cup tapioca pearls, washed and drained
- ½ cup water
- ½ cup sugar
- Zest of ½ lemon, grated

- 1 and ¼ cups milk

Directions:
1. In your pressure cooker, mix tapioca with water, sugar, milk and lemon zest, stir, cover and cook on High for 8 minutes.
2. Transfer to bowls and serve for breakfast.

Nutrition: calories 140, fat 2, fiber 1, carbs 20, protein 4

Breakfast Chestnut Butter

Preparation time: 10 minutes
Cooking time: 20 minutes
Servings: 2

Ingredients:
- ½ pound chestnuts
- A splash of rum liquor
- 1 ounce sugar
- 2 ounces water

Directions:
1. In your pressure cooker, mix chestnuts with sugar and water, stir, cover and cook on High for 20 minutes.
2. Blend well using an immersion blender, add rum, blend again and serve for breakfast.

Nutrition: calories 200, fat 3, fiber 1, carbs 3, protein 8

Breakfast Couscous Salad

Preparation time: 10 minutes
Cooking time: 5 minutes
Servings: 2

Ingredients:
- ½ tablespoon butter
- 1 cup chicken stock
- 3 ounces couscous
- 1 red bell pepper, chopped
- A pinch of salt and black pepper

Directions:
1. Set your pressure cooker on sauté mode, add butter and melt it.
2. Add stock, bell pepper, couscous, salt and pepper, stir, cover and cook on High for 5 minutes.
3. Fluff couscous with a fork, divide into 2 bowls and serve as a breakfast.

Nutrition: calories 163, fat 3, fiber 2, carbs 3, protein 7

Couscous and Mint

Preparation time: 10 minutes
Cooking time: 7 minutes
Servings: 4

Ingredients:
- 1 cup pearl couscous
- 2 tablespoons extra virgin olive oil
- 1 small yellow onion, thinly sliced
- 1 and ½ cups veggie stock
- 2 tablespoons mint leaves, finely chopped

Directions:
1. Set your pressure cooker on sauté mode, add oil, heat it up, add onion, stir and cook for 2 minutes.
2. Add couscous and stock, stir, cover and cook on High for 5 minutes.
3. Fluff with a fork, divide into bowls, sprinkle mint on top and serve for breakfast.

Nutrition: calories 170, fat 7, fiber 3, carbs 20, protein 6

Quince Jam

Preparation time: 10 minutes
Cooking time: 10 minutes
Servings: 6

Ingredients:
- 2 pounds quince, grated
- Juice of 1 lemon
- ¼ cup water
- 10 cloves
- 2 pounds sugar

Directions:
1. In your pressure cooker, mix quince with sugar, lemon juice, water and cloves, stir, cover and cook on High for 10 minutes.
2. Serve on toasted bread for breakfast.

Nutrition: calories 90, fat 3, fiber 1, carbs 14, protein 4

Veggie and Couscous Breakfast

Preparation time: 10 minutes
Cooking time: 20 minutes
Servings: 2

Ingredients:
- 2 bay leaves
- 1 tablespoon olive oil
- 1 small onion, chopped
- 1 cup carrot, grated
- 1 and ¾ cup water
- 1 and ¾ cup couscous
- ½ teaspoon garam masala
- A pinch of salt and black pepper
- 1 tablespoon cilantro, chopped
- 1 tablespoon lemon juice

Directions:

1. Set your pressure cooker on sauté mode, add oil, heat it up, add onion and bay leaves, stir and cook for 2 minutes.
2. Add carrot and bell pepper, stir and cook for 1 minute.
3. Add garam masala, water, salt, pepper and couscous, stir, cover and cook on Manual for 10 minutes.
4. Fluff couscous mix with a fork, add cilantro and lemon juice, stir, divide into 2 bowls and serve for breakfast.

Nutrition: calories 164, fat 3, fiber 1, carbs 2, protein 3

Potato and Salmon Breakfast

Preparation time: 10 minutes
Cooking time: 25 minutes
Servings: 2

Ingredients:
- 2 salmon fillets
- ½ pound small potatoes, diced
- A pinch of salt and black pepper
- 1 teaspoon canola oil
- 1 small yellow onion, chopped
- ½ small red bell pepper, chopped
- ½ cup spinach
- 2 garlic cloves, minced
- ½ tablespoon dill, chopped
- 2 cups water+ 2 tablespoons

Directions:
1. Put 2 cups water in your pressure cooker, add the steamer basket, add potatoes, cover and cook on High for 15 minutes.
2. Drain potatoes, transfer them to a bowl and clean the pot.
3. Add the oil, set on Sauté mode, add salmon fillets, season with a pinch of salt, cook for 2 minutes on each side, transfer to a plate, cool them down and flake with a fork.
4. Heat the pressure cooker again on sauté mode, add bell pepper, garlic and onion, stir and cook for 3 minutes more.
5. Return potatoes, salmon, dill, spinach, salt, pepper and 2 tablespoons water, stir gently, cover and cook on High for 5 minutes.
6. Divide between plates and serve for breakfast.

Nutrition: calories 193, fat 3, fiber 1, carbs 3, protein 7

Rhubarb Breakfast Spread

Preparation time: 10 minutes
Cooking time: 10 minutes
Servings: 6

Ingredients:
- 8 ounces rhubarb, chopped
- 1 tablespoon cider vinegar
- 1/3 cup honey
- ¼ cup raisins
- ¼ cup water

Directions:
1. In your pressure cooker, mix rhubarb with vinegar, honey, water and raisins, stir, cover and cook on High for 10 minutes.
2. Pulse using an immersion blender, transfer to bowls and serve for breakfast.

Nutrition: calories 100, fat 2, fiber 3, carbs 17, protein 2

Strawberry and Rhubarb Breakfast Compote

Preparation time: 10 minutes
Cooking time: 30 minutes
Servings: 6

Ingredients:
- 1/3 cup water
- 3 tablespoons honey
- 2 pounds rhubarb, chopped
- 6 mint leaves, chopped
- 1 pound strawberries, chopped

Directions:
1. Put rhubarb and water in your pressure cooker, cover, cook on High for 10 minutes, add strawberries and honey and stir.
2. Set cooker in sauté mode, cook compote for 20 minutes, mix with mint, divide into bowls and serve for breakfast.

Nutrition: calories 100, fat 1, fiber 4, carbs 15, protein 2

Main Dish Recipes

Chicken Curry

Preparation time: 10 minutes
Cooking time: 45 minutes
Servings: 2

Ingredients:
- 1 bay leaf
- 1 tablespoon butter
- A small cinnamon piece
- 1 cup onion, chopped
- A pinch of cumin seeds
- ½ tablespoon garlic, minced
- 1 tablespoon tomato paste
- ½ tablespoon ginger, grated
- A pinch of turmeric powder
- 1 tablespoon coriander powder
- A pinch of salt and black pepper
- A pinch of cayenne pepper
- 1 pound chicken thighs
- 1 cup potato, cubed
- ¼ cup water
- 1 teaspoon garam masala
- 1 tablespoon cashew paste
- 2 tablespoons cilantro, chopped

Directions:
1. Set your pressure cooker on sauté mode, add butter, melt it, add cumin, bay leaf and cinnamon and stir.
2. Also add ginger, onion and garlic, stir and sauté for 6 minutes more.
3. Add tomato paste, stir and cook for 3 minutes more.
4. Add turmeric, coriander, cayenne, salt, pepper, chicken and the water, stir, cover and cook on High for 15 minutes.
5. Add garam masala and potatoes, cover and cook on Manual for 6 minutes more.
6. Add cashew paste and cilantro, stir, divide into bowls and serve.

Nutrition: calories 312, fat 2, fiber 2, carbs 10, protein 17

Beef Stew

Preparation time: 10 minutes
Cooking time: 25 minutes
Servings: 2

Ingredients:
- 1 pound beef meat, cubed
- 1 tablespoon olive oil
- 1 tablespoon flour
- A pinch of salt and black pepper
- 1 small yellow onion, chopped
- 1 garlic clove, minced

- 3 tablespoons red wine
- 1 celery stalk, chopped
- 2 small carrots, chopped
- ½ pound red potatoes, chopped
- ½ tablespoon tomato paste
- 1 cup beef stock
- 2 tablespoons parsley, chopped

Directions:
1. In a bowl, mix beef meat with salt, pepper and flour and toss.
2. Set your pressure cooker on sauté mode, add the oil and heat it up.
3. Add beef, brown on all sides, transfer to a bowl and leave aside.
4. Add wine to your pressure cooker and cook on Sauté mode for a couple more minutes.
5. Return beef to the pot, add carrots, garlic, onions, potatoes, celery, stock and tomato paste, stir, cover and cook on High for 20 minutes.
6. Add parsley, stir your stew, divide into 2 bowls and serve.

Nutrition: calories 312, fat 2, fiber 2, carbs 4, protein 6

Juicy Roast

Preparation time: 10 minutes
Cooking time: 1 hour
Servings: 4

Ingredients:
- 1 pound chuck roast
- 4 garlic cloves, minced
- 1 cup chicken stock
- 1 tablespoon soy sauce
- 1 tablespoon olive oil

Directions:
1. Set your pressure cooker on sauté mode, add oil, heat it up, add chuck roast and brown for 10 minutes on each side.
2. Add garlic to the pot, stir and cook for a couple more minutes.
3. Add stock and soy sauce, stir, cover and cook on High for 45 minutes.
4. Leave roast to cool down a bit, slice, divide between plates and serve with cooking juices on top.

Nutrition: calories 343, fat 6, fiber 6, carbs 25, protein 18

Mac and Cheese

Preparation time: 10 minutes
Cooking time: 15 minutes
Servings: 4

Ingredients:
- 16 ounces macaroni
- 4 tablespoons butter
- 4 cups water
- 14 ounces cheddar cheese, grated
- 12 ounces evaporated milk

Directions:
1. In your pressure cooker, mix macaroni with water, stir, cover and cook on High for 4 minutes.
2. Drain macaroni and clean the pot.
3. Add the butter to your pressure cooker, set it on sauté mode, melt it, add macaroni and stir well.
4. Add cheese and milk and cook for 10 minutes stirring often.
5. Divide into bowls and serve.

Nutrition: calories 321, fat 6, fiber 8, carbs 16, protein 4

Vegetarian Lentils Soup

Preparation time: 10 minutes
Cooking time: 30 minutes
Servings: two

Ingredients:
- 1 teaspoon olive oil
- ½ cup yellow onion, chopped
- ½ cup carrot, chopped
- 1/3 cup celery, chopped
- 1 tablespoon garlic, minced
- ½ teaspoon turmeric, ground
- 1 teaspoon cumin, ground
- ½ teaspoon thyme, dried
- A pinch of salt and black pepper
- 2 cups veggie stock
- ½ cup lentils
- 3 cups baby spinach

Directions:
1. Set your pressure cooker on sauté mode, add the oil, heat it up, add onion, celery and carrot, stir and cook for 5 minutes.
2. Add turmeric, garlic, cumin, thyme, salt and pepper, stir and cook for 1 minute more.
3. Add lentils and stock, stir, cover and cook on Manual for 12 minutes.
4. Add spinach, stir, ladle into bowls and serve.

Nutrition: calories 235, fat 1, fiber 2, carbs 4, protein 7

Crispy Chicken

Preparation time: 10 minutes
Cooking time: 25 minutes
Servings: 2

Ingredients:
- 1 pound chicken breasts, skinless and boneless
- ½ teaspoon oregano, dried
- ½ teaspoon chili powder
- ½ tablespoon cumin, ground
- A pinch of salt and black pepper
- Zest and juice from ½ orange
- 2 tablespoon chicken stock

- 2 garlic cloves, minced
- 1 small yellow onion, chopped
- 1 tablespoon adobo sauce
- 2 tablespoons cilantro, chopped
- 1 tablespoon olive oil

For the sauce:
- ½ tablespoon milk
- 3 tablespoon mayonnaise
- 1 chipotle pepper
- A pinch of salt and garlic powder
- 2 tortillas for serving

Directions:
1. In a bowl, mix chili powder with oregano, cumin, salt, pepper and chicken breasts and toss.
2. Set your pressure cooker on sauté mode, add oil, heat it up, add chicken breasts, brown for 1 minute on each side and transfer to a plate.
3. Add garlic and onion to your pressure cooker, stir and cook for 2 minutes.
4. Return chicken to your pressure cooker, add orange juice and zest, stock, adobo sauce, bay leaf and cilantro, stir, cover and cook on High for 10 minutes.
5. Transfer chicken breasts to a cutting board, cool down, shred using a fork, transfer to a bowl, drizzle some of the cooking liquid from the cooker and toss.
6. Spread chicken on a lined baking sheet, introduce in preheated broiler and cook broil for 10 minutes.
7. Meanwhile, in your blender, mix milk with mayo, chipotle pepper, salt and garlic powder and pulse well.
8. Divide chicken on tortillas, add the sauce you've just made, roll and serve them.

Nutrition: calories 242, fat 2, fiber 2, carbs 6, protein 8

BBQ Ribs

Preparation time: 10 minutes
Cooking time: 25 minutes
Servings: 3

Ingredients:
- 1 cup water, for the pressure cooker
- 1 rack baby back ribs
- 4 tablespoons BBQ sauce
- Salt to the taste
- Black pepper to the taste
- A pinch of chili powder

Directions:
1. In a bowl, mix ribs with bbq sauce, salt, pepper and chili powder and toss well.
2. Add the water to your pressure cooker, add steamer basket, add ribs inside, cover and cook on High for 25 minutes.
3. Divide them between plates and serve.

Nutrition: calories 362, fat 7, fiber 7, carbs 18, protein 12

Chili Beef

Preparation time: 10 minutes
Cooking time: 35 minutes

Servings: 4

Ingredients:
- 1 pound beef, ground
- 1 green bell pepper, chopped
- 26 ounces tomatoes, chopped
- 4 teaspoons chili powder
- 1 yellow onion, chopped

Directions:
1. Set your pressure cooker on sauté mode, add beef, stir and brown for 3 minutes.
2. Add onion, stir and cook for 2 minutes more.
3. Add bell pepper, tomatoes and chili powder, stir, cover and cook on High for 30 minutes.
4. Divide chili into bowls and serve.

Nutrition: calories 300, fat 9, fiber 7, carbs 28, protein 3

Rice and Beans

Preparation time: 10 minutes
Cooking time: 50 minutes
Servings: 2

Ingredients:
- ½ yellow onion, chopped
- 1 small red bell pepper, chopped
- 1 celery stalk, chopped
- 1 garlic clove, minced
- 1/3 pound red kidney beans
- A pinch of salt and black pepper
- A pinch of white pepper
- ½ teaspoon thyme, chopped
- 1/3 teaspoon hot sauce
- 1 bay leaf
- 3 cups water
- ½ pound chicken sausage, sliced
- 3 cups rice, already cooked

Directions:
1. In your pressure cooker, mix onion with bell pepper, celery, garlic, beans, salt, black pepper, white pepper, thyme, hot sauce, bay leaf and water, stir, cover and cook on High for 28 minutes.
2. Add sausage, stir, cover cooker again and cook on Manual for 15 minutes more.
3. Divide rice on 2 plates, add beans mix on top and serve.

Nutrition: calories 194, fat 2, fiber 2, carbs 7, protein 10

Turkey Meatballs

Preparation time: 10 minutes
Cooking time: 10 minutes
Servings: 2

Ingredients:

- ½ pound turkey meat, ground
- 2 tablespoons green onion, chopped
- 2 saltine crackers, crushed
- 1 and ½ tablespoons buttermilk
- A pinch of salt and black pepper
- ½ tablespoon canola oil
- ½ tablespoon sesame seeds

For the sauce:
- 1 garlic clove, minced
- 4 tablespoons soy sauce
- 2 tablespoon rice vinegar
- 1 teaspoon ginger, grated
- 1 tablespoon canola oil
- 1 and ½ tablespoon brown sugar
- A pinch of black pepper
- ½ tablespoon cornstarch

Directions:
1. In a bowl, mix turkey with crackers, green onions, salt, pepper and buttermilk, stir, shape 8 meatballs and leave them aside.
2. In another bowl, mix soy sauce with vinegar, garlic, ginger, 1 tablespoon canola, brown sugar, black pepper and cornstarch and stir well.
3. Set your pressure cooker on sauté mode, add ½ tablespoon canola oil, heat it up, add meatballs and brown them for 2 minutes on each side.
4. Add the sauce, cover and cook on High for 10 minutes.
5. Divide between 2 plates and serve with sesame seeds sprinkled on top.

Nutrition: calories 293, fat 4, fiber 1, carbs 2, protein 9

Shredded Chicken

Preparation time: 10 minutes
Cooking time: 15 minutes
Servings: 4

Ingredients:
- 2 pounds chicken drumsticks
- 1 tablespoon peanut oil
- 10 red chilies, dried and chopped
- ¼ cup dark soy sauce
- 2 tablespoons balsamic vinegar

Directions:
1. Set your pressure cooker on sauté mode, add peanut oil, heat it up, add chilies, stir and cook them for 3 minutes.
2. Add chicken pieces, soy sauce and vinegar, stir, cover and cook on High for 12 minutes.
3. Transfer meat to a cutting board, cool down a bit, shred, return to cooker and toss with cooking sauce.
4. Divide between plates and serve with a side salad.

Nutrition: calories 261, fat 7, fiber 3, carbs 20, protein 4

Beef Stew

Preparation time: 10 minutes
Cooking time: 36 minutes
Servings: 4

Ingredients:
- 2 pounds beef stew meat
- 1 cup baby carrots
- 4 cups beef stock
- 1 jar corn salsa
- 6 ounces canned garbanzo beans, drained

Directions:
1. Set your pressure cooker on sauté mode, add beef, stir and brown for 8 minutes on each side.
2. Add salsa, stock, beans and baby carrots, stir, cover and cook on High for 20 minutes.
3. Divide into bowls and serve.

Nutrition: calories 281, fat 6, fiber 12, carbs 26, protein 6

Cinnamon Pho

Preparation time: 10 minutes
Cooking time: 40 minutes
Servings: 2

Ingredients:
- 1 pound chicken pieces, bone in and skin on
- A small ginger piece, grated
- 1 small onion, cut into quarters
- ½ tablespoon coriander seeds, toasted
- ½ teaspoon cardamom pods
- ½ cardamom pods
- 2 cloves
- ½ lemongrass stalk, chopped
- ½ cinnamon stick
- 2 tablespoons fish sauce
- ½ bok choy, chopped
- ½ daikon root, cut with a spiralizer
- 1 tablespoon green onions, chopped

Directions:
1. In your pressure cooker, mix chicken with ginger, onion, coriander seeds, cardamom, cloves, lemongrass, fish sauce, daikon, bok choy and water to cover them all, stir, cover and cook on High for 30 minutes.
2. Strain soup into another pot, shred chicken and divide into 2 bowls.
3. Add strained soup and green onions and serve.

Nutrition: calories 182, fat 2, fiber 3, carbs 6, protein 7

Black Bean Soup

Preparation time: 10 minutes
Cooking time: 40 minutes
Servings: 2

Ingredients:
- 1 small yellow onion, chopped
- 1 green bell pepper, chopped
- 1 red bell pepper, chopped
- 3 ounces tomatoes, chopped
- 1 celery stalk, chopped
- ½ pound black beans
- A pinch of salt and black pepper
- 1/3 teaspoon hot sauce
- ½ tablespoon chili powder
- 1 teaspoon paprika
- ½ tablespoon cumin
- 1 bay leaf
- 2 cups veggie stock

Directions:
1. In your pressure cooker, mix onion with red bell pepper, green bell pepper, tomatoes, celery, black beans, salt, pepper, hot sauce, chili powder, cumin, paprika, bay leaf and stock, stir, cover and cook on High for 40 minutes.
2. Ladle into 2 soup bowls and serve.

Nutrition: calories 300, fat 2, fiber 1, carbs 2, protein 3

Pork Chops and Tomato Sauce

Preparation time: 10 minutes
Cooking time: 20 minutes
Servings: 4

Ingredients:
- 4 pork chops, boneless
- 1 tablespoon soy sauce
- ¼ teaspoon sesame oil
- 1 and ½ cups tomato paste
- 1 yellow onion
- 8 mushrooms, sliced

Directions:
1. In a bowl, mix pork chops with soy sauce and sesame oil, toss and leave aside for 10 minutes.
2. Set your pressure cooker on sauté mode, add pork chops and brown them for 5 minutes on each side.
3. Add onion, stir and cook for 1-2 minutes more.
4. Add tomato paste and mushrooms, toss, cover and cook on High for 8-9 minutes.
5. Divide everything between plates and serve.

Nutrition: calories 300, fat 7, fiber 7, carbs 18, protein 4

Chicken Dish

Preparation time: 10 minutes
Cooking time: 30 minutes
Servings: 8

Ingredients:
- 7 cups water
- 1 cup jasmine rice
- 6 chicken drumsticks
- 1 tablespoon ginger, grated
- 2 tablespoons green onions, chopped

Directions:
1. In your pressure cooker, mix rice with water, chicken and ginger, stir, cover and cook on High for 30 minutes.
2. Add onions, stir, divide into bowls and serve.

Nutrition: calories 251, fat 7, fiber 4, carbs 12, protein 4

Chickpea Curry

Preparation time: 10 minutes
Cooking time: 25 minutes
Servings: 2

Ingredients:
- 1 cup chickpeas, soaked for 8 hours and drained
- 1 cup water
- ½ cup tomatoes, chopped
- 1 tablespoon olive oil
- 4 tablespoons red onion, chopped
- 1 garlic clove, minced
- A pinch of chili powder
- A pinch of garam masala
- A pinch of turmeric powder
- 1 bay leaf
- ½ tablespoon curry powder
- ½ tablespoon lemon juice
- A pinch of salt and black pepper
- 1 tablespoon cilantro, chopped

Directions:
1. Put the oil in your pressure cooker, set on sauté mode, heat it up, add garlic and onion, stir and cook for 2 minutes.
2. Add tomatoes, stir and cook for 4 minutes more.
3. Add chili powder, garam masala, turmeric, bay leaf and curry powder, stir and cook for 1 minute more.
4. Add chickpeas and water, stir, cover and cook on High for 10 minutes.
5. Discard bay leaf, add lemon juice and cilantro, some salt and pepper, stir, divide into bowls and serve.

Nutrition: calories 310, fat 1, fiber 2, carbs 4, protein 10

Beef Dish

Preparation time: 10 minutes
Cooking time: 1 hour
Servings: 2

Ingredients:
- 1 pound beef roast, cubed
- 2 garlic cloves, minced
- 1 small yellow onion, chopped
- 2 ounces green chilies, chopped
- 1 teaspoon oregano, dried
- A pinch of salt and black pepper
- 1 chipotle pepper, chopped
- Juice from 1 lime
- 1 tablespoon coconut vinegar
- 2 teaspoons cumin, ground
- ½ cup water

Directions:
1. In your pressure cooker, mix beef with garlic, onion, green chilies, oregano, salt, pepper, chipotle pepper, lime juice, vinegar, cumin and water, stir, cover and cook on Manual for 1 hour.
2. Divide into bowls and serve.

Nutrition: calories 254, fat 1, fiber 2, carbs 3, protein 9

Beef and Broccoli

Preparation time: 10 minutes
Cooking time: 15 minutes
Servings: 4

Ingredients:
- 1 and ½ pounds flank steak, cut into thin strips
- 1 tablespoon olive oil
- 1 tablespoon tamari sauce
- 1 cup beef stock
- 1 pound broccoli, florets separated

Directions:
1. In a bowl, mix steak strips with oil and tamari, toss and leave aside for 10 minutes.
2. Set your pressure cooker on sauté mode, add beef strips and brown them for 4 minutes on each side.
3. Add stock, stir, cover and cook on High for 8 minutes.
4. Add broccoli, stir, cover cooker again and cook on High for 4 minutes more.
5. Divide everything between plates and serve.

Nutrition: calories 312, fat 5, fiber 12, carbs 20, protein 4

Fast Salmon

Preparation time: 10 minutes
Cooking time: 5 minutes
Servings: 4

Ingredients:
- 4 salmon fillets, boneless
- 1 bunch dill, chopped

- 1 tablespoon butter
- ¼ cup lemon juice
- A pinch of salt
- 1 cup water, for the pressure cooker

Directions:
1. Put the water in your pressure cooker, add lemon juice, add steamer basket, add salmon inside, season with some salt, sprinkle dill and drizzle melted butter, cover cooker and cook on Manual for 5 minutes.
2. Divide salmon between plates and serve with a side dish.

Nutrition: calories 412, fat 12, fiber 8, carbs 27, protein 12

Coconut Quinoa

Preparation time: 10 minutes
Cooking time: 1 minute
Servings: 2

Ingredients:
- ½ cup quinoa
- 6 ounces coconut milk
- 2 tablespoons water
- Zest and juice from ½ lime
- A pinch of salt
- 1 tablespoon cilantro, chopped

Directions:
1. In your pressure cooker, mix quinoa with coconut milk, water, lime zest and lime juice and salt, stir, cover and cook on High for 1 minute.
2. Leave quinoa aside for 10 minutes, fluff with a fork, divide into 2 bowls, add cilantro and serve.

Nutrition: calories 200, fat 1, fiber 2, carbs 3, protein 4

Chicken Wrap

Preparation time: 10 minutes
Cooking time: 10 minutes
Servings: 2

Ingredients:
- ½ pound chicken, ground
- 1 small yellow onion, chopped
- 2 teaspoons garlic, minced
- A pinch of ginger, grated
- A pinch of allspice, ground
- 4 tablespoons water chestnuts
- 2 tablespoons soy sauce
- 2 tablespoons chicken stock
- 2 tablespoons balsamic vinegar
- 2 tortillas for serving

Directions:

1. In your pressure cooker, mix chicken meat with onion, garlic, ginger, allspice, chestnuts, soy sauce, stock and vinegar, stir a bit, cover and cook on Manual for 10 minutes.
2. Divide chicken mix on 2 tortillas, wrap and serve.

Nutrition: calories 231, fat 4, fiber 3, carbs 6, protein 10

Steamed Tilapia

Preparation time: 10 minutes
Cooking time: 10 minutes
Servings: 4

Ingredients:
- 1 pound tilapia fillets
- 1 tablespoon Chinese black bean paste
- 3 tablespoons soy sauce
- ¼ cup scallions, chopped
- 1 tablespoon peanut oil
- 2 cups water, for the pressure cooker

Directions:
1. In a bowl, mix soy sauce with black bean paste and whisk well.
2. Add fish, toss and leave aside for 10 minutes.
3. Set your pressure cooker on sauté mode, add oil, heat it up, add scallions, stir, cook for a couple of minutes and transfer to a bowl.
4. Clean the pot, add the water, add steamer basket, add fish fillets inside, sprinkle scallions on top, cover cooker and cook on High for 3 minutes.
5. Divide everything between plates and serve with a side salad.

Nutrition: calories 152, fat 2, fiber 7, carbs 12, protein 5

Lemon Pepper Salmon

Preparation time: 10 minutes
Cooking time: 10 minutes
Servings: 4

Ingredients:
- 1 cup water, for the pressure cooker
- 1 lemon, sliced
- 1 pound salmon fillets, boneless and skin on
- Black pepper to the taste
- 3 teaspoons butter, melted
- 1 red bell pepper, julienned

Directions:
1. Put the water in your pressure cooker, add steamer basket, add salmon fillets, season them with black pepper, drizzle melted butter all over, divide bell pepper and lemon slices on top, cover and cook on High for 7 minutes.
2. Divide salmon and bell pepper on plates, top with lemon slices and serve.

Nutrition: calories 281, fat 8, fiber 4, carbs 16, protein 6

Tikka Masala

Preparation time: 10 minutes

Cooking time: 22 minutes
Servings: 2

Ingredients:
- ½ pound chicken breasts, skinless and boneless
- ½ tablespoon butter
- ½ tablespoon olive oil
- 1 small yellow onion, chopped
- A pinch of salt and black pepper
- ½ tablespoon garam masala
- ½ teaspoon coriander, ground
- ½ teaspoon turmeric
- ½ teaspoon chili powder
- 3 garlic cloves, minced
- 1 inch ginger piece, grated
- 7 ounces canned tomatoes, crushed
- 1 and ½ tablespoon yogurt
- 1 tablespoon almond butter

Directions:
1. Add the butter and the oil to your pressure cooker, set it on sauté mode, heat it up, add onion, stir and cook for 5 minutes.
2. Add chili powder, salt, pepper, garam masala, coriander, turmeric, ginger, garlic and tomatoes, stir and cook for 1 minute more.
3. Add chicken breasts, cover and cook on Manual for 16 minutes.
4. Transfer meat to a cutting board, shred using 2 forks and leave aside for now.
5. Blend the mix from the cooker using an immersion blender, add yogurt and almond butter and stir gently.
6. Return chicken to the pot, stir a bit, divide into 2 bowls and serve.

Nutrition: calories 300, fat 4, fiber 4, carbs 7, protein 8

Lemon and Olive Chicken

Preparation time: 10 minutes
Cooking time: 16 minutes
Servings: 2

Ingredients:
- 2 chicken breasts, skinless and boneless
- A pinch of salt and black pepper
- A pinch of cumin, ground
- 3 tablespoons butter
- Juice from ½ lemon
- 2 lemon slices
- ½ cup chicken stock
- ½ cup green olives, pitted
- 3 tablespoons red onion, chopped

Directions:
1. Set your pressure cooker on sauté mode, add chicken breasts, season with salt, pepper and cumin and brown for 3 minutes on each side.

2. Add butter, lemon juice, lemon slices, stock, olives and onion, stir, cover and cook on High for 10 minutes.
3. Divide chicken mixture between 2 plates and serve.

Nutrition: calories 265, fat 3, fiber 4, carbs 6, protein 9

Fish Soup

Preparation time: 10 minutes
Cooking time: 8 minutes
Servings: 4

Ingredients:
- 1 pound white fish fillets, boneless, skinless and cubed
- 1 carrot, chopped
- 1 cup bacon, chopped
- 4 cups chicken stock
- 2 cups heavy cream

Directions:
1. In your pressure cooker, mix fish with carrot, bacon and stock, stir, cover and cook on High for 5 minutes.
2. Add heavy cream, stir, set the cooker on sauté mode, cook for 3 minutes more, ladle into bowls and serve.

Nutrition: calories 271, fat 7, fiber 16, carbs 30, protein 5

Chili Mahi Mahi

Preparation time: 10 minutes
Cooking time: 5 minutes
Servings: 2

Ingredients:
- 2 tablespoons butter
- 2 mahi mahi fillets, boneless
- ¼ cup enchilada sauce
- Salt to the taste
- Black pepper to the taste
- 1 cup water, for the pressure cooker

Directions:
1. Put the water in your pressure cooker, add steamer basket, add mahi mahi fillets inside, drizzle melted butter, season with salt and pepper and spread enchilada sauce all over them.
2. Cover pot, cook on High for 5 minutes.
3. Divide fish and sauce between plates and serve.

Nutrition: calories 200, fat 5, fiber 12, carbs 27, protein 7

Chicken and Tomatillo Salsa

Preparation time: 10 minutes
Cooking time: 28 minutes
Servings: 2

Ingredients:

- 4 chicken drumsticks, skin removed
- A pinch of salt and black pepper
- ½ tablespoon cider vinegar
- ½ teaspoon oregano, dried
- ½ teaspoon olive oil
- 1 cup tomatillo sauce
- 2 tablespoons cilantro, chopped
- 1 small jalapeno, chopped

Directions:
1. Add the oil to your pressure cooker, set on sauté mode, add chicken drumsticks, season with salt, pepper and oregano and brown for 4 minutes on each side.
2. Add tomatillo sauce, jalapeno and half of the cilantro, stir, cover and cook on High for 20 minutes.
3. Add the rest of the cilantro, stir again, divide between 2 plates and serve.

Nutrition: calories 264, fat 5, fiber 2, carbs 5, protein 9

Chicken with Dates

Preparation time: 10 minutes
Cooking time: 30 minutes
Servings: 2

Ingredients:
- 4 chicken thighs, skinless and boneless
- A pinch of salt and black pepper
- ½ tablespoon olive oil
- 1 teaspoon cumin, ground
- 1 teaspoon smoked paprika
- 1 teaspoon coriander, ground
- 1 garlic clove, minced
- ½ yellow onion, chopped
- 1 carrot, chopped
- 14 ounces tomatoes, chopped
- 4 tablespoons chicken stock
- 4 medjol dates, chopped
- ½ lemon, cut into wedges
- 4 tablespoons green olives, pitted
- 2 tablespoons pine nuts
- Chopped mint for serving

Directions:
1. In a bowl, mix chicken thighs with salt, pepper, oil, cumin, paprika and coriander and toss.
2. Set your pressure cooker on sauté mode, add chicken and brown for 5 minutes on each side.
3. Add garlic, onion, carrot, tomatoes, stock, dates and olives, stir, cover and cook on High for 20 minutes.
4. Divide into bowls, sprinkle pine nuts and mint on top and serve.

Nutrition: calories 283, fat 5, fiber 4, carbs 7, protein 8

Cod and Orange Sauce

Preparation time: 10 minutes

Cooking time: 7 minutes
Servings: 4

Ingredients:
- 4 cod fillets, boneless
- A small ginger piece, grated
- Juice from 1 orange
- 4 spring onions
- 1 cup white wine

Directions:
1. In your pressure cooker, mix wine with ginger, spring onions and orange juice, stir, add steamer basket, add cod fillets inside, cover and cook on High for 7 minutes.
2. Divide fish on plates, drizzle orange juice all over and serve.

Nutrition: calories 172, fat 5, fiber 3, carbs 7, protein 7

Garlic Shrimp

Preparation time: 10 minutes
Cooking time: 3 minutes
Servings: 3

Ingredients:
- 2 pounds shrimp, deveined and peeled
- 2 tablespoons olive oil
- ½ cup chicken stock
- ½ cup white wine
- 1 tablespoon garlic, minced

Directions:
1. Set your pressure cooker on sauté mode, add oil, heat it up, add garlic, stir and cook for 30 seconds.
2. Add shrimp, wine and stock, stir, cover and cook on High for 3 minutes.
3. Divide into bowls and serve.

Nutrition: calories 190, fat 2, fiber 4, carbs 7, protein 2

Beef Curry

Preparation time: 1 hour
Cooking time: 55 minutes
Servings: 2

Ingredients:
For the marinade:
- 1 tablespoon coconut oil
- ½ teaspoon garlic powder
- ½ teaspoon turmeric powder
- ½ teaspoon ginger powder
- A pinch of salt and black pepper

For the curry:
- 1 pound beef roast, cubed
- 1 and ½ teaspoon coconut oil

- 1 small onion, chopped
- ½ cup coconut milk
- 2 kaffir lime leaves
- ½ cinnamon stick
- 1 small plantain, peeled and cut into medium chunks
- ½ tablespoon coriander, chopped

Directions:
1. In a bowl, mix beef with 1 tablespoon oil, garlic powder, turmeric powder, ginger powder, salt and pepper, toss and leave aside for 1 hour.
2. Set your pressure cooker on sauté mode, add 1 and ½ teaspoons oil, heat it up, add beef, stir and brown for 5 minutes on each side.
3. Add coconut milk, onion, lime leaves and cinnamon, stir, cover and cook on Manual for 35 minutes.
4. Set the cooker on Sauté mode again, add plantain, stir and simmer curry for a few more minutes.
5. Divide into bowls, sprinkle coriander on top and serve.

Nutrition: calories 213, fat 4, fiber 2, carbs 6, protein 9

Beef and Artichokes

Preparation time: 10 minutes
Cooking time: 15 minutes
Servings: 2

Ingredients:
- ½ tablespoon olive oil
- 1 pound beef, ground
- 1 small yellow onion, chopped
- ½ teaspoon garlic powder
- ½ teaspoon oregano, dried
- ½ teaspoon dill, dried
- ½ teaspoon onion powder
- A pinch of salt and black pepper
- 10 ounces frozen artichoke hearts
- 1/3 cup water
- ½ teaspoon apple cider vinegar
- 3 tablespoons avocado mayonnaise

Directions:
1. Add the oil to your pressure cooker, set on sauté mode, heat it up, add onion, stir and cook for 5 minutes.
2. Add beef, salt, pepper, oregano, dill, garlic and onion powder, stir and cook for 3 minutes.
3. Add water and artichokes, stir, cover and cook on Manual for 7 minutes more.
4. Drain excess water, add vinegar and mayo, stir, divide into bowls and serve.

Nutrition: calories 300, fat 4, fiber 4, carbs 6, protein 12

Shrimp Boil

Preparation time: 10 minutes
Cooking time: 35 minutes
Servings: 4

Ingredients:
- 1 cup chicken stock
- 1 tablespoon old bay seasoning
- 1 teaspoon red pepper, crushed
- 1 sweet onion, chopped
- 2 pounds shrimp, peeled and deveined

Directions:
1. In your pressure cooker, mix stock with old bay seasoning, red pepper, onion and shrimp, stir, cover and cook on Low for 30 minutes.
2. Divide into bowls and serve.

Nutrition: calories 162, fat 2, fiber 4, carbs 6, protein 4

Fast Shrimp Scampi

Preparation time: 10 minutes
Cooking time: 4 minutes
Servings: 4

Ingredients:
- 1 pound shrimp, peeled and deveined
- 2 shallots, chopped
- 2 tablespoons butter
- 1 cup chicken stock
- Juice of 1 lemon

Directions:
1. Set your pressure cooker on sauté mode, add butter, heat it up, add shallots, stir and cook for 1-2 minutes.
2. Add shrimp, lemon juice and stock, stir, cover and cook on High for 2 minutes more.
3. Divide into bowls and serve.

Nutrition: calories 182, fat 5, fiber 7, carbs 12, protein 5

Pork Roast

Preparation time: 10 minutes
Cooking time: 35 minutes
Servings: 2

Ingredients:
- 1 pound pork roast
- A pinch of chili powder
- A pinch of onion powder
- A pinch of garlic powder
- A pinch of salt and black pepper
- ½ tablespoon olive oil
- 1 cup water
- 3 tablespoons apple juice

Directions:

1. In a bowl, mix roast with chili powder, onion powder, garlic powder, salt and pepper and rub well.
2. Add the oil to your pressure cooker, set on sauté mode, add roast and brown for 5 minutes on each side.
3. Add apple juice and water, stir a bit, cover and cook on High for 25 minutes.
4. Slice roast, divide between 2 plates and drizzle cooking juices all over.

Nutrition: calories 321, fat 4, fiber 2, carbs 4, protein 6

Pork and Pineapple Delight

Preparation time: 1 hour
Cooking time: 50 minutes
Servings: 2

Ingredients:
- 1 tablespoon olive oil
- 1 pound pork, cubed
- A pinch of salt and black pepper
- ½ tablespoon soy sauce
- 2 tablespoon cassava flour
- A pinch of cloves, ground
- A pinch of turmeric powder
- A pinch of ginger powder
- 1 small yellow onion, cut into medium chunks
- 1 garlic clove, minced
- ½ teaspoon cinnamon, ground
- ½ cup pineapple, peeled and cut into medium chunks
- 1 tablespoon dates, pitted and chopped
- 1 bay leaf
- ½ cup beef stock
- ½ bunch Swiss chard, chopped

Directions:
1. In a bowl, mix pork with soy sauce, salt, pepper, flour, cloves, ginger powder and turmeric powder, toss and leave aside for 1 hour.
2. Set your pressure cooker on sauté mode, add the oil, heat it up, add onion and garlic, stir, cook for 2 minutes and transfer to a bowl.
3. Add pork cubes to your pressure cooker and brown them for 5 minutes on each side.
4. Return garlic and onion, also add cinnamon, pineapple, stock, dates and bay leaf, stir, cover and cook on High for 35 minutes.
5. Set the cooker on Simmer mode, add Swiss chard, cook for 1-2 minutes more, discard bay leaf, divide pork and pineapple mixture into bowls and serve.

Nutrition: calories 310, fat 4, fiber 1, carbs 6, protein 12

Delicious and Simple Octopus

Preparation time: 10 minutes
Cooking time: 15 minutes
Servings: 4

Ingredients:
- 2 pounds octopus, rinsed

- Water, for the pressure cooker
- Salt to the taste
- Black pepper to the taste
- A pinch of chili powder
- ¼ teaspoon sweet paprika

Directions:
1. Season octopus with salt and pepper, add to the pot, add water to cover, also add chili powder and paprika, stir a bit, cover and cook on High for 15 minutes.
2. Cut octopus and serve with a simple side salad.

Nutrition: calories 112, fat 6, fiber 3, carbs 7, protein 3

Teriyaki Scallops

Preparation time: 10 minutes
Cooking time: 4 minutes
Servings: 3

Ingredients:
- 1 tablespoon avocado oil
- 1 pound sea scallops
- 3 tablespoons maple syrup
- ½ cup coconut aminos
- 1 tablespoon chives, chopped

Directions:
1. Set your pressure cooker on sauté mode, add oil, heat it up, add scallops and sear them for 1 minute on each side.
2. Add maple syrup, aminos and chives, toss, cover cooker and cook on High for 2 minutes.
3. Divide between plates and serve scallops right away.

Nutrition: calories 300, fat 5, fiber 7, carbs 8, protein 12

Squash and Apple Soup

Preparation time: 10 minutes
Cooking time: 15 minutes
Servings: 2

Ingredients:
- ½ butternut squash, peeled and cubed
- A drizzle of olive oil
- A pinch of ginger powder
- 1 small apple, peeled, cored and chopped
- 2 cups veggie stock
- A pinch of salt and white pepper

Directions:
1. Add the oil to your pressure cooker, set on sauté mode, heat it up, add squash cubes and brown them for 5 minutes.
2. Add ginger powder, apple, stock, salt and pepper, stir, cover and cook on High for 15 minutes,
3. Puree everything using an immersion blender, divide soup into 2 bowls and serve.

Nutrition: calories 183, fat 1, fiber 2, carbs 3, protein 6

Chicken and Veggie Soup

Preparation time: 10 minutes
Cooking time: 30 minutes
Servings: 2

Ingredients:
- ½ pound chicken breast, skinless and boneless
- ½ yellow onion, chopped
- ½ tablespoon olive oil
- 1 garlic clove, minced
- 2 and ½ cups chicken stock
- 1 small bay leaf
- A pinch of thyme, dried
- 1 teaspoon Worcestershire sauce
- A pinch of salt and black pepper
- ½ carrot, chopped
- 1 celery stalk, chopped
- ½ zucchini, cubed
- ½ cup broccoli florets, roughly chopped
- 1 tablespoon parsley, chopped

Directions:
1. Add the oil to your pressure cooker, set on sauté mode, add garlic and onion, stir and cook for 3 minutes.
2. Add chicken breasts, brown for 3 minutes on each side and mix with bay leaf, stock, thyme, salt, pepper and Worcestershire sauce.
3. Stir, cover cooker and cook on High for 15 minutes.
4. Transfer meat to a cutting board, cool it down, cut into medium cubes and return to the pot.
5. Add celery, zucchini and carrots, cover cooker and cook on High for 5 minutes more.
6. Add broccoli, set the cooker on simmer mode, stir for a couple of minutes more, ladle into bowls, sprinkle parsley on top and serve.

Nutrition: calories 241, fat 2, fiber 1, carbs 4, protein 10

Mussels and White Wine Sauce

Preparation time: 10 minutes
Cooking time: 6 minutes
Servings: 4

Ingredients:
- 3 pounds mussels, debearded and cleaned
- 6 tablespoons butter
- 4 shallots, chopped
- 1 and ½ cups chicken stock
- 1 cup white wine

Directions:
1. Set the cooker on sauté mode, add butter and melt it.
2. Add shallots, stir and cook them for 2 minutes.

3. Add wine, stir and cook for 1 minute more.
4. Add mussels and stock, stir, cover and cook on High for 3 minutes more.
5. Discard unopened mussels, divide the rest and the wine into bowls and serve.

Nutrition: calories 200, fat 2, fiber 4, carbs 6, protein 5

Beet Soup

Preparation time: 10 minutes
Cooking time: 52 minutes
Servings: 6

Ingredients:
- 8 cups beets, peeled and chopped
- 3 cups cabbage, chopped
- 6 cups chicken stock
- 1 yellow onion, chopped
- A pinch of salt
- 1 cup water, for the pressure cooker

Directions:
1. Add the water to your pressure cooker, add steamer basket, add beets, cover and cook on High for 7 minutes.
2. Discard water, return beets to the pot, also add cabbage, onion, salt and stock, stir, cover and cook on Manual for 45 minutes.
3. Ladle soup into bowls and serve.

Nutrition: calories 152, fat 6, fiber 4, carbs 6, protein 8

Chicken and Kale Soup

Preparation time: 10 minutes
Cooking time: 15 minutes
Servings: 2

Ingredients:
- ½ tablespoon olive oil
- 3 ounces pork chorizo, chopped
- 2 chicken thighs, boneless, skinless and chopped
- ½ yellow onion, chopped
- 1 garlic clove, minced
- 1 cup chicken stock
- 3 ounces tomatoes, chopped
- 1 small bay leaf
- 1 gold potato, peeled and cubed
- 1 ounce baby kale
- 3 ounces canned chickpeas, drained
- A pinch of salt and black pepper

Directions:
1. Set your pressure cooker on sauté mode, add the oil, heat it up, add chicken, chorizo and onion, stir and cook for 5 minutes.
2. Add garlic, stock, bay leaf, tomatoes, potato and kale, stir, cover and cook on high for 5 minutes.

3. Discard bay leaf, add chickpeas, salt and pepper, set the cooker on simmer mode and cook soup until potatoes are done.
4. Ladle into bowls and serve.

Nutrition: calories 200, fat 4, fiber 1, carbs 3, protein 7

Chicken and Fennel Soup

Preparation time: 10 minutes
Cooking time: 30 minutes
Servings: 2

Ingredients:
- ½ pound chicken breast, skinless, boneless and cubed
- 1 small yellow onion, chopped
- ½ fennel bulb, chopped
- 2 green onions, chopped
- ½ cup spinach
- 1 cup chicken stock
- 1 garlic clove, minced
- A pinch of salt and black pepper
- 2 cup water
- 1 small bay leaf
- ½ tablespoon oregano, dried

Directions:
1. In your pressure cooker, mix chicken with onion, fennel, green onions, spinach, stock, garlic, water, bay leaf, oregano, salt and pepper, stir, cover and cook on Soup mode for 30 minutes.
2. Stir soup one more time, ladle into 2 bowls and serve.

Nutrition: calories 212, fat 4, fiber 2, carbs 6, protein 6

Onion Cream

Preparation time: 10 minutes
Cooking time: 40 minutes
Servings: 4

Ingredients:
- 3 pounds mixed onions, chopped
- 2 quarts chicken stock
- 6 tablespoons butter
- ½ cup dry sherry
- 1 teaspoon cider vinegar

Directions:
1. Set the cooker on sauté mode, add butter, melt it, add onions, stir and cook for 3 minutes.
2. Cover cooker and cook onions on High for 20 minutes more.
3. Add sherry, vinegar and stock, stir, cover and cook on High for 13 minutes.
4. Blend soup a bit using an immersion blender, ladle into bowls and serve.

Nutrition: calories 300, fat 12, fiber 5, carbs 20, protein 6

Black Bean Soup

Preparation time: 10 minutes
Cooking time: 20 minutes
Servings: 4

Ingredients:
- 45 ounces canned black beans and juice
- ½ cup cilantro, chopped
- 2 and ½ cups salsa
- 1 garlic clove
- 2 teaspoons cumin, ground

Directions:
1. In your pressure cooker, mix salsa with black beans, cilantro, garlic, and cumin, stir, cover and cook on High for 15 minutes.
2. Stir soup one more time, ladle into bowls and serve.

Nutrition: calories 184, fat 8, fiber 9, carbs 20, protein 7

Onion Soup

Preparation time: 10 minutes
Cooking time: 25 minutes
Servings: 2

Ingredients:
- 1 tablespoon avocado oil
- ½ tablespoon balsamic vinegar
- 4 cups yellow onion, chopped
- A pinch of salt and black pepper
- 3 cups pork stock
- 1 bay leaf
- 1 thyme sprigs, chopped

Directions:
1. Set your pressure cooker on sauté mode, add the oil and heat it up.
2. Add onion, some salt and pepper, stir and sauté for 15 minutes.
3. Add vinegar, thyme, bay leaf and stock, cover and cook on High for 10 minutes.
4. Discard bay leaf, blend soup using an immersion blender, ladle into 2 bowls and serve.

Nutrition: calories 210, fat 2, fiber 3, carbs 4, protein 6

Chicken and Red Cabbage Soup

Preparation time: 10 minutes
Cooking time: 35 minutes
Servings: 2

Ingredients:
- ½ pound chicken pieces
- 1 garlic clove, minced
- 1 small red onion, chopped
- ½ small red cabbage, chopped
- A pinch of salt and black pepper
- 1 carrot, chopped

- ½ teaspoon ginger powder
- ½ teaspoon cinnamon powder
- ½ teaspoon turmeric powder
- ½ teaspoon white peppercorns
- ½ tablespoon tamarind paste
- Juice from 1/3 lime
- Lime wedges for serving
- 1/3 pineapple, peeled and cubed
- 1 sprigs onion, chopped

Directions:
1. In your pressure cooker, mix chicken with carrot, red onion, salt, pepper, cabbage, garlic, peppercorns and water to cover everything.
2. Cover your pressure cooker and cook on Soup mode for 30 minutes.
3. Transfer chicken to a cutting board, cool it down, shred using 2 forks and return to the pot.
4. In a small bowl, mix 1 tablespoon soup with tamarind paste, stir and pour into the pot.
5. Add, cinnamon, ginger, turmeric, pineapple and lime juice, stir soup, set your pressure cooker on sauté mode and cook for 10 minutes more.
6. Ladle into 2 bowls, sprinkle sprigs onion on top and serve with lime wedges on the side.

Nutrition: calories 212, fat 1, fiber 3, carbs 4, protein 6

Minestrone Soup

Preparation time: 10 minutes
Cooking time: 6 minutes
Servings: 4

Ingredients:
- 27 ounces tomato paste
- 15 ounces canned cannellini beans, drained
- 2 cups veggie stock
- 1 cup orzo pasta, already cooker
- Grated parmesan for serving

Directions:
1. In your pressure cooker, mix tomato paste with beans and stock, stir, cover and cook on High for 6 minutes.
2. Add pasta, stir, ladle into bowls and serve with parmesan sprinkled on top.

Nutrition: calories 254, fat 2, fiber 7, carbs 12, protein 4

Swiss Chard Soup

Preparation time: 10 minutes
Cooking time: 6 minutes
Servings: 4

Ingredients:
- 8 cups Swiss chard, chopped
- 3 leeks, chopped
- Salt to the taste
- 1 cup coconut milk
- 1 and ½ cups chicken stock

Directions:
1. In your pressure cooker, mix chard with leeks, salt, stock and coconut milk, stir, cover and cook on High for 6 minutes.
2. Blend using an immersion blender, ladle into bowls and serve.

Nutrition: calories 142, fat 4, fiber 4, carbs 6, protein 7

Turkey Soup

Preparation time: 10 minutes
Cooking time: 12 minutes
Servings: 2

Ingredients:
- ½ pound turkey, ground
- ½ tablespoon olive oil
- ½ cup cauliflower florets
- 1 garlic clove, minced
- ½ cup yellow onion, chopped
- 10-ounce marinara sauce

- 2 cups chicken stock
- 1 cup water
- ½ cabbage head, chopped

Directions:
1. Add the oil to your pressure cooker, set on sauté mode, heat it up, add turkey, garlic and onion, stir and sauté for 5 minutes.
2. Add cauliflower, stock, water, marinara sauce and cabbage, stir, cover and cook on High for 6 minutes.
3. Ladle into bowls and serve.

Nutrition: calories 212, fat 1, fiber 3, carbs 3, protein 4

Red Pepper Soup

Preparation time: 10 minutes
Cooking time: 40 minutes
Servings: 2

Ingredients:
- ½ cauliflower head, florets separated
- 2 green onions, chopped
- 2 garlic cloves, minced
- 2 roasted red peppers, chopped
- 4 ounces canned tomatoes, chopped
- 1 carrot, chopped
- 1 red bell pepper, chopped
- 2 tablespoons Swiss chard, chopped
- 1 teaspoon onion powder
- 1 teaspoon garlic powder
- ½ tablespoon smoked paprika
- A pinch of cumin, dried
- 1 tablespoon apple cider vinegar
- 2 cups chicken stock
- A pinch of salt and black pepper

Directions:
1. Add the oil to your pressure cooker, set on sauté mode, heat it up, add red bell pepper, onion, carrot and garlic, stir and cook for 3 minutes.
2. Add onion powder, garlic powder, paprika, cumin, vinegar, salt and pepper, stir and cook for 1 minute more.
3. Add roasted peppers, tomatoes, cauliflower, Swiss chard and stock, stir, cover and cook on Soup mode for 30 minutes.
4. Stir soup one more time, ladle into 2 bowls and serve.

Nutrition: calorie 212, fat 4, fiber 1, carbs 3, protein 4

Broccoli and Cheese Soup

Preparation time: 10 minutes
Cooking time: 10 minutes
Servings: 8

Ingredients:

- 4 cups broccoli florets
- 3 and ½ cups chicken stock
- 1 cup heavy cream
- 3 cups cheddar cheese, grated
- 4 garlic cloves, minced

Directions:
1. Set your pressure cooker on sauté mode, add garlic and cook it for 1 minute.
2. Add broccoli, stock and cream, stir, cover and cook on High for 8-9 minutes.
3. Add cheese, stir until it melts, ladle into bowls and serve.

Nutrition: calories 291, fat 20, fiber 1, carbs 8, protein 13

Potato Soup

Preparation time: 10 minutes
Cooking time: 15 minutes
Servings: 8

Ingredients:
- 3 pounds potatoes, peeled and cubed
- 1 pint milk
- A pinch of salt
- 12 green onions, chopped
- 1 cup cheddar cheese, shredded

Directions:
1. In your pressure cooker, mix potatoes with milk and salt, stir, cover and cook on High for 12 minutes.
2. Add cheddar cheese and green onions, stir, set the cooker on sauté mode, cook until cheese melts, ladle everything into bowls and serve.

Nutrition: calories 314, fat 12, fiber 4, carbs 17, protein 5

Potato Soup

Preparation time: 10 minutes
Cooking time: 30 minutes
Servings: 2

Ingredients:
- 4 potatoes, peeled and cubed
- 1 carrot, chopped
- 4 ounces roasted garlic paste
- 3 tablespoons celery, chopped
- 2 tablespoons baby spinach leaves, chopped
- 1 yellow onion, chopped
- ½ cup chicken stock
- A pinch of salt and black pepper
- A pinch of smoked paprika
- ½ tablespoon chia seeds
- A pinch of red pepper, crushed

Directions:

1. In your pressure cooker, mix potatoes with carrot, garlic paste, celery, spinach, onion, stock, salt, pepper, paprika, chia seeds and red pepper, stir, cover and cook on Soup mode for 30 minutes.
2. Blend soup a bit using an immersion blender, ladle into 2 bowls and serve.

Nutrition: calories 213, fat 4, fiber 1, carbs 4, protein 4

Meatloaf

Preparation time: 10 minutes
Cooking time: 45 minutes
Servings: 2

Ingredients:
- ½ pound beef, ground
- 1 egg white
- 3 tablespoons breadcrumbs
- ½ yellow onion, chopped
- 3 black olives, pitted and sliced
- 2 basil leaves, chopped
- 1 tablespoon ketchup
- A pinch of salt and black pepper
- ½ teaspoon garlic, minced
- ½ tablespoon flaxseed, ground
- Cooking spray
- 1 cup water

For the glaze:
- ½ tablespoon brown mustard
- ½ tablespoon brown sugar
- 2 tablespoons ketchup

Directions:
1. In a bowl, mix beef with egg white, breadcrumbs, onion, olives, basil, 1 tablespoon ketchup, salt, pepper, garlic and flaxseed and stir really well.
2. Grease a meatloaf pan with cooking spray, add beef mixture and spread well.
3. In another bowl, mix mustard with sugar and 2 tablespoons ketchup, whisk well and brush your meatloaf with this.
4. Add the water to your pressure cooker, add the trivet, add the meatloaf pan, cover and cook on Manual for 45 minutes.
5. Leave meatloaf aside to cool down, slice, divide between 2 plates and serve.

Nutrition: calories 321, fat 5, fiber 2, carbs 4, protein 7

Cream of Spinach

Preparation time: 10 minutes
Cooking time: 10 minutes
Servings: 8

Ingredients:
- ½ pound mushrooms, sliced
- 1 yellow onion, chopped
- 1 and ¾ cup chicken stock
- 20 ounces cream of mushroom soup

- 20 ounces spinach, chopped

Directions:
1. In your pressure cooker, mix mushrooms with onion, cream of mushroom and stock, stir, cover and cook on High for 5 minutes.
2. Add spinach, stir, cover and cook on High for 5 minutes more.
3. Pulse using an immersion blender, divide into bowls and serve.

Nutrition: calories 172, fat 4, fiber 8, carbs 20, protein 4

Soup

Preparation time: 10 minutes
Cooking time: 5 minutes
Servings: 4

Ingredients:
- 1 ounce prosciutto, chopped
- 1 cup apple juice
- 4 cups cantaloupe, chopped
- ¼ teaspoon salt
- 1 tablespoon chives, chopped

Directions:
1. Set your pressure cooker on sauté mode, add prosciutto, stir, cook for 3 minutes and transfer to a bowl
2. Add apple juice, cantaloupe, salt and chives to the pot, stir, cover and cook on High for 2 minutes.
3. Blend using an immersion blender, ladle into bowls, sprinkle prosciutto on top and serve.

Nutrition: calories 100, fat 1, fiber 1, carbs 8, protein 2

Bean Casserole

Preparation time: 10 minutes
Cooking time: 15 minutes
Servings: 2

Ingredients:
- ½ pound lima beans, soaked for 10 hours and drained
- 3 tablespoons brown sugar
- 3 tablespoons butter
- ½ tablespoon dry mustard
- 4 cups water
- ½ tablespoon dark karo syrup
- A pinch of salt
- ½ cup sour cream

Directions:
1. In your pressure cooker, mix soaked beans with the water and some salt, cover and cook on Manual for 4 minutes.
2. Drain beans and return them to your pressure cooker.
3. Add sugar, butter, mustard, karo syrup, salt and sour cream, stir, cover and cook on Manual for 10 minutes more.
4. Divide between 2 plates and serve.

Nutrition: calories 212, fat 2, fiber 1, carbs 4, protein 10

Flavored Pasta

Preparation time: 10 minutes
Cooking time: 20 minutes
Servings: 2

Ingredients:
- 1 pound penne pasta
- 1 small shallot, chopped
- 1 small yellow onion, chopped
- 2 garlic cloves, minced
- 7 white mushrooms, sliced
- 1 small zucchini squash, sliced
- A pinch of basil, dried
- A pinch of oregano, dried
- A drizzle of olive oil
- A pinch of salt and black pepper

For the sauce:
- 3 ounces tomato paste
- ½ cup chicken stock
- 1 cup water
- 1 tablespoon soy sauce
- ½ tablespoon Worcestershire sauce
- ½ tablespoon fish sauce

Directions:
1. Set your pressure cooker on sauté mode, add a drizzle of oil, heat it up, add shallot, onion and garlic, stir and cook for 3 minutes.
2. Add salt, pepper, mushroom, zucchini, oregano and basil, stir, cook for 1 more minute and transfer to a bowl.
3. Add stock and water to your pressure cooker and stir really well.
4. Add soy sauce, Worcestershire sauce and fish sauce and stir really well.
5. Add pasta and tomato paste, cover and cook on High for 4 minutes.
6. Divide pasta on 2 plates, add veggie mix, drizzle the sauce from the cooker all over and serve.

Nutrition: calories 310, fat 4, fiber 1, carbs 3, protein 6

Mussels Bowls

Preparation time: 5 minutes
Cooking time: 6 minutes
Servings: 4

Ingredients:
- 2 pounds mussels, scrubbed and debearded
- 12 ounces dark beer
- 1 tablespoon olive oil
- 8 ounces spicy sausage
- 1 tablespoon paprika

Directions:
1. Set your pressure cooker on Sauté mode, add oil, heat it up, add sausages and cook for 4 minutes.
2. Add paprika, beer and mussels, stir, cover and cook on Low for 2 minutes.
3. Discard unopened mussels, divide everything into bowls and serve.

Nutrition: calories 162, fat 4, fiber 6, carbs 9, protein 6

Artichokes and Citrus Sauce

Preparation time: 10 minutes
Cooking time: 20 minutes
Servings: 4

Ingredients:
- 4 artichokes, trimmed and stems removed
- 1 tablespoon tarragon, chopped
- 2 cups chicken stock
- Lemon zest from 2 lemons, grated+ lemon pulp
- ½ cup olive oil

Directions:
1. Set your pressure cooker on sauté mode, add stock, oil, tarragon, lemon zest and lemon pulp, stir and heat up for 2-3 minutes.
2. Add artichokes, toss them a bit, cover and cook on High for 18 minutes.
3. Divide artichokes on plates, drizzle citrus sauce on top and serve.

Nutrition: calories 172, fat 3, fiber 4, carbs 12, protein 4

Beans Chili

Preparation time: 10 minutes
Cooking time: 50 minutes
Servings: 2

Ingredients:
- ½ cup mixed red, yellow and orange bell peppers, chopped
- ½ pound beef, ground
- 1 yellow onion, chopped
- 3 garlic cloves, minced
- 6 ounces canned tomatoes, chopped
- 2 cups kidney beans
- ½ tablespoon honey
- 2 teaspoons cocoa powder
- A pinch of salt and black pepper
- 1 teaspoon sweet paprika
- 1 teaspoon coriander
- 1 and ½ tablespoons chili powder
- ½ tablespoon cumin

Directions:
1. Set your pressure cooker on sauté mode, add beef, stir and brown for a few minutes.
2. Add onion and bell pepper, stir and cook for 2 minutes more.

3. Add garlic, tomatoes, beans, honey, cocoa powder, salt, pepper, paprika, coriander, chili powder and cumin, stir, cover and cook on Manual for 40 minutes.
4. Ladle into 2 bowls and serve hot.

Nutrition: calories 242, fat 3, fiber 1, carbs 3, protein 4

Pasta and Spinach

Preparation time: 10 minutes
Cooking time: 10 minutes
Servings: 2

Ingredients:
- 1/3 pound fusilli pasta
- 2 garlic cloves, minced
- 1 and ½ cups spinach, roughly chopped
- A pinch of salt and black pepper
- 1 and ½ tablespoons butter
- 1 and ½ cups water
- 2 tablespoon parmesan, grated

Directions:
1. In your pressure cooker, mix pasta with water.
2. Add spinach and garlic, cover and cook on High for 6 minutes.
3. Add parmesan, salt, pepper and butter, stir, cover and leave aside for 5 minutes.
4. Divide between 2 plates and serve.

Nutrition: calories 293, fat 1, fiber 2, carbs 7, protein 8

Chicken and Potatoes Mix

Preparation time: 10 minutes
Cooking time: 40 minutes
Servings: 4

Ingredients:
- 6 chicken thighs
- 1 teaspoon vegetable oil
- ½ cup white wine
- 15 ounces canned tomatoes, chopped
- 1 and ½ pounds potatoes, chopped

Directions:
1. Set your pressure cooker on Sauté mode, add oil, heat it up, add chicken, stir and brown them for 4 minutes on each side.
2. Add wine, tomatoes and potatoes, stir, cover and cook on High for 30 minutes.
3. Divide into bowls and serve.

Nutrition: calories 251, fat 10, fiber 2, carbs 8, protein 27

Cajun Sausage Mix

Preparation time: 15 minutes
Cooking time: 30 minutes
Servings: 8

Ingredients:
- 1 pound smoked sausage, sliced
- 1 pound red beans, dried, soaked overnight and drained
- 2 tablespoons Cajun seasoning
- ½ green bell pepper, chopped
- 5 cups water

Directions:
1. In your pressure cooker, mix beans with sausage, Cajun seasoning, bell pepper and water, stir, cover and cook on High for 30 minutes.
2. Divide mix into bowls and serve right away.

Nutrition: calories 210, fat 5, fiber 10, carbs 26, protein 12

Pea and Ham Soup

Preparation time: 10 minutes
Cooking time: 17 minutes
Servings: 2

Ingredients:
- 2 and ½ cups water
- 1 cup peas
- A pinch of salt and black pepper
- 4 tablespoons ham, chopped
- 1 small yellow onion, chopped

Directions:
1. In your pressure cooker, mix peas with water, salt, pepper, ham and onion, stir, cover and cook on High for 17 minutes.
2. Stir soup one more time, ladle into bowls and serve.

Nutrition: calories 193, fat 2, fiber 5, carbs 6, protein 9

Lamb Casserole

Preparation time: 10 minutes
Cooking time: 35 minutes
Servings: 2

Ingredients:
- ½ pound rack of lamb
- ½ pound baby potatoes
- 1 carrot, chopped
- ½ onion, chopped
- 1 celery stalk, chopped
- 1 tomato, chopped
- 1 cup chicken stock
- 2 garlic cloves, minced
- A pinch of salt and black pepper
- 1 teaspoon sweet paprika
- 1 teaspoon cumin, ground
- A pinch of oregano, dried
- A pinch of rosemary, dried
- 1 tablespoon ketchup
- 1 tablespoon red wine

Directions:
1. In your pressure cooker, mix lamb with baby potatoes, carrot, onion, celery, tomato, stock, garlic, salt, pepper, paprika, cumin, oregano, rosemary, ketchup and wine, cover and cook on Manual for 35 minutes.
2. Divide everything between 2 plates and serve.

Nutrition: calories 278, fat 5, fiber 4, carbs 6, protein 10

Turkey Mix

Preparation time: 10 minutes
Cooking time: 20 minutes
Servings: 4

Ingredients:
- 4 turkey wings
- 2 tablespoons olive oil
- 1 and ½ cups cranberries
- 1 cup orange juice
- 1 bunch thyme, roughly chopped

Directions:
1. Set your pressure cooker on Sauté mode, add oil, heat up, add turkey wings, brown them on all sides and transfer them to a bowl.
2. Add cranberries and thyme to your pressure cooker, stir and cook for 2 minutes.
3. Add orange juice, return turkey wings to pot, stir, cover, cook on High for 20 minutes and transfer turkey pieces to plates.
4. Set the cooker on sauté mode again, heat up the sauce for a couple of minutes more, drizzle over turkey winds and serve right away.

Nutrition: calories 293, fat 10, fiber 4, carbs 12, protein 20

Chicken Fall Stew

Preparation time: 10 minutes
Cooking time: 15 minutes
Servings: 4

Ingredients:
- 4 chicken thighs
- 2 cups mushrooms, sliced
- ½ teaspoon onion powder
- ½ cup water
- 1 teaspoon Dijon mustard

Directions:
1. Set your pressure cooker on sauté mode, add chicken and onion powder, stir, cook for 2 minutes on each side and transfer to a bowl.
2. Add mushrooms to your pressure cooker, stir and sauté them for 2 minutes more.
3. Return chicken to the pot, also add water and mustard, stir well, cover and cook on High for 10 minutes.
4. Divide between plates and serve right away.

Nutrition: calories 243, fat 8, fiber 4, carbs 10, protein 18

BBQ Ribs

Preparation time: 10 minutes
Cooking time: 40 minutes
Servings: 2

Ingredients:
- 1 rack baby back ribs
- 4 tablespoons BBQ sauce
- Salt and black pepper to the taste

- 1 cup water

Directions:
1. Season ribs with salt and pepper.
2. Add the water to your pressure cooker, add the trivet, add ribs inside, cover and cook on High for 25 minutes.
3. Transfer ribs to a baking sheet, brush with BBQ sauce, introduce in the oven at 450 degrees F and bake for 15 minutes.
4. Divide between 2 plates and serve.

Nutrition: calories 264, fat 3, fiber 1, carbs 8, protein 7

Jambalaya

Preparation time: 10 minutes
Cooking time: 25 minutes
Servings: 2

Ingredients:
- ½ tablespoon olive oil
- 1/3 pound chicken breasts, chopped
- 1/3 pound shrimp
- ½ cup mixed bell peppers, chopped
- ½ cup yellow onion, chopped
- ½ tablespoon garlic, minced
- 2 cups chicken stock
- ½ cup rice
- ½ cup tomatoes, crushed
- 2 teaspoons Creole seasoning
- 2 teaspoons Worcestershire sauce
- 1/3 pound sausage, cooked and sliced

Directions:
1. Add the oil to your pressure cooker, set it on sauté mode, heat it up, add chicken and half of the Creole seasoning, toss, brown for a few minutes on each side and transfer to a bowl.
2. Add bell pepper, onion and garlic to your pressure cooker and sauté them for 2 minutes.
3. Add rice, stir and cook for 2 minutes more.
4. Add the rest of the Creole seasoning, tomato, Worcestershire sauce and chicken, cover and cook on Rice mode.
5. Add sausage and shrimp, cover and cook on Manual for 2 minutes.
6. Divide between 2 plates and serve hot.

Nutrition: calories 312, fat 1, fiber 4, carbs 5, protein 12

Pork and Lemon Sauce

Preparation time: 10 minutes
Cooking time: 1 hour
Servings: 4

Ingredients:
- 1 and ½ pounds pork shoulder, chopped
- 3 garlic cloves, minced
- Juice of 1 lemon

- ½ cup water
- 2 tablespoons coconut aminos

Directions:
1. Set your pressure cooker on Sauté mode, heat it up, add pork, salt and pepper, stir and brown for 5 minutes on each side.
2. Add garlic, aminos, water and lemon juice, stir, cover and cook on High for 50 minutes.
3. Divide pork and sauce between plates and serve.

Nutrition: calories 330, fat 4, fiber 2, carbs 16, protein 24

Fennel Cream

Preparation time: 10 minutes
Cooking time: 15 minutes
Servings: 4

Ingredients:
- 2 fennel bulbs, chopped
- 3 cups water
- 2 bay leaves
- 2 tablespoon olive oil
- 4 teaspoons parmesan cheese, grated

Directions:
1. In your pressure cooker, mix fennel with bay leaves, oil and water, stir, cover and cook on High for 15 minutes.
2. Add cheese, blend a bit using an immersion blender, ladle into bowls and serve.

Nutrition: calories 226, fat 3, fiber 3, carbs 9, protein 5

Cod and Beer

Preparation time: 10 minutes
Cooking time: 30 minutes
Servings: 2

Ingredients:
- ½ pound cod fillet, boneless and skinless
- ½ cup beer
- 2 potatoes, peeled and roughly chopped
- ½ red bell pepper, chopped
- ½ tablespoon olive oil
- ½ tablespoon oyster sauce
- A pinch of salt
- ½ tablespoon rock candy

Directions:
1. Put fish in your pressure cooker.
2. Add beer, potatoes, bell pepper, oil, oyster sauce, salt and rock candy, cover and cook on Manual for 30 minutes.
3. Divide between 2 plates and serve.

Nutrition: calories 221, fat 2, fiber 1, carbs 4, protein 7

Salmon with Lemon

Preparation time: 10 minutes
Cooking time: 10 minutes
Servings: 2

Ingredients:
- ¾ cup water
- 2 parsley sprigs, chopped
- 2 dill sprigs, chopped
- 2 basil leaves, chopped
- 2 teaspoons olive oil
- A pinch of salt and black pepper
- ½ lemon, sliced
- 1 zucchini, chopped
- 1 red bell pepper, chopped
- 1 carrot, chopped
- 2 salmon fillets, skin on and boneless

Directions:
1. Put the water in your pressure cooker, add dill, basil and parsley and place the trivet inside.
2. Add salmon fillets, season with salt and pepper, drizzle the oil all over and top with lemon slices.
3. Cover the cooker and Steam fish for 3 minutes.
4. Divide salmon between 2 plates and keep warm for now.
5. Set your pressure cooker on sauté mode, add zucchini, bell pepper and carrot, stir and sauté for 4 minutes.
6. Divide next to salmon and serve.

Nutrition: calories 243, fat 4, fiber 1, carbs 3, protein 7

Cauliflower Salad

Preparation time: 10 minutes
Cooking time: 5 minutes
Servings: 10

Ingredients:
- 21 ounces cauliflower, florets separated
- 1 cup red onion, chopped
- 2 tablespoons balsamic vinegar
- 1 teaspoon stevia
- 1 cup mayonnaise
- ½ cup water, for the pressure cooker

Directions:
1. Put the water in your pressure cooker, add steamer basket, add cauliflower, cover cooker and cook on High for 5 minutes.
2. Transfer cauliflower to a bowl, add onion, stevia and vinegar and toss.
3. Add mayo, toss well, divide between plates and serve.

Nutrition: calories 171, fat 6, fiber 2, carbs 6, protein 3

Collard Greens Stew

Preparation time: 10 minutes
Cooking time: 30 minutes
Servings: 4

Ingredients:
- 2 cups bacon, chopped
- 1 pound collard greens, trimmed
- A pinch of salt and black pepper
- ½ cup chicken stock
- 3 tablespoons tomato paste

Directions:
1. Set your pressure cooker on sauté mode, add bacon, stir and brown for 5 minutes.
2. Add collard greens, salt, pepper, tomato paste and water, cover the cooker and cook on High for 20 minutes.
3. Divide into bowls and serve.

Nutrition: calories 325, fat 2, fiber 5, carbs 9, protein 4

Chinese Fish

Preparation time: 20 minutes
Cooking time: 10 minutes
Servings: 2

Ingredients:
For the marinade:
- 1 tablespoon rice wine
- 1 and ½ tablespoons soy sauce
- ½ tablespoon Chinese black bean paste
- ½ teaspoon garlic, minced
- ½ teaspoon ginger, minced
- 2 tilapia fillets, skinless and boneless

For the veggies:
- 2 cups water
- 2 tablespoons ginger, grated
- ½ tablespoon peanut oil
- 2 tablespoons cilantro, chopped
- 2 tablespoons green onions, chopped

Directions:
1. In a bowl, mix wine with soy sauce, black bean paste, garlic, ½ teaspoon ginger and the fish, toss well and leave aside for 20 minutes.
2. Add the water to your pressure cooker, add the steamer basket, place fish inside, cover and cook on Low for 2 minutes.
3. Meanwhile, heat up a pan with the oil over medium high heat, add 2 tablespoons ginger, cilantro and green onions, stir and cook for 2 minutes.
4. Add reserved marinade from the fish, stir well and cook for a couple more minutes.
5. Divide fish on 2 plates, add veggie mix on the side and serve.

Nutrition: calories 158, fat 1, fiber 2, carbs 3, protein 3

Salmon and Risotto

Preparation time: 10 minutes
Cooking time: 15 minutes
Servings: 2

Ingredients:
- 2 salmon fillets, boneless
- 1 and ½ cups water
- Juice from 1/3 lemon

For the rice:
- 1 small yellow onion, chopped
- 12 ounces mushrooms, sliced
- 1 cup artichokes, chopped
- ½ tablespoon garlic, minced
- 1 cup Arborio rice
- 2 tablespoons white wine
- 2 cups chicken stock
- ½ cup parmesan, grated
- 1 teaspoon olive oil

Directions:
1. Put the water in your pressure cooker, add the steamer basket, add the fish inside, drizzle lemon juice, cover, Steam for 3 minutes, divide between 2 plates and leave aside for now.
2. Clean your pressure cooker, add the oil and set it on Sauté mode.
3. Heat up the oil, add onion, garlic and mushrooms, stir and cook for 3 minutes.
4. Add artichokes, wine, ice and stock, stir, cover and cook on Manual for 7 minutes.
5. Add parmesan, stir a bit, divide next to salmon and serve right away.

Nutrition: calories 212, fat 3, fiber 2, carbs 4, protein 7

Spicy Chicken Wings

Preparation time: 10 minutes
Cooking time: 14 minutes
Servings: 4

Ingredients:
- 3 pounds chicken wings pieces
- 1 tablespoon Worcestershire sauce
- 4 tablespoons butter
- 4 tablespoons cayenne pepper sauce
- A pinch of salt
- 3 ounces water, for the pressure cooker

Directions:
1. Put the water in your pressure cooker, add steamer basket, add chicken wings, cover and cook on High for 8 minutes.
2. In a bowl, mix butter with Worcestershire sauce, pepper sauce and salt and whisk really well.
3. Brush chicken pieces with this mix, return them to steamer basket, cover cooker again and cook on High for 5 minutes more.
4. Divide between plates and serve with a side salad.

Nutrition: calories 201, fat 6, fiber 3, carbs 12, protein 4

Rich Chicken Salad

Preparation time: 10 minutes
Cooking time: 5 minutes
Servings: 2

Ingredients:
- 1 chicken breast, skinless and boneless
- 1 cup water for the pressure cooker,
- 2 garlic cloves, minced
- 2 tablespoons olive oil
- 1 tablespoon balsamic vinegar
- Mixed salad greens

Directions:
1. Add the water to your pressure cooker, add steamer basket, add chicken inside, cover, cook at High for 5 minutes, transfer to a cutting board, cool down, cut in thin strips, add to a bowl and mix with salad greens.
2. In a bowl, mix garlic with vinegar and olive oil, whisk very well, drizzle over chicken, toss, divide between plates and serve.

Nutrition: calories 173, fat 2, fiber 4, carbs 10, protein 6

Salmon Casserole

Preparation time: 10 minutes
Cooking time: 13 minutes
Servings: 2

Ingredients:
- 2 cups milk
- 2 salmon fillets, boneless
- 2 cups chicken stock
- ¼ cup olive oil
- A pinch of salt and black pepper
- 1 teaspoon garlic, minced
- 2 cups mixed peas and corn
- 4 ounces cream of celery soup
- ¼ teaspoon dill, chopped
- ¼ teaspoon cilantro, chopped
- 1 tablespoon parmesan, grated

Directions:
1. Add the oil to your pressure cooker, set on sauté mode, heat it up, add salmon and cook for a couple of minutes.
2. Flake salmon a bit, add garlic and chicken stock and stir.
3. Add milk, cream of celery, peas and corn, dill, cilantro, salt and pepper, stir gently, cover and cook on Manual for 8 minutes.
4. Add parmesan, divide between 2 plates and serve.

Nutrition: calories 312, fat 2, fiber 3, carbs 6, protein 7

Salmon and Chili Sauce

Preparation time: 10 minutes
Cooking time: 5 minutes
Servings: 2

Ingredients:
- 2 salmon fillets
- 1 cup water
- A pinch of salt and black pepper
- 1 jalapeno, chopped
- 2 garlic cloves, minced
- Juice from 1 lime
- 1 tablespoon olive oil
- 1 tablespoon honey
- 1 tablespoon hot water
- 1 tablespoon parsley, chopped
- ½ teaspoon cumin, ground
- ½ teaspoon sweet paprika

Directions:
1. IN a bowl, mix jalapeno with lime juice, garlic, honey, oil, 1 tablespoon water, parsley, paprika and cumin, whisk really well and leave aside for now.
2. Put 1 cup water in your pressure cooker, add the steamer basket, add salmon fillets inside, season with a pinch of salt and pepper, cover cooker and cook on Steam mode for 5 minutes.
3. Divide salmon on 2 plates, drizzle the sauce all over and serve.

Nutrition: calories 212, fat 2, fiber 3, carbs 4, protein 9

Calamari Stew

Preparation time: 10 minutes
Cooking time: 32 minutes
Servings: 3

Ingredients:
- 1 pound calamari, tentacles separated and cut into strips
- 7 ounces canned tomatoes, chopped
- ½ bunch parsley, chopped
- ¼ cup white wine
- 1 tablespoon olive oil

Directions:
1. Set your pressure cooker on Sauté mode, add oil and calamari, stir and cook for 9 minutes.
2. Add wine, tomatoes and half of the parsley, stir, cover and cook on High for 25 minutes.
3. Add the rest of the parsley, stir, divide into bowls and serve.

Nutrition: calories 160, fat 4, fiber 2, carbs 7, protein 7

Lamb Ribs and Sauce

Preparation time: 10 minutes
Cooking time: 30 minutes
Servings: 2

Ingredients:
- 4 lamb ribs
- 1 carrot, chopped
- 6 ounces veggie stock
- 1 tablespoon olive oil
- 1 tablespoon white flour

Directions:
1. Set your pressure cooker on Sauté mode, add the oil, heat it up, add lamb and brown it for a few minutes on all sides.
2. Add flour, carrot and stock stir, cover the pot, cook on High for 20 minutes.
3. Serve lamb with carrots on the side and cooking juices drizzled all over.

Nutrition: calories 200, fat 4, fiber 6, carbs 14, protein 25

Salmon and Veggies

Preparation time: 10 minutes
Cooking time: 5 minutes
Servings: 2

Ingredients:
- 2 medium salmon fillets, boneless
- ½ teaspoon cumin, ground
- ½ teaspoon sweet paprika
- 1 carrot, chopped
- 1 celery stalk, chopped
- 1 yellow onion, roughly chopped
- 1 cup broccoli florets, roughly chopped
- 2 tablespoon dry sherry
- A pinch of salt and black pepper
- 1 cup water

Directions:
1. In a heatproof pan, mix carrot with celery, onion, broccoli, salt and pepper and toss a bit.
2. Add salmon fillets on top, season them with salt, pepper, cumin and paprika and add dry sherry at the end.
3. Add the water to your pressure cooker, add the trivet, place the pan with the fish inside, cover and cook on High for 5 minutes.
4. Divide fish and veggies between 2 plates and serve.

Nutrition: calories 214, fat 2, fiber 5, carbs 7, protein 10

Pasta with Salmon and Pesto

Preparation time: 10 minutes
Cooking time: 9 minutes
Servings: 2

Ingredients:
- 8 ounces pasta
- 2 cups water
- 6 ounces smoked salmon, flaked

- A pinch of salt and black pepper
- ½ teaspoon lemon zest, grated
- ½ teaspoon lemon juice
- 2 tablespoons butter

For the pesto:
- 2 tablespoons walnuts
- 1 garlic clove
- 5 cups spinach leaves
- 2 tablespoons olive oil
- ½ cup parmesan, grated
- 1 tablespoon lemon zest, grated
- ½ cup heavy cream

Directions:
1. In your food processor, mix walnuts with garlic, spinach, olive oil, 1 tablespoon lemon zest, parmesan and ½ cup heavy cream, pulse well and leave aside for now.
2. Put the pasta in your pressure cooker, add the water and butter, cover and cook on High for 4 minutes.
3. Drain pasta into a bowl and clean your pressure cooker.
4. Set your pressure cooker on sauté mode, add salmon, a pinch of salt and pepper, ½ teaspoon lemon zest, lemon juice and pasta, stir and cook for 2 minutes.
5. Add pesto, toss well divide between plates and serve.

Nutrition: calories 216, fat 1, fiber 4, carbs 7, protein 8

Spicy Salmon

Preparation time: 10 minutes
Cooking time: 5 minutes
Servings: 2

Ingredients:
- 2 salmon fillets, boneless
- Juice from ½ lemon
- ½ lemon, sliced
- 1 tablespoon chili pepper, minced
- A pinch of salt and black pepper
- 1 cup water

Directions:
1. In a bowl, mix salmon with lemon juice, chili pepper, salt and pepper and toss.
2. Add the water to your pressure cooker, add the steamer basket, place fish inside, cover with lemon slices, cover the cooker and cook on High for 5 minutes.
3. Divide between 2 plates and serve with a side salad.

Nutrition: calories 153, fat 1, fiber 2, carbs 3, protein 7

Mediterranean Cod

Preparation time: 10 minutes
Cooking time: 15 minutes
Servings: 2

Ingredients:

- 2 cod fillets, boneless
- 1 and ½ tablespoon butter
- Juice from 1/3 lemon
- 1 small yellow onion, chopped
- A pinch of salt and black pepper
- ½ teaspoon oregano, dried
- 12 ounces canned tomatoes, chopped

Directions:
1. Set your pressure cooker on sauté mode, add the butter and melt it.
2. Add onion, tomatoes, salt, pepper, oregano and lemon juice, stir and cook for 10 minutes.
3. Add fish, cover the cooker and cook on High for 5 minutes.
4. Divide everything between 2 plates and serve.

Nutrition: calories 211, fat 1, fiber 2, carbs 2, protein 6

Pork Tenderloin and Pomegranate Sauce

Preparation time: 10 minutes
Cooking time: 40 minutes
Servings: 4

Ingredients:
- 2 pounds pork tenderloin, trimmed
- ¼ cup sugar
- 3 cups pomegranate juice
- A pinch of salt
- A pinch of black pepper

Directions:
1. Set your pressure cooker on sauté mode, add pomegranate juice, heat it up, add sugar, stir and cook until sugar starts to melt.
2. Add pork, salt and pepper, toss a bit, cover and cook on High for 40 minutes.
3. Leave pork to cool down, slice, divide between plates and serve with pomegranate sauce on top.

Nutrition: calories 215, fat 4, fiber 1, carbs 20, protein 24

Lemon Lamb Chops

Preparation time: 10 minutes
Cooking time: 15 minutes
Servings: 4

Ingredients:
- ½ teaspoon oregano, dried
- 2 tablespoons lemon juice
- 1 teaspoon olive oil
- 8 lamb chops, trimmed
- 1 cup chicken stock

Directions:
1. In your pressure cooker, mix lamb chops with oregano, lemon juice, oil and stock, toss well, cover and cook on High for 15 minutes.
2. Divide lamb chops between plates and serve right away.

Nutrition: calories 220, fat 10, fiber 1, carbs 2, protein 28

Chicken and Salsa

Preparation time: 10 minutes
Cooking time: 15 minutes
Servings: 4

Ingredients:
- 4 chicken breasts, skinless and boneless
- ½ cup water
- 16 ounces salsa
- 1 and ½ tablespoons parsley, chopped
- 1 teaspoon chili powder

Directions:
1. In your pressure cooker, mix chicken with water, salsa, parsley and chili powder, stir, cover and cook on High for 15 minutes.
2. Divide everything between plates and serve.

Nutrition: calories 187, fat 4, fiber 2, carbs 16, protein 10

Green Beans Stew

Preparation time: 10 minutes
Cooking time: 10 minutes
Servings: 4

Ingredients:
- 1 tablespoon olive oil
- 2 garlic cloves, minced
- 1 pound green beans
- 14 ounces canned tomatoes, chopped
- 1 tablespoon basil, chopped

Directions:
1. Set the pressure cooker on Sauté mode, add oil, heat it up, add garlic, stir and cook for 2 minutes.
2. Add tomatoes and green beans cover cooker and cook on High for 5 minutes.
1. Sprinkle basil, toss, divide between plates and serve.

Nutrition: calories 100, fat 3, fiber 5, carbs 10, protein 2

Fish and Orange Sauce

Preparation time: 10 minutes
Cooking time: 7 minutes
Servings: 2

Ingredients:
- 2 cod fillets, boneless
- Zest and juice from ½ orange
- 1 inch ginger, grated
- A drizzle of olive oil
- 2 sprigs onions, chopped
- ½ cup fish stock
- A pinch of salt and black pepper

Directions:
1. Season with salt and pepper, drizzle oil and rub well.
2. In your pressure cooker, mix stock with orange zest, juice, ginger and sprigs onions and stir.
3. Add the steamer basket, place fish inside, cover cooker and cook on High for 7 minutes.
4. Divide between 2 plates and serve with the orange sauce drizzled all over.

Nutrition: calories 212, fat 2, fiber 1, carbs 3, protein 4

Shrimp

Preparation time: 10 minutes
Cooking time: 2 minutes
Servings: 2

Ingredients:
- 1 pound shrimp
- 1 tablespoon olive oil

- 1 tablespoon butter
- ½ tablespoon garlic, minced
- ¼ cup white wine
- ¼ cup chicken stock
- ½ tablespoon lemon juice
- 1 tablespoon parsley, chopped
- A pinch of salt and black pepper
- Your favorite pasta, already cooked for serving

Directions:
1. Set your pressure cooker on sauté mode, add butter and oil, heat them up, add garlic, stir and cook for 1 minute.
2. Add stock and wine and stir.
3. Add shrimp and parsley, cover and cook on High for 2 minutes.
4. Divide shrimp on plates and serve with pasta on the side.

Nutrition: calories 198, fat 1, fiber 2, carbs 3, protein 5

Spinach Pasta

Preparation time: 5 minutes
Cooking time: 15 minutes
Servings: 4

Ingredients:
- 1 pound spinach
- 1 pound fusilli pasta
- 2 garlic cloves, minced
- A drizzle of olive oil
- ½ cup veggie stock

Directions:
1. Set pressure cooker on Sautee, add olive oil, heat it up, add spinach and garlic, stir and cook for 6-8 minutes.
2. Add pasta and stock, stir, cover and cook on Low for 6 minutes.
3. Stir again, divide between plates and serve.

Nutrition: calories 214, fat 1, fiber 4, carbs 15, protein 6

Chickpeas Cakes

Preparation time: 10 minutes
Cooking time: 25 minutes
Servings: 6

Ingredients:
- 1 cup dried chickpeas, soaked for 8 hours and drained
- 1 teaspoon cumin
- 1 teaspoon garlic powder
- 3 tablespoons tomato paste
- ½ cup whole wheat flour
- 1 cup water, for the pressure cooker + water for boiling the chickpeas

Directions:

1. Put chickpeas in your pressure cooker, add water to cover, cumin and garlic powder, stir, cover and cook on High for 15 minutes.
2. Transfer chickpeas to your food processor, pulse very well, add tomato paste and flour, blend again and shape 6 cakes out of this mix.
3. Add 1 cup water to your pressure cooker, add steamer basket, add chickpeas inside, cover and cook on High for 10 minutes.
4. Serve chickpeas cakes right away with a side salad.

Nutrition: calories 110, fat 1, fiber 4, carbs 20, protein 3

Side Dish Recipes

Baked Sweet Potatoes

Preparation time: 10 minutes
Cooking time: 10 minutes
Servings: 2

Ingredients:
- 2 big sweet potatoes, scrubbed
- 1 cup water
- A pinch of salt and black pepper
- ½ teaspoon smoked paprika
- ½ teaspoon cumin, ground

Directions:
1. Put the water in your pressure cooker, add the steamer basket, add sweet potatoes inside, cover and cook on High for 10 minutes.
2. Split potatoes, add salt, pepper, paprika and cumin, divide them between plates and serve as a side dish.

Nutrition: calories 152, fat 2, fiber 3, carbs 4, protein 4

Broccoli Pasta

Preparation time: 10 minutes
Cooking time: 4 minutes
Servings: 2

Ingredients:
- 2 cups water
- ½ pound pasta
- 8 ounces cheddar cheese, grated
- ½ cup broccoli
- ½ cup half and half

Directions:
1. Put the water and the pasta in your pressure cooker.
2. Add the steamer basket, add the broccoli, cover the cooker and cook on High for 4 minutes.
3. Drain pasta, transfer it as well as the broccoli, and clean the pot.
4. Set it on sauté mode, add pasta and broccoli, cheese and half and half, stir well, cook for 2 minutes, divide between plates and serve as a side dish for chicken.

Nutrition: calories 211, fat 4, fiber 2, carbs 6, protein 7

Cauliflower Rice

Preparation time: 10 minutes
Cooking time: 12 minutes
Servings: 2

Ingredients:
- 1 tablespoon olive oil
- ½ cauliflower head, florets separated
- A pinch of salt and black pepper

- A pinch of parsley flakes
- ¼ teaspoon cumin, ground
- ¼ teaspoon turmeric powder
- ¼ teaspoon paprika
- 1 cup water
- ½ tablespoon cilantro, chopped
- Juice from 1/3 lime

Directions:
1. Put the water in your pressure cooker, add the steamer basket, add cauliflower florets, cover and cook on High for 2 minutes.
2. Discard water, transfer cauliflower to a plate and leave aside.
3. Clean your pressure cooker, add the oil, set on sauté mode and heat it up.
4. Add cauliflower, mash using a potato masher, add salt, pepper, parsley, cumin, turmeric, paprika, cilantro and lime juice, stir well, cook for 10 minutes more, divide between 2 plates and serve as a side dish.

Nutrition: calories 191, fat 1, fiber 2, carbs 4, protein 5

Refried Beans

Preparation time: 10 minutes
Cooking time: 35 minutes
Servings: 2

Ingredients:
- 1 pound pinto beans, soaked for 20 minutes and drained
- 1 cup onion, chopped
- 2 garlic cloves, minced
- 1 teaspoon oregano, dried
- ½ jalapeno, chopped
- 1 teaspoon cumin, ground
- A pinch of salt and black pepper
- 1 and ½ tablespoon olive oil
- 2 cups chicken stock

Directions:
1. In your pressure cooker, mix oil with onion, jalapeno, garlic, oregano, cumin, salt, pepper, stock and beans, stir, cover and cook on Manual for 30 minutes.
2. Stir beans one more time, divide them between 2 plates and serve as a side dish.

Nutrition: calories 200, fat 1, fiber 3, carbs 7, protein 7

Sweet Brussels Sprouts

Preparation time: 10 minutes
Cooking time: 4 minutes
Servings: 2

Ingredients:
- ½ pounds Brussels sprouts
- 2 teaspoon buttery spread
- ½ teaspoon orange zest, grated
- 1 tablespoon orange juice

- ½ tablespoon maple syrup
- A pinch of salt and black pepper

Directions:
1. In your pressure cooker, mix Brussels sprouts with buttery spread, orange zest, orange juice, maple syrup, salt and pepper, stir, cover and cook on High for 4 minutes.
2. Divide between 2 plates and serve as a side dish.

Nutrition: calories 65, fat 2, fiber 3, carbs 10, protein 3

Roasted Potatoes

Preparation time: 10 minutes
Cooking time: 15 minutes
Servings: 2

Ingredients:
- ½ pound potatoes, cut into wedges
- ¼ teaspoon onion powder
- ½ teaspoon garlic powder
- 2 tablespoons avocado oil
- A pinch of salt and black pepper
- ½ cup chicken stock

Directions:
1. Set your pressure cooker on sauté mode, add the oil and heat it up.
2. Add potatoes, onion powder, garlic powder, salt and pepper, stir and sauté for 8 minutes.
3. Add stock, cover and cook on High for 7 minutes more.
4. Divide between 2 plates and serve as a side dish.

Nutrition: calories 192, fat 1, fiber 4, carbs 8, protein 8

Squash Risotto

Preparation time: 10 minutes
Cooking time: 13 minutes
Servings: 2

Ingredients:
- 1 small yellow onion, chopped
- A drizzle of olive oil
- 1 garlic clove, minced
- ½ red bell pepper, chopped
- 1 cup butternut squash, chopped
- 1 cup Arborio rice
- 1 and ½ cups veggie stock
- 3 tablespoons dry white wine
- 4 ounces mushrooms, chopped
- A pinch of salt and black pepper
- A pinch of oregano, dried
- ¼ teaspoon coriander, ground
- 1 and ½ cups mixed kale and spinach
- 1 tablespoon nutritional yeast

Directions:
1. Set your pressure cooker on sauté mode, add the oil and heat it up.
2. Add onion, bell pepper, squash and garlic, stir and cook for 5 minutes.
3. Add rice, stock, wine, salt, pepper, mushrooms, oregano and coriander, stir, cover and cook on High for 5 minutes.
4. Add mixed kale and spinach, parsley and yeast, stir and leave aside for 5 minutes.
5. Divide between 2 plates and serve as a side dish.

Nutrition: calories 163, fat 1, fiber 2, carbs 3, protein 6

Cabbage Side Dish

Preparation time: 10 minutes
Cooking time: 10 minutes
Servings: 2

Ingredients:
- ½ pound turkey sausage, sliced
- ½ cabbage head, shredded
- 2 garlic cloves, minced
- ½ yellow onion, chopped
- 1 teaspoon sugar
- 1 teaspoon balsamic vinegar
- 1 teaspoon mustard
- A drizzle of olive oil
- A pinch of salt and black pepper

Directions:
1. Set your pressure cooker on sauté mode, add the oil and heat it up.
2. Add onion, sausage and garlic, stir and sauté for 5 minutes.
3. Add cabbage, sugar, vinegar, mustard, salt and pepper, stir, cover and cook on High for 5 minutes more.
4. Divide between 2 plates and serve.

Nutrition: calories 200, fat 3, fiber 1, carbs 8, protein 3

Beans and Chorizo

Preparation time: 10 minutes
Cooking time: 42 minutes
Servings: 2

Ingredients:
- ½ tablespoon vegetable oil
- 3 ounces chorizo, chopped
- ½ pound black beans
- ½ yellow onion, chopped
- 3 garlic cloves, minced
- ½ orange
- 1 bay leaf
- 1 quart chicken stock
- A pinch of salt and black pepper
- 1 tablespoon cilantro, chopped

Directions:
1. Set your pressure cooker on sauté mode, add the oil and heat it up.
2. Add chorizo, stir and cook for 2 minutes.
3. Add garlic, onion, beans, orange, bay leaf, salt, pepper and stock, stir, cover and cook on High for 40 minutes.
4. Discard bay leaf and orange, add cilantro, stir, divide between plates and serve as a side dish.

Nutrition: calories 224, fat 1, fiber 2, carbs 7, protein 10

Spanish Rice

Preparation time: 10 minutes
Cooking time: 12 minutes
Servings: 2

Ingredients:
- ½ tablespoon olive oil
- ½ tablespoon butter
- ½ cup rice
- ½ cup chicken stock
- ½ cup tomato sauce
- 1 teaspoon chili powder
- ½ teaspoon cumin, ground
- ¼ teaspoon oregano, dried
- A pinch of salt and black pepper
- 2 tablespoons tomatoes, chopped

Directions:
1. Put the oil in your pressure cooker, set on sauté mode and heat it up.
2. Add rice, stir and cook for 4 minutes.
3. Add stock, tomato sauce, chili powder, cumin, oregano, tomatoes, salt and pepper, stir, cover and cook on High for 8 minutes.
4. Stir rice one more time, divide between 2 plates and serve as a side dish.

Nutrition: calories 174, fat 1, fiber 2, carbs 6, protein 8

Spaghetti Squash Delight

Preparation time: 10 minutes
Cooking time: 33 minutes
Servings: 2

Ingredients:
- 1 cup water
- 1 small spaghetti squash
- ½ cup apple juice
- 1 tablespoon duck fat
- A pinch of salt and black pepper

Directions:
1. Put the water in your pressure cooker, add the steamer basket, add the squash inside, cover and cook on High for 30 minutes.

2. Cut squash in half, scoop seeds and take out squash spaghetti.
3. Clean the pressure cooker, set it on sauté mode, add duck fat and heat it up.
4. Add apple juice, salt and pepper, stir and simmer for 3 minutes.
5. Divide squash spaghetti between 2 plates, drizzle the sauce all over, toss a bit and serve as a side dish.

Nutrition: calories 183, fat 3, fiber 3, carbs 7, protein 8

Artichokes Side Dish

Preparation time: 10 minutes
Cooking time: 20 minutes
Servings: 2

Ingredients:
- 2 artichokes, trimmed and tops cut off
- 1 cup water
- 1 lemon wedges

Directions:
1. Rub artichokes with the lemon wedge.
2. Add the water to your pressure cooker, add the steamer basket, place artichokes inside, cover and cook on High for 20 minutes.
3. Divide between 2 plates and serve as a side dish.

Nutrition: calories 100, fat 1, fiber 1, carbs 1, protein 3

Cabbage and Cream

Preparation time: 10 minutes
Cooking time: 10 minutes
Servings: 2

Ingredients:
- ½ cup bacon, chopped
- ½ yellow onion, chopped
- 1 cup beef stock
- 1 pound Savoy cabbage, chopped
- A pinch of nutmeg, ground
- ½ cup coconut milk
- 1 small bay leaf
- 1 tablespoon parsley flakes
- A pinch of salt

Directions:
1. Set your pressure cooker on sauté mode, add bacon and onion, stir and cook for 3 minutes.
2. Add stock, bay leaf and cabbage, cover the cooker and cook on Manual for 4 minutes.
3. Set the cooker on sauté mode again, add coconut milk, nutmeg and a pinch of salt, discard bay leaf, stir cabbage and simmer for 4 minutes.
4. Sprinkle parsley flakes at the end, divide between 2 plates and serve.

Nutrition: calories 229, fat 2, fiber 4, carbs 9, protein 6

Carrots and Kale

Preparation time: 10 minutes

Cooking time: 11 minutes
Servings: 2

Ingredients:
- 10 ounces kale, roughly chopped
- 1 tablespoon butter
- 3 carrots, sliced
- 1 yellow onion, chopped
- 4 garlic cloves, minced
- ½ cup chicken stock
- A pinch of salt and black pepper
- A splash of balsamic vinegar
- ¼ teaspoon red pepper flakes

Directions:
1. Set your pressure cooker on sauté mode, add butter and melt it.
2. Add onion and carrots, stir and cook for 3 minutes.
3. Add garlic, stir and cook for 1 minute more.
4. Add kale and stock, cover and cook on High for 7 minutes.
5. Add vinegar and pepper flakes, stir, divide between 2 plates and serve.

Nutrition: calories 183, fat 2, fiber 3, carbs 6, protein 8

Beets Side Dish

Preparation time: 10 minutes
Cooking time: 25 minutes
Servings: 2

Ingredients:
- 2 beets
- 1 tablespoon balsamic vinegar
- ½ bunch parsley, chopped
- A pinch of salt and black pepper
- 1 small garlic clove, minced
- ½ tablespoon olive oil
- 1 tablespoon capers
- 1 cup water

Directions:
1. Put the water in your pressure cooker, add the steamer basket, add beets inside, cover and cook on High for 25 minutes.
2. Transfer beets to a cutting board, leave aside to cool down, peel, slice and transfer to a bowl.
3. In another bowl, mix parsley with salt, pepper, garlic, oil and capers and whisk really well.
4. Divide beets on plates, drizzle vinegar all over, add parsley dressing and serve as a side dish.

Nutrition: calories 76, fat 2, fiber 1, carbs 4, protein 1

Sweet Potato Puree

Preparation time: 10 minutes
Cooking time: 20 minutes
Servings: 2

Ingredients:
- 2 tablespoons butter
- A pinch of sea salt and black pepper
- 1 pounds sweet potatoes, roughly chopped
- A pinch of baking soda
- ½ teaspoon chipotle powder, dried
- 2 tablespoons brown sugar
- 3 tablespoons water

Directions:
1. Set your pressure cooker on sauté mode, add the butter and melt it.
2. Add sweet potatoes, baking soda, sugar, chipotle powder, water, salt and pepper, stir, cover and cook on High for 16 minutes.
3. Mash using a potato masher, divide between 2 plates and serve as a side dish.

Nutrition: calories 121, fat 1, fiber 2, carbs 3, protein 7

Beet and Cabbage Mix

Preparation time: 10 minutes
Cooking time: 20 minutes
Servings: 2

Ingredients:
- 1 small apple, cored and chopped
- 2 cups chicken stock
- ½ small green cabbage head, chopped
- ½ yellow onion, chopped
- 1 beet, chopped
- 1 carrot, chopped
- ½ tablespoons ginger, grated
- ½ teaspoon gelatin
- 1 tablespoon parsley
- A pinch of salt

Directions:
1. In your pressure cooker, mix apple with beet, cabbage, onion, carrot, ginger, gelatin, stock, salt and parsley, stir, cover and cook on High for 20 minutes.
2. Divide between 2 plates and serve as a side dish.

Nutrition: calories 100, fat 1, fiber 2, carbs 2, protein 4

Broccoli and Garlic

Preparation time: 10 minutes
Cooking time: 15 minutes
Servings: 2

Ingredients:
- 1 broccoli head, florets separated
- 5 garlic cloves, minced

- ½ cup water
- 1 tablespoon olive oil
- 1 tablespoon rice wine
- A pinch of salt and black pepper

Directions:
1. Put the water in your pressure cooker, add the steamer basket, add broccoli, cover cooker and cook on High for 10 minutes.
2. Transfer broccoli to a bowl filled with ice water, cool it down, drain and transfer to a bowl.
3. Clean your pressure cooker, set on sauté mode, add the oil and heat it up.
4. Add garlic, stir and cook for 1-2 minutes.
5. Add salt, pepper and wine, stir and cook for 1 minute more.
6. Add broccoli, stir, cook everything for 1-2 minutes more, divide between plates and serve as a side dish.

Nutrition: calories 121, fat 2, fiber 1, carbs 2, protein 4

Creamy Corn

Preparation time: 10 minutes
Cooking time: 10 minutes
Servings: 2

Ingredients:
- 4 ounces cream cheese
- ½ cup milk
- 30 ounces canned corn, drained
- ½ stick butter
- ½ tablespoon sugar
- A pinch of salt and black pepper

Directions:
1. In your pressure cooker, mix corn with cream cheese, milk, butter, sugar, salt and pepper, stir, cover and cook on Low for 10 minutes.
2. Divide between plates and serve as a side dish.

Nutrition: calories 211, fat 2, fiber 4, carbs 6, protein 4

Rice and Quinoa

Preparation time: 10 minutes
Cooking time: 13 minutes
Servings: 2

Ingredients:
- 1 cup sprouted rice and quinoa
- 1 and ½ cups water
- A pinch of salt and white pepper
- ½ teaspoon cumin, ground
- A pinch of smoked paprika

Directions:
1. In your pressure cooker, mix rice and quinoa with water, salt, pepper, cumin and paprika, stir, cover and cook on High for 13 minutes.

2. Fluff with a fork, divide between 2 plates and serve as a side dish.

Nutrition: calories 100, fat 1, fiber 2, carbs 2, protein 6

Mushrooms Side Dish

Preparation time: 10 minutes
Cooking time: 6 minutes
Servings: 2

Ingredients:
- 1 and ½ tablespoons olive oil
- 2 small garlic cloves, minced
- ½ pound mushrooms, sliced
- 1 and ½ tablespoons balsamic vinegar
- 1 and ½ tablespoons white wine
- A pinch of salt and black pepper

Directions:
1. Set your pressure cooker on sauté mode, add the oil and heat it up.
2. Add garlic and mushrooms, stir and cook for 3 minutes.
3. Add wine and vinegar, stir, cover and cook on High for 2 minutes.
4. Add salt and pepper, stir, divide between 2 plates and serve as a side dish.

Nutrition: calories 121, fat 2, fiber 3, carbs 4, protein 5

Mashed Potatoes

Preparation time: 10 minutes
Cooking time: 8 minutes
Servings: 2

Ingredients:
- 2 big potatoes, peeled and cubed
- ½ cup chicken stock
- 1 garlic clove, minced
- 2 tablespoons milk
- 1 and ½ tablespoon butter
- 1 rosemary sprigs, chopped
- 1 tablespoon sour cream
- A pinch of salt and black pepper

Directions:
1. In your pressure cooker, mix potatoes with stock, garlic and rosemary, cover and cook on High for 8 minutes.
2. Transfer potatoes to a bowl, mash using a potato masher, add milk, butter, salt and pepper and whisk really well.
3. Add sour cream, stir mashed potatoes again, divide between 2 plates and serve as a side dish.

Nutrition: calories 165, fat 3, fiber 2, carbs 4, protein 5

Mushrooms and Asparagus

Preparation time: 10 minutes
Cooking time: 4 minutes
Servings: 2

Ingredients:
- ½ pound asparagus crowns
- 4 tablespoons mushrooms, sliced
- 3 tablespoons chicken stock
- Salt and black pepper to the taste

Directions:
1. In your pressure cooker, mix asparagus with mushrooms, stock, salt and pepper, stir, cover and cook on Low for 2 minutes.
2. Divide between 2 plates and serve as a side dish.

Nutrition: calories 110, fat 1, fiber 1, carbs 2, protein 4

Onion, Celery and Bread Side Dish

Preparation time: 10 minutes
Cooking time: 20 minutes
Servings: 2

Ingredients:
- ½ yellow onion, chopped
- ½ cup celery, chopped
- 3 tablespoons butter
- 1 cup chicken stock
- A pinch of salt and black pepper
- 1 small sourdough bread, cubed and toasted
- ½ teaspoon poultry seasoning
- 1 and ½ cups water

Directions:
1. Put the stock in a small cooker and bring to a simmer over medium heat.
2. Add butter, onion and celery, stir and simmer for 5 minutes.
3. Add salt, pepper and poultry seasoning, stir and take off heat.
4. In a bowl, mix bread cubes with stock mix, stir well, pour everything into a Bundt pan and cover with tin foil.
5. Add the water to your pressure cooker, add the trivet, place pan inside, cover cooker and cook on high for 15 minutes.
6. Divide between 2 plates and serve as a side dish.

Nutrition: calories 192, fat 2, fiber 2, carbs 6, protein 6

Cranberry Side Dish

Preparation time: 10 minutes
Cooking time: 7 minutes
Servings: 2

Ingredients:
- ½ pound cranberries, fresh

- ½ cup sugar
- 2 tablespoons lime zest, grated
- Juice from ½ orange

Directions:
1. In your pressure cooker, mix cranberries with sugar, lime zest and orange juice, stir, cover and cook on High for 7 minutes.
2. Serve as a side dish for a tasty steak.

Nutrition: calories 100, fat 0, fiber 0, carbs 0, protein 2

Green Beans and Bacon

Preparation time: 10 minutes
Cooking time: 3 minutes
Servings: 2

Ingredients:
- 1 cup water
- ½ pound green beans, trimmed
- 2 tablespoon bacon, chopped
- 2 teaspoons butter
- A pinch of salt and black pepper

Directions:
1. Put the water in your pressure cooker, add the steamer basket, add green beans, cover and cook on High for 3 minutes.
2. Transfer beans to a bowl, add butter and stir until it melts.
3. Add bacon, salt and pepper, toss, divide between 2 plates and serve as a side dish.

Nutrition: calories 142, fat 2, fiber 4, carbs 6, protein 6

Beans and Avocado Salsa

Preparation time: 10 minutes
Cooking time: 45 minutes
Servings: 2

Ingredients:
- ½ pound pinto beans, soaked and drained
- 1 tablespoon olive oil
- ½ yellow onion, chopped
- ½ poblano pepper, chopped
- ½ red bell pepper, chopped
- ½ green bell pepper, chopped
- ½ tablespoon garlic, minced
- ½ tablespoon cumin, ground
- 1 teaspoon oregano, dried
- 1 and ½ cups veggie stock
- A pinch of salt and black pepper

For the salsa:
- 2 tablespoons lime juice
- 1 avocado, peeled, pitted and chopped
- ½ red onion, chopped

- ½ poblano pepper, chopped
- 1 tablespoon olive oil

Directions:
3. Put beans, stock and ½ tablespoon oil in your pressure cooker, cover and cook on High for 30 minutes.
4. Meanwhile, heat up a pan with ½ tablespoon oil over medium high heat, add ½ poblano pepper, yellow onion, green and red bell pepper, stir and cook for 5 minutes.
5. Add oregano, garlic, salt, pepper and cumin, stir and cook for 2 minutes more.
6. Drain beans, clean your pressure cooker, add beans and set the cooker on sauté mode.
7. Add bell peppers, mix, stir, cover and cook on High for 6 minutes.
8. In a bowl, mix avocado with ½ red onion, ½ poblano pepper, 1 tablespoon oil, lime juice, and whisk really well.
9. Add this to beans, toss and serve as a side dish.

Nutrition: calories 182, fat 2, fiber 2, carbs 6, protein 6

Spicy Zucchini

Preparation time: 10 minutes
Cooking time: 1 minute
Servings: 2

Ingredients:
- 2 zucchinis, sliced
- 1/3 cup water
- ½ tablespoon butter
- 1 tablespoon Cajun seasoning
- ½ teaspoon smoked paprika
- ½ teaspoon garlic powder

Directions:
1. In your pressure cooker, mix zucchini slices with butter, water, Cajun seasoning, paprika and garlic powder, stir, cover and cook on High for 1 minute.
2. Divide between 2 plates and serve as a side dish.

Nutrition: calories 113, fat 1, fiber 1, carbs 1, protein 2

Mexican Zucchini Side Dish

Preparation time: 10 minutes
Cooking time: 15 minutes
Servings: 2

Ingredients:
- ½ tablespoon olive oil
- 1 poblano pepper, cut into thin strips
- 1 small yellow onion, chopped
- 1 teaspoon butter
- ½ tablespoon garlic, minced
- ½ zucchini, roughly chopped
- ½ yellow squash, peeled and roughly chopped
- A pinch of salt and black pepper
- 3 tablespoons chicken stock

- ¼ teaspoon cumin, ground
- ½ tablespoon sour cream

Directions:
4. Set your pressure cooker on sauté mode, add the oil and heat it up.
5. Add poblano strips, stir and cook for 10 minutes
6. Add butter, garlic and onion, stir and cook for 2 minutes more.
7. Add zucchini, squash, salt, pepper, cumin and stock, stir, cover and cook on Low for 2 minutes more
8. Add sour cream, toss to coat, divide between 2 plates and serve as a side dish.

Nutrition: calories 104, fat 1, fiber 2, carbs 3, protein 1

Zucchini and Mushrooms

Preparation time: 10 minutes
Cooking time: 6 minutes
Servings: 2

Ingredients:
- ½ tablespoon olive oil
- 1 cup yellow onion, chopped
- 1 garlic clove, minced
- 4 ounces mushrooms, sliced
- 1 teaspoon basil, dried
- A pinch of salt and black pepper
- 2 zucchinis, sliced
- 5 ounces tomatoes and juice, crushed

Directions:
1. Add the oil to your pressure cooker, set on sauté mode and heat it up.
2. Add mushroom, garlic and onion, stir and cook for 4 minutes.
3. Add salt, pepper and basil and stir.
4. Add zucchinis and toss a bit,
5. Add tomatoes, cover and cook on Low for 1 minute.
6. Divide between 2 plates and serve as a side dish.

Nutrition: calories 142, fat 2, fiber 2, carbs 5, protein 5

Yellow Squash and Zucchini

Preparation time: 10 minutes
Cooking time: 6 minutes
Servings: 2

Ingredients:
- 1 cup zucchini, sliced
- 1 cup yellow squash, peeled, sliced and then roughly chopped
- ½ teaspoon Italian seasoning
- A pinch of salt and black pepper
- ½ teaspoon garlic powder
- 2 tablespoons butter
- ½ cup veggie stock

- 2 tablespoons parmesan, grated
- 2 tablespoons pork rinds, crushed

Directions:
1. Set your pressure cooker on sauté mode, add the garlic and heat it up.
2. Add zucchini, squash, Italian seasoning, salt, pepper and garlic powder, stir and sauté for 5 minutes.
3. Add stock, cover and cook on Low for 1 minute.
4. Add parmesan and pork rinds, toss a bit, divide between 2 plates and serve as a side dish.

Nutrition: calories 121, fat 2, fiber 3, carbs 3, protein 5

Bell Peppers Stir Fry

Preparation time: 10 minutes
Cooking time: 15 minutes
Servings: 2

Ingredients:
- 2 red bell peppers, cut into medium strips
- 1 tablespoon olive oil
- 4 small potatoes, cubed
- ½ teaspoon cumin seeds
- 1 tablespoon water
- 3 garlic cloves, minced
- ½ teaspoon dry mango powder
- 1 tablespoon cilantro, chopped
- ¼ teaspoon turmeric powder
- ½ teaspoon cayenne pepper
- 2 teaspoons coriander powder

Directions:
1. Set your pressure cooker on sauté mode, add the oil and heat it up.
2. Add garlic and cumin, stir and cook for 1 minute.
3. Add potatoes, bell peppers, turmeric, water, cayenne and coriander, stir, cover and cook on High for 2 minutes.
4. Add mango powder and cilantro, toss a bit, divide between 2 plates and serve as a side dish.

Nutrition: calories 124, fat 2, fiber 1, carbs 3, protein 4

Bell Peppers and Sausages

Preparation time: 10 minutes
Cooking time: 25 minutes
Servings: 2

Ingredients:
- 5 sausages, sliced
- 2 green bell peppers, cut into strips
- 14 ounces canned tomatoes, chopped
- 6 ounces tomato sauce
- ½ cup water
- ½ tablespoon basil, chopped
- 1 teaspoon garlic powder

- ½ tablespoon Italian seasoning

Directions:
1. In your pressure cooker, mix sausage slices with bell pepper strips, tomatoes, tomato sauce, water, basil, garlic powder and Italian seasoning, stir a bit, cover and cook on High for 25 minutes.
2. Divide between 2 plates and serve as a side dish.

Nutrition: calories 176, fat 3, fiber 2, carbs 4, protein 6

Mixed Veggies Side Dish

Preparation time: 10 minutes
Cooking time: 10 minutes
Servings: 2

Ingredients:
- 2 tablespoons olive oil
- ½ sweet onion, sliced
- 1 tablespoon garlic, crushed
- 1 tablespoon tomato paste
- 1 small eggplant, cut into small cubes
- 1 small green bell pepper, cut into small chunks
- 1 small red bell pepper, cut into small chunks
- 1 small green zucchini, chopped
- ½ yellow squash, peeled and cubed
- 6 ounces canned tomatoes, chopped
- 1 teaspoon Italian seasoning
- A pinch of salt and black pepper
- 1/3 cup veggie stock

Directions:
1. Set your pressure cooker on sauté mode, add the oil and heat it up.
2. Add onions, stir and cook for 3 minutes.
3. Add tomato paste and garlic, stir and cook for a few seconds more.
4. Add eggplant, green bell pepper, red bell pepper, zucchini, squash, tomatoes, salt, pepper, Italian seasoning and stock, stir, cover and cook on High for 7 minutes.
5. Divide between 2 plates and serve as a side dish.

Nutrition: calories 126, fat 2, fiber 2, carbs 4, protein 7

Braised Endives

Preparation time: 10 minutes
Cooking time: 10 minutes
Servings: 2

Ingredients:
- ½ pounds Belgian endives, halved
- A pinch of salt and black pepper
- ½ tablespoon olive oil
- 1 small garlic clove, minced
- A pinch of nutmeg, ground
- 2 teaspoons brown sugar

- 2 ounces water

Directions:
1. Set your pressure cooker on sauté mode, add the oil and heat it up.
2. Add endives, cook for 2 minutes and mix with garlic, nutmeg and sugar.
3. Stir gently, cook for 1 minute, add water, cover and cook on High for 7 minutes.
4. Divide between 2 plates and serve as a side dish.

Nutrition: calories 172, fat 2, fiber 1, carbs 2, protein 4

Bok Choy Side Dish

Preparation time: 10 minutes
Cooking time: 15 minutes
Servings: 2

Ingredients:
- ½ tablespoon peanut oil
- 1 small garlic clove, minced
- 1 small ginger piece, grated
- ½ pound baby bok choy, trimmed
- A pinch of salt and black pepper
- 1/3 cup water
- A pinch of red pepper flakes
- ½ tablespoon soy sauce
- ½ tablespoon rice vinegar
- ½ teaspoon sesame oil

Directions:
1. Put the peanut oil in your pressure cooker, set the cooker on sauté mode and heat it up.
2. Add garlic and ginger, stir and cook for 3 minutes.
3. Add bok choy, salt, pepper and water, cover and cook on High for 5 minutes.
4. In a bowl, mix vinegar with sesame oil and soy sauce and whisk really well.
5. Divide bok choy between 2 plates, drizzle the sauce all over, sprinkle red pepper flakes and serve as a side dish.

Nutrition: calories 100, fat 1, fiber 2, carbs 3, protein 3

Bok Choy and Rice

Preparation time: 10 minutes
Cooking time: 5 minutes
Servings: 2

Ingredients:
- ½ tablespoon olive oil
- 2 tablespoons yellow onion, chopped
- 1 garlic clove, minced
- 1 cup Arborio rice
- 3 tablespoons white wine
- 2 cups veggie stock
- 1 and ½ cups bok choy, trimmed and roughly chopped
- A pinch of red pepper flakes
- A pinch of salt and black pepper

Directions:
1. set your pressure cooker on sauté mode, add the oil, heat it up, add onion and garlic, stir and cook for 1 minute.
2. Add rice and wine, stir and cook for 1 minute more.
3. Add stock, cover cooker and cook on High for 4 minutes.
4. Add bok choy, salt, pepper and pepper flakes, stir everything, divide between 2 plates and serve as a side dish.

Nutrition: calories 100, fat 2, fiber 1, carbs 3, protein 4

Collard Greens and Bacon

Preparation time: 10 minutes
Cooking time: 30 minutes
Servings: 2

Ingredients:
- 1 cup bacon, chopped
- ½ pound collard greens, trimmed
- A pinch of salt and black pepper
- 4 tablespoons water

Directions:
4. Set your pressure cooker on sauté mode, add bacon, stir and brown for 5 minutes.
5. Add collard greens, salt, pepper and water, cover the cooker and cook on High for 20 minutes.
6. Divide between 2 plates and serve as a side dish.

Nutrition: calories 165, fat 2, fiber 2, carbs 3, protein 5

Collard Greens Side Dish

Preparation time: 10 minutes
Cooking time: 6 minutes
Servings: 2

Ingredients:
- 1 bunch collard greens, trimmed and cut into medium strips
- ½ yellow onion, roughly chopped
- 1 tablespoon water
- 2 garlic cloves, minced
- ½ cup water
- A pinch of salt
- A pinch of red pepper flakes

Directions:
1. Set your pressure cooker on sauté mode, add 1 tablespoon water and onion, stir and cook for 2 minutes.
2. Add pepper flakes, salt and garlic, stir and cook for 1 minute more.
3. Add collard greens and 1 cup water, stir, cover and cook on High for 3 minutes.
4. Divide between 2 plates and serve as a side dish.

Nutrition: calories 87, fat 1, fiber 2, carbs 2, protein 3

Spicy Collard Greens

Preparation time: 10 minutes
Cooking time: 30 minutes
Servings: 2

Ingredients:
- 1 bunch collard greens, cut into strips
- 2 cups chicken stock
- 2 bacon slices, chopped
- 1 garlic clove, minced
- 1 small jalapeno, chopped
- 2 teaspoons Creole seasoning
- A splash of apple cider vinegar

Directions:
1. Set your pressure cooker on sauté mode, add bacon, stir and cook for 4 minutes.
2. Add garlic, stir and cook for 1 minute more.
3. Add jalapeno, collard greens, Creole seasoning and stock, stir, cover and cook on High for 25 minutes.
4. Divide between plates, add a splash of vinegar all over and serve as a side dish.

Nutrition: calories 103, fat 1, fiber 1, carbs 2, protein 3

Rice and Edamame

Preparation time: 10 minutes
Cooking time: 12 minutes
Servings: 2

Ingredients:
- 1 small yellow onion, chopped
- ½ tablespoon olive oil
- ½ tablespoon butter
- 1 cup white rice
- 2 cups chicken stock
- A pinch of salt and black pepper
- 3 tablespoons white wine
- ½ cup edamame

Directions:
1. Set your pressure cooker on sauté mode, add the oil and the butter and heat them up.
2. Add onion, stir and cook for 3 minutes.
3. Add rice, stir and cook for 2 minutes more.
4. Add wine, stock, salt, pepper and edamame, stir, cover and cook on High for 7 minutes.
5. Stir rice one more time, divide between plates and serve.

Nutrition: calories 110, fat 1, fiber 1, carbs 2, protein 4

Poached Fennel

Preparation time: 10 minutes
Cooking time: 10 minutes
Servings: 2

Ingredients:
- 2 fennel bulbs, sliced
- A pinch of salt and white pepper
- 1 tablespoon butter
- 1 tablespoon white flour
- 1 and ½ cups milk
- A pinch of nutmeg, ground

Directions:
1. Set your pressure cooker on sauté mode, add the butter and heat it up.
2. Add fennel slices, stir and brown for a few minutes more.
3. Add salt, pepper, nutmeg, flour and milk, toss well, cover cooker and cook on High for 6 minutes.
4. Divide fennel on 2 plates and serve as a side dish.

Nutrition: calories 76, fat 1, fiber 2, carbs 2, protein 4

Fennel and Shallots

Preparation time: 10 minutes
Cooking time: 10 minutes
Servings: 2

Ingredients:
- 1 big fennel bulb, sliced
- A pinch of salt and black pepper
- ½ pound shallots, sliced
- 2 tablespoons olive oil
- ½ cup orange juice
- 1 teaspoon parsley, chopped
- ½ teaspoon orange zest, grated

Directions:
1. Set your pressure cooker on sauté mode, add the oil and heat it up.
2. Add shallots, stir and cook for 4 minutes.
3. Add fennel, salt, pepper, orange juice and zest and parsley, stir a bit, cover and cook on high for 7 minutes.
4. Divide fennel mix on 2 plates and serve as a side dish.

Nutrition: calories 92, fat 1, fiber 1, carbs 2, protein 3

Pea Rice

Preparation time: 10 minutes
Cooking time: 10 minutes
Servings: 2

Ingredients:
- 2 tablespoons butter
- 1 yellow onion, chopped
- 2 celery sticks, chopped
- A pinch of salt and black pepper
- 1 cup white rice

- 1 cup baby peas
- 2 garlic cloves, minced
- Zest from ½ lemon, grated
- 2 cup veggie stock
- 2 tablespoons lemon juice
- 1 ounce parmesan, grated

Directions:
1. Set your pressure cooker on sauté mode, add the butter and melt it.
2. Add onion, salt, pepper and celery, stir and cook for 4 minutes.
3. Add peas, rice, garlic, lemon zest, stock, salt and pepper, stir, cover and cook on High for 5 minutes.
4. Add lemon juice and parmesan, stir again, divide between plates and serve as a side dish.

Nutrition: calories 198, fat 3, fiber 5, carbs 6, protein 7

Rice with Fennel

Preparation time: 10 minutes
Cooking time: 15 minutes
Servings: 2

Ingredients:
- ½ brown onion, chopped
- 1 tablespoon olive oil
- 1 small fennel bulb, chopped
- ½ small asparagus bunch, chopped
- A pinch of salt and black pepper
- 1 garlic clove, minced
- 1 cup Arborio rice
- 3 tablespoons white wine
- Zest from 1/3 lemon, grated
- 1 cup veggie stock
- 1 cup chicken stock
- 1 tablespoon butter
- 2 tablespoons parmesan, grated

Directions:
1. Set your pressure cooker on sauté mode, add the oil and heat it up.
2. Add onion, stir and cook for 5 minutes.
3. Add asparagus, fennel, salt and garlic and stir.
4. Add rice, wine, lemon zest, chicken stock and chicken stock, stir, cover and cook on High for 5 minutes.
5. Add parmesan and butter, stir rice, divide between 2 plates and serve as a side dish.

Nutrition: calories 183, fat 3, fiber 1, carbs 3, protein 4

Coconut Cabbage

Preparation time: 10 minutes
Cooking time: 10 minutes
Servings: 2

Ingredients:

- ½ tablespoon coconut oil
- ½ brown onion, chopped
- A pinch of salt and black pepper
- 1 garlic clove, minced
- ½ chili pepper, chopped
- ½ tablespoon mustard seeds
- ½ tablespoon curry powder
- ½ tablespoon turmeric powder
- ½ cabbage head, shredded
- ½ carrot, chopped
- 1 tablespoon lime juice
- 4 tablespoons coconut, desiccated
- ½ tablespoon olive oil
- 3 tablespoons water

Directions:
1. Set your pressure cooker on sauté mode, add the coconut oil and heat it up.
2. Add onion, a pinch of salt and black pepper, stir and cook for 3 minutes.
3. Add chili pepper garlic, mustard seeds, curry powder, turmeric powder, cabbage, carrot, lime juice, coconut, olive oil and water, stir, cover and cook on High for 6 minutes.
4. Stir cabbage one more time, divide between 2 plates and serve as a side dish.

Nutrition: calories 200, fat 2, fiber 3, carbs 4, protein 6

Corn on the Cob

Preparation time: 10 minutes
Cooking time: 5 minutes
Servings: 2

Ingredients:
- 3 cobs of corn, halved
- ½ cup water
- 1 and ½ tablespoons butter
- 1 small garlic clove, minced
- 1 teaspoon sweet paprika
- 1 teaspoon onion powder
- A pinch of cayenne pepper
- 1 teaspoon oregano, dried
- A pinch of salt and black pepper
- ½ lime, cut into wedges
- 1 tablespoon cilantro, chopped

Directions:
1. Put the water in your pressure cooker, add the steamer basket, add corn inside, cover and cook on High for 3 minutes.
2. Transfer corn to a plate and clean up your pressure cooker.
3. Set the cooker on sauté mode, add the butter and melt it.
4. Add garlic, stir and cook for a few seconds.
5. Add corn, paprika, onion powder, cayenne, oregano, salt and pepper, stir and sauté for 2 minutes.
6. Sprinkle cilantro on top and serve as a side dish with lime wedges on the side.

Nutrition: calories 127, fat 3, fiber 1, carbs 4, protein 4

Steamed Leeks

Preparation time: 10 minutes
Cooking time: 7 minutes
Servings: 2

Ingredients:
- 2 leeks, trimmed and cut into halves lengthwise
- 1/3 cup water
- A pinch of salt and black pepper
- ½ tablespoon butter

Directions:
1. Put the water in your pressure cooker, add the steamer basket, add leeks inside, season with salt and pepper, cover and cook on High for 5 minutes.
2. Clean your pressure cooker and transfer leeks to a plate.
3. Set the cooker on sauté mode, add the butter, melt it, add leeks, stir, cook for a couple of minutes, divide between 2 plates and serve as a side dish.

Nutrition: calories 100, fat 1, fiber 2, carbs 2, protein 4

Sautéed Escarole

Preparation time: 10 minutes
Cooking time: 5 minutes
Servings: 2

Ingredients:
- 4 cups escarole, roughly chopped
- 2 garlic cloves, minced
- 2 tablespoons water
- 1 tablespoon olive oil
- ¼ teaspoon red pepper flakes
- A pinch of salt and black pepper
- 2 tablespoons parmesan, grated

Directions:
1. Set your pressure cooker on sauté mode, add the oil and heat it up.
2. Add garlic and pepper flakes, stir and cook for 2 minutes.
3. Add escarole, water, salt and pepper, cover and cook on High for 3 minutes.
4. Add parmesan, toss, divide between 2 plates and serve as a side dish.

Nutrition: calories 93, fat 1, fiber 2, carbs 2, protein 3

Stir Fried Okra

Preparation time: 10 minutes
Cooking time: 10 minutes
Servings: 2

Ingredients:
- 1 onion, chopped
- 1 pound okra, cut into medium pieces

- 1 tablespoon olive oil
- 1 tomato, chopped
- ½ teaspoon cumin seeds
- 2 garlic cloves, minced
- ¼ teaspoon turmeric powder
- 1 teaspoon coriander powder
- A pinch of cayenne pepper
- A pinch of salt and black pepper
- 1 teaspoon lemon juice

Directions:
1. Set your pressure cooker on sauté mode, add the oil and heat it up.
2. Add garlic and cumin seeds, stir and cook for 1 minute.
3. Add onion, stir and cook for 2 minutes.
4. Add okra, tomato, turmeric, coriander, cayenne, salt, pepper and lemon juice, stir, cover and cook on Low for 5 minutes.
5. Divide between 2 plates and serve as a side dish.

Nutrition: calories 92, fat 1, fiber 1, carbs 2, protein 3

Snack and Appetizer Recipes

Flavored Parmesan Mushrooms

Preparation time: 10 minutes
Cooking time: 10 minutes
Servings: 4

Ingredients:
- 1 and ½ pounds cremini mushrooms, sliced
- 3 tablespoons olive oil
- ¼ cup parmesan, grated
- ¼ cup lemon juice
- Salt to the taste
- 1 cup water, for the pressure cooker

Directions:
1. In a bowl, mix mushrooms with oil, lemon juice, parmesan and salt and toss well.
2. Add the water to your pressure cooker, add steamer basket, add mushrooms inside, cover and cook on High for 10 minutes.
3. Divide between plates and serve as a side dish.

Nutrition: calories 128, fat 4, fiber 4, carbs 9, protein 4

Buttery Potatoes

Preparation time: 10 minutes
Cooking time: 15 minutes
Servings: 4

Ingredients:
- 3 pounds red potatoes, halved
- 2 tablespoons butter
- ½ teaspoon basil
- ¼ cup parmesan, grated
- Salt to the taste
- 1 cup water, for the pressure cooker

Directions:
1. Put the water in your pressure cooker, add potatoes, cover, cook on High for 10 minutes, drain and transfer to a bowl.
2. Clean the pot, set it on sauté mode, add butter, melt it, add potatoes, basil, salt and parmesan, toss, cook for 5 minutes, divide between plates and serve as a side dish.

Nutrition: calories 137, fat 3, fiber 6, carbs 10, protein 3

Beef Dip

Preparation time: 10 minutes
Cooking time: 20 minutes
Servings: 2

Ingredients:

- ½ cup mushrooms, chopped
- ½ yellow onion, chopped
- 2 tablespoons beer
- ½ pound beef, ground
- A pinch of salt and black pepper
- ½ teaspoon garlic powder
- 2 ounces cream cheese
- ½ tablespoons white flour
- ½ cup cheddar cheese, shredded

Directions:
1. Set your pressure cooker on sauté mode, add the oil, heat it up, add mushrooms, beef and onion, stir and cook for 5 minutes.
2. Add salt, pepper, garlic powder and beer, cover and cook on High for 10 minutes.
3. Add cream cheese and flour, stir, turn the cooker on sauté mode again and cook for 5 minutes.
4. Add cheddar cheese, toss a bit, transfer to a bowl and serve at a casual gathering.

Nutrition: calories 212, fat 2, fiber 3, carbs 6, protein 7

Potato Wedges

Preparation time: 10 minutes
Cooking time: 10 minutes
Servings: 2

Ingredients:
- 1 cup water
- A pinch of salt and black pepper
- A pinch of baking soda
- 1 teaspoon onion powder
- ½ teaspoon garlic powder
- A pinch of cayenne pepper
- ½ teaspoon oregano, dried
- 2 big potatoes, cut into medium wedges
- 3 quarts sunflower oil+ 2 tablespoons
- 1 cup flour
- 3 tablespoons cornstarch
- ½ cup buttermilk

Directions:
1. Put the water in your pressure cooker, add some salt and the baking soda, stir and place the steamer basket inside.
2. In a bowl, mix onion powder with garlic powder, salt, pepper, oregano and cayenne and stir.
3. Add potatoes, toss them well, add them to the pot, cover and cook on High for 2 minutes.
4. In a bowl, mix cornstarch with flour and stir.
5. In another bowl, mix buttermilk with a pinch of baking soda and whisk.
6. Drain potato wedges, dredge them in flour mix and then dip them in buttermilk.
7. Heat up a large pan with 3 quarts water over medium high heat, add potato wedges, cook them for 4 minutes and transfer them to paper towels.
8. Drain grease, transfer wedges to a bowl and serve them as a snack.

Nutrition: calories 284, fat 1, fiber 2, carbs 5, protein 7

Green Beans Fries

Preparation time: 10 minutes
Cooking time: 9 minutes
Servings: 4

Ingredients:
- 1 cup water, for the pressure cooker
- 1 and ½ pounds green beans, trimmed
- 1 cup panko
- ½ cup parmesan, grated
- Salt to the taste
- 2 eggs, whisked

Directions:
1. Put the water in your pressure cooker, add steamer basket, add green beans, cover, cook on High for 5 minutes and transfer to a bowl.
2. In a bowl, mix panko with parmesan and salt and stir.
3. Put the eggs in a separate bowl.
4. Dredge green beans in panko and then in eggs mix.
5. Set the cooker on sauté mode, heat it up, add green beans fries, cook them for 2-3 minutes on each side, arrange them on plates and serve as a side dish.

Nutrition: calories 174, fat 3, fiber 6, carbs 7, protein 7

Mixed Veggies

Preparation time: 10 minutes
Cooking time: 10 minutes
Servings: 4

Ingredients:
- 2 cups butternut squash, roughly chopped
- 1 red onion, cut into wedges
- 2 tablespoons olive oil
- 1 red bell pepper, chopped
- 2 tablespoons balsamic vinegar
- 1 cup water, for the pressure cooker

Directions:
1. In a bowl, mix squash with red onion, oil, bell pepper and vinegar and toss well.
2. Add the water to your pressure cooker, add steamer basket, add mixed veggies inside, cover and cook on High for 10 minutes.
3. Divide mixed veggies between plates and serve as a side dish.

Nutrition: calories 128, fat 3, fiber 7, carbs 9, protein 8

BBQ Chicken Wings

Preparation time: 10 minutes
Cooking time: 25 minutes
Servings: 2

Ingredients:
- 2 pounds chicken wings
- ½ cup BBQ sauce
- 1 cup water

Directions:
1. Put the water in your pressure cooker, add the steamer basket, add chicken wings, cover and cook on High for 5 minutes.
2. Put BBQ sauce in a bowl, add chicken wings, toss them well and spread on a lined baking sheet.
3. Introduce in the oven at 450 degrees F and bake for 18 minutes.
4. Serve as an appetizer for a casual snack.

Nutrition: calories 263, fat 3, fiber 5, carbs 8, protein 8

Beef Meatballs

Preparation time: 10 minutes
Cooking time: 30 minutes
Servings: 2

Ingredients:
- 1 tablespoon olive oil
- ½ yellow onion, chopped
- 1 garlic clove, minced
- 7 ounces tomato sauce
- ½ cup water
- ½ tablespoon Worcestershire sauce
- ½ pound beef, ground
- 4 tablespoons rice
- A pinch of salt and black pepper

Directions:
1. Set your pressure cooker on sauté mode, add the oil and heat it up.
2. Add half of the garlic and onion, stir and cook for 4 minutes.
3. Add water, Worcestershire sauce and tomato sauce, stir and bring to a simmer.
4. Meanwhile, in a bowl, mix beef with rice, salt, pepper, the rest of the garlic and onion and stir well.
5. Shape meatballs out of this mix, add the to your pressure cooker, cover and cook on High for 15 minutes.
6. Transfer meatballs on a platter and serve as an appetizer.

Nutrition: calories 221, fat 2, fiber 3, carbs 4, protein 7

Corn Side Dish

Preparation time: 10 minutes
Cooking time: 12 minutes
Servings: 4

Ingredients:
- 6 ounces cream cheese
- 2 cups corn kernels
- ¼ cup butter

- 1/3 cup milk
- 3 garlic cloves, minced

Directions:
1. Set the cooker on sauté mode, add butter, melt it, add garlic, stir and cook for 2 minutes.
2. Add corn, stir and cook for 2 minutes more.
3. Add cream cheese and milk, stir, cover and cook on Manual for 7 minutes.
4. Toss creamy corn one more time, divide between plates and serve as a side dish.

Nutrition: calories 200, fat 3, fiber 7, carbs 10, protein 3

Tomatoes Side Salad

Preparation time: 10 minutes
Cooking time: 6 minutes
Servings: 4

Ingredients:
- 15 ounces canned garbanzo beans, drained
- 2 pints mixed cherry tomatoes, halved
- ¼ teaspoon parsley, chopped
- 1 tablespoons sherry vinegar
- 2 tablespoons olive oil

Directions:
1. Set your pressure cooker on sauté mode, add oil, heat it up, add garbanzo beans and tomatoes, stir and cook for 3 minutes.
2. Add parsley and vinegar, stir, cover and cook on High for 3 minutes more.
3. Divide everything between plates and serve as a side dish.

Nutrition: calories 132, fat 3, fiber 4, carbs 7, protein 5

Stuffed Chicken Breasts

Preparation time: 10 minutes
Cooking time: 30 minutes
Servings: 2

Ingredients:
- 2 chicken breasts, skinless, boneless and butterflied
- 1 ounce ham, chopped
- 6 asparagus spears
- 14 bacon strips
- 4 mozzarella slices
- A pinch of salt and black pepper
- 3 cups water

Directions:
1. Flatten chicken breasts with a meat mallet and place them on a plate.
2. In a bowl, mix 2 cups water with a pinch of salt and whisk well.
3. Add chicken breasts, cover and leave aside for 30 minutes.
4. Pat dry chicken breasts and place them on a cutting board.
5. Add 2 slices of mozzarella on each, divide ham and asparagus as well.
6. Season with a pinch of salt and pepper and roll chicken breasts.

7. Line bacon slices on a cutting board, add rolled chicken breasts and wrap each in bacon.
8. Secure with toothpicks and place all rolls on a plate.
9. Add 1 cup water to your pressure cooker, add the trivet, add chicken rolls inside, cover and cook on High for 10 minutes.
10. Arrange on a platter and serve as an appetizer.

Nutrition: calories 231, fat 4, fiber 5, carbs 7, protein 8

Vidalia Onions Mix

Preparation time: 10 minutes
Cooking time: 15 minutes
Servings: 4

Ingredients:
- 4 Vidalia onions, sliced
- 1 tablespoon sage, chopped
- ½ cup cornbread stuffing cubes
- 2 tablespoons butter
- ¼ cup chicken stock

Directions:
1. Set your pressure cooker on sauté mode, add butter, melt it, add onions and sage, toss a bit and cook for 3 minutes,
2. Add stock, stir, cover and cook on High for 7 minutes.
3. Add cornbread stuffing cubes, set the cooker in sauté mode again, toss and cook everything for 3-4 minutes more.
4. Divide everything between plates and serve as a side dish.

Nutrition: calories 146, fat 4, fiber 6, carbs 8, protein 5

Parmesan Zucchini Fries

Preparation time: 10 minutes
Cooking time: 8 minutes
Servings: 4

Ingredients:
- 4 zucchinis, cut into quarters lengthwise
- ½ teaspoon oregano, dried
- ½ cup parmesan, grated
- 2 tablespoons olive oil
- 2 tablespoons parsley, chopped
- 1 cup water, for the pressure cooker

Directions:
1. In a bowl, mix parmesan with parsley and oregano and toss.
2. In another bowl, mix zucchini fries with the oil and toss well.
3. Combine zucchini fries with parmesan mix and toss well.
4. Put the water in your pressure cooker, add steamer basket, add zucchini fries inside, cover and cook on High for 8 minutes.
5. Arrange on plates and serve as a side dish.

Nutrition: calories 162, fat 3, fiber 5, carbs 5, protein 4

Baby Back Ribs Appetizer

Preparation time: 10 minutes
Cooking time: 40 minutes
Servings: 2

Ingredients:
- 2 carrots, chopped
- 1 rack baby back ribs
- 3 drops liquid smoke
- 2 tablespoons brown sugar
- 2 teaspoon chili powder
- A pinch of salt and black pepper
- 1 teaspoon garlic powder
- 1 teaspoon onion powder
- 1 teaspoon cinnamon powder
- ½ teaspoon fennel seeds, ground
- ½ teaspoon cumin seeds
- A pinch of cayenne pepper

For the sauce:
- 1 cup ketchup
- 3 garlic cloves, minced
- 1 yellow onion, chopped
- 1/8 cup maple syrup
- ½ cup water
- 1/8 cup honey
- 2 tablespoons apple cider vinegar
- 2 tablespoons mustard
- 1 tablespoon brown sugar

Directions:
1. In a bowl, mix ribs with carrots, liquid smoke and toss.
2. Add 2 tablespoons brown sugar, chili powder, a pinch of salt, black pepper, onion powder, garlic powder, cinnamon powder, cumin seeds, fennel seeds and cayenne and toss really well.
3. In another bowl, mix onion with garlic, ketchup, water, maple syrup, honey, vinegar, mustard and 1 tablespoon sugar and whisk really well.
4. Add this to your pressure cooker, add ribs, cover and cook on High for 25 minutes.
5. Transfer ribs to a platter and leave aside.
6. Turn your pressure cooker on Sauté mode again and simmer sauce for a few minutes until it thickens.
7. Serve your ribs with the sauce on the side.

Nutrition: calories 242, fat 5, fiber 5, carbs 8, protein 12

Tomatoes and Corn Side Salad

Preparation time: 10 minutes
Cooking time: 7 minutes
Servings: 6

Ingredients:
- 6 sweet corn ears, shucked

- 4 tomatoes, roughly chopped
- ¼ cup mint leaves
- 1 tablespoons olive oil
- 3 ounces goat cheese, crumbled
- 1 and ½ cups water, for the pressure cooker

Directions:
1. Put the water in your pressure cooker, add corn, cover, cook on High for 5 minutes, drain and transfer to a bowl.
2. Clean the pot, set it on sauté mode, add oil, heat it up, add corn and tomatoes, stir and cook for 2 minutes.
3. Add mint, stir, cook for 2 minutes more, divide between plates and serve with cheese on top.

Nutrition: calories 122, fat 3, fiber 3, carbs 6, protein 4

Tomatoes and Burrata Side Salad

Preparation time: 10 minutes
Cooking time: 3 minutes
Servings: 4

Ingredients:
- 4 tomatoes, different colors, cut into wedges
- 2 tablespoons olive oil
- 5 ounces burrata cheese, shredded
- ½ teaspoon oregano, dried
- 1 tablespoon water

Directions:
1. In your pressure cooker, mix tomatoes with oil, oregano and water, toss a bit, cover and cook on High for 3 minutes.
2. Divide on plates, add burrata on top and serve an as a side dish.

Nutrition: calories 111, fat 2, fiber 3, carbs 3, protein 3

Crispy Chicken

Preparation time: 10 minutes
Cooking time: 20 minutes
Servings: 2

Ingredients:
- 6 chicken thighs
- 1 yellow onion, chopped
- 4 garlic cloves, minced
- 1 cup water
- A pinch of rosemary, chopped
- A pinch of salt and black pepper
- 1 and ½ cups panko bread crumbs
- 2 tablespoons olive oil
- 2 tablespoons butter
- 1 cup flour
- 2 eggs, whisked

Directions:
1. In your pressure cooker, mix garlic with onion, rosemary and water and stir.
2. Put the steamer basket in your pressure cooker, add chicken thighs, cover and cook on High for 9 minutes.
3. Meanwhile, heat up a pan with 2 tablespoons oil, 2 tablespoons butter and panko, stir and cook for a couple of minutes.
4. Pat dry chicken thighs and season them with salt and pepper.
5. Coat chicken with flour, dip in eggs, coat in panko and place on a lined baking sheet.
6. Introduce in the oven at 400 degrees F and bake for 5 minutes.
7. Arrange on a platter and serve as an appetizer.

Nutrition: calories 222, fat 4, fiber 5, carbs 8, protein 7

Boiled Peanuts

Preparation time: 10 minutes
Cooking time: 1 hour
Servings: 2

Ingredients:
- ½ pound raw peanuts
- 2 tablespoons salt
- ½ tablespoon Cajun seasoning
- 2 garlic cloves, minced
- 1 small jalapeno, chopped

Directions:
1. Put peanuts in your pressure cooker, add salt and water to cover.
2. Add the trivet over peanuts, cover cooker and cook on High for 1 hour.
3. Transfer peanuts to a bowl, add Cajun seasoning, jalapeno and garlic, toss well and serve as a snack.

Nutrition: calories 195, fat 4, fiber 1, carbs 4, protein 3

Sweet Pearl Onion Mix

Preparation time: 10 minutes
Cooking time: 5 minutes
Servings: 4

Ingredients
- 1 pound pearl onions, peeled
- A pinch of salt
- ½ cup water
- 4 tablespoons balsamic vinegar
- 1 tablespoon sugar

Directions:
1. In your pressure cooker, mix pearl onions with salt, water, vinegar and sugar, stir, cover and cook on Low for 5 minutes.
2. Toss onions again, divide them between plates and serve as a side dish.

Nutrition: calories 130, fat 2, fiber 1, carbs 7, protein 1

Arborio Rice Side Salad

Preparation time: 10 minutes
Cooking time: 4 minutes
Servings: 4

Ingredients:
- 2 cups Arborio rice
- 4 cups water
- A pinch of salt
- 1 cup black olives in oil, pitted and sliced
- 1 bunch basil, chopped

Directions:
1. In your pressure cooker, mix rice with water, cover, cook on High for 4 minutes, drain and transfer to a salad bowl.
2. Add a pinch of salt, olives and basil, toss well, divide between plates and serve as a side salad.

Nutrition: calories 120, fat 4, fiber 2, carbs 5, protein 2

Roasted Hummus

Preparation time: 10 minutes
Cooking time: 1 hour and 30 minutes
Servings: 2

Ingredients:
- 3 cups water
- ½ pound garbanzo beans
- A pinch of salt
- 1 small yellow onion, chopped
- 2 garlic cloves, minced
- 1 tablespoon olive oil
- A pinch of cumin, ground
- 2 tablespoons lemon juice
- ½ tablespoon sesame oil
- ½ cup sesame seeds, toasted

Directions:
1. Put the beans in your pressure cooker, add the water and some salt, cover and cook on High for 1 hour and 30 minutes.
2. Meanwhile, heat up a pan with the oil over medium high heat, add onion and garlic, stir and cook for 2 minutes.
3. Transfer beans to your food processor, add garlic and onion, cumin, lemon juice, sesame seeds and sesame oil and pulse really well.
4. Transfer hummus to a bowl and serve as an appetizer.

Nutrition: calories 253, fat 4, fiber 2, carbs 4, protein 8

Brussels Sprouts and Chestnuts

Preparation time: 10 minutes
Cooking time: 5 minutes

Servings: 5

Ingredients:
- 2 pounds Brussels sprouts, halved
- 3 tablespoons olive oil
- 1 cup jarred chestnuts, halved
- 1 splash of red vinegar
- ¼ cup veggie stock

Directions:
1. Set your pressure cooker on sauté mode, add oil, heat it up, add Brussels sprouts, stir and cook for 2 minutes.
2. Add chestnuts, stock and vinegar, stir, cover and cook on High for 3 minutes.
3. Divide everything between plates and serve as a side dish.

Nutrition: calories 182, fat 3, fiber 4, carbs 6, protein 4

Spinach Side Dish

Preparation time: 10 minutes
Cooking time: 5 minutes
Servings: 3

Ingredients:
- 1 teaspoon olive oil
- ½ teaspoon garam masala
- ½ teaspoon turmeric powder
- ½ cup veggie stock
- 6 ounces spinach leaves

Directions:
1. Set your pressure cooker on sauté mode, add oil, heat it up, add spinach, stir and toss for 1-2 minutes.
2. Add garam masala, turmeric and stock, stir, cover and cook on High for 3 minutes
3. Divide between plates and serve as a side dish.

Nutrition: calories 100, fat 3, fiber 1, carbs 6, protein 1

Brown Rice Salad

Preparation time: 10 minutes
Cooking time: 20 minutes
Servings: 2

Ingredients:
- ½ cup brown rice
- ½ cup mung beans
- ½ teaspoon cumin seeds
- 4 cups water
- 1 teaspoon lemon juice

Directions:

1. In your pressure cooker, mix mung beans with rice, water, lemon juice and cumin, stir, cover and cook on High for 13 minutes.
2. Divide between plates and serve as a side dish.

Nutrition: calories 170, fat 6, fiber 7, carbs 12, protein 4

Brussels Sprouts Side Salad

Preparation time: 10 minutes
Cooking time: 5 minutes
Servings: 4

Ingredients:
- 1 pound Brussels sprouts, halved
- ½ cup pecans, chopped
- 1/3 cup olive oil
- 3 tablespoons balsamic vinegar
- 2 teaspoons Dijon mustard

Directions:
1. Set your pressure cooker on sauté mode, add oil, heat it up, add sprouts, stir and cook for 2 minutes.
2. Add pecans, vinegar and mustard, toss, cover and cook on High for 3 minutes.
3. Divide Brussels sprouts mix on plates and serve as a side dish.

Nutrition: calories 167, fat 4, fiber 4, carbs 6, protein 4

Pasta Appetizer Salad

Preparation time: 10 minutes
Cooking time: 4 minutes
Servings: 2

Ingredients:
- 4 bacon slices, cooked and crumbled
- 2 cups water
- ½ pound gemelli pasta
- A pinch of salt and black pepper
- 4 tablespoons mayonnaise
- 2 tablespoons sour cream
- ½ teaspoon lemon juice
- 2 tablespoons red onion, chopped
- ½ teaspoon Worcestershire sauce
- ½ teaspoon sugar
- 1 teaspoon apple cider vinegar
- 2 ounces cheddar cheese, grated
- 5 ounces peas

Directions:
1. In your pressure cooker, mix pasta with a pinch of salt and water, cover and cook on High for 4 minutes.
2. Drain pasta and transfer to a bowl.
3. Add peas, salt, pepper, bacon, red onion, mayo, sour cream, lemon juice, Worcestershire sauce, sugar, vinegar and cheddar cheese, toss well and serve as an appetizer.

Nutrition: calories 213, fat 4, fiber 3, carbs 4, protein 8

Kidney Beans and Corn Side Dish

Preparation time: 10 minutes
Cooking time: 10 minutes
Servings: 2

Ingredients:
- 1 cup kidney beans, already cooked
- ½ cup corn
- 1 small red onion, chopped
- ½ teaspoon chili powder
- 1 and ½ cups chicken stock

Directions:
1. In your pressure cooker, mix beans with corn, onion, chili powder and stock, stir, cover and cook on High for 10 minutes.
2. Divide between plates and serve as a side dish.

Nutrition: calories 203, fat 7, fiber 5, carbs 9, protein 2

Eggplant and Cashews Mix

Preparation time: 10 minutes
Cooking time: 15 minutes
Servings: 3

Ingredients:
- 2 tablespoons cashews, chopped
- 1 tablespoon coriander seeds
- 4 baby eggplants, roughly chopped
- 1 cup veggie stock
- 1 teaspoon lime juice

Directions:
1. In your pressure cooker, mix eggplants with stock and coriander, stir, cover and cook on High for 10 minutes.
2. Add cashews and lime juice, stir, divide between plates and serve as a side dish.

Nutrition: calories 170, fat 4, fiber 4, carbs 7, protein 3

Honey Chicken Appetizer

Preparation time: 10 minutes
Cooking time: 10 minutes
Servings: 2

Ingredients:
- 2 pound chicken wings pieces
- ½ cup ketchup
- ½ tablespoon liquid smoke
- 3 tablespoons brown sugar
- 1 garlic clove, minced

- 2 tablespoons onion, chopped
- 3 tablespoons water
- 2 tablespoons bourbon
- 1 teaspoon smoked paprika
- A pinch of cayenne pepper
- A pinch of salt and black pepper
- 1 and ½ tablespoons honey

Directions:
1. In your pressure cooker, mix ketchup with smoke, sugar, garlic, onion, water, bourbon, paprika, salt, pepper, cayenne and honey, whisk well, set on sauté mode and simmer for a few minutes.
2. Add chicken wings, toss, cover and cook on High for 5 minutes.
3. Transfer chicken wings to a lined baking sheet, introduce in the oven at 400 degrees F and roast for 5 minutes.
4. Serve as an appetizer.

Nutrition: calories 243, fat 4, fiber 4, carbs 7, protein 9

Shiitake Mushrooms Mix

Preparation time: 10 minutes
Cooking time: 10 minutes
Servings: 4

Ingredients:
- 1 pound shiitake mushroom caps, quartered
- 3 tablespoons butter
- 2 cups edamame
- 2 teaspoons ginger
- 1 cup veggie stock

Directions:
1. Set your pressure cooker on sauté mode, add butter, melt it, add ginger, stir and cook for 30 seconds.
2. Add mushrooms, stir and cook for 1-2 minutes.
3. Add edamame and stock, stir, cover and cook on High for 8 minutes.
4. Divide between plates and serve as a side dish.

Nutrition: calories 164, fat 3, fiber 6, carbs 8, protein 3

Green Cabbage and Tomatoes Side Dish

Preparation time: 10 minutes
Cooking time: 5 minutes
Servings: 4

Ingredients:
- 3 tablespoons olive oil
- 1 green cabbage head, chopped
- 15 ounces canned tomatoes, chopped
- ½ cup yellow onion, chopped
- 2 teaspoons turmeric powder

Directions:
1. Set your pressure cooker on Sauté mode, add oil, heat it up, add onion, stir and cook for 2 minutes
2. Add cabbage, tomatoes and turmeric, stir, cover, cook on High for 4 minutes, divide between plates and serve as a side dish.

Nutrition: calories 152, fat 5, fiber 8, carbs 9, protein 7

Radishes Side Salad

Preparation time: 10 minutes
Cooking time: 8 minutes
Servings: 3

Ingredients:
- 7 ounces red radishes, halved
- ½ cup veggie stock
- 2 tablespoons sour cream
- 2 bacon slices, chopped
- 1 tablespoon green onions, chopped

Directions:
1. Set your pressure cooker on sauté mode, add bacon, stir and cook for a couple of minutes.
2. Add radishes and stock, stir, cover and cook on High for 4 minutes.
3. Add sour cream and green onions, stir, cover cooker again, cook on High for 2 minutes more, divide between plates and serve as a side dish.

Nutrition: calories 187, fat 6, fiber 3, carbs 10, protein 8

Turnip Mash

Preparation time: 10 minutes
Cooking time: 5 minutes
Servings: 4

Ingredients:
- 4 turnips, peeled and chopped
- ½ cup chicken stock
- Salt to the taste

- 1 yellow onion, chopped
- ¼ cup heavy cream

Directions:
1. In your pressure cooker, mix turnips with stock and onion, stir, cover, cook on High for 5 minutes and blend using an immersion blender.
2. Add salt and cream blend again, divide between plates and serve as a side dish.

Nutrition: calories 140, fat 3, fiber 3, carbs 7, protein 3

Garlic Beets Salad

Preparation time: 10 minutes
Cooking time: 20 minutes
Servings: 4

Ingredients:
- 3 beets, washed
- 2 cups water, for the pressure cooker
- 1 tablespoon olive oil
- Salt to the taste
- 2 garlic cloves, minced
- 1 teaspoon lemon juice

Directions:
1. Put the water in your pressure cooker, add steamer basket, add beets inside, cover, cook on High for 15 minutes, drain, transfer them to a cutting board, peel and cut them in medium cubes.
2. Clean your pressure cooker, set it on sauté mode, add oil, heat it up, add beets, stir and cook for 4 minutes.
3. Add garlic, lemon juice and salt, toss, divide between plates and serve as a side dish.

Nutrition: calories 121, fat 1, fiber 2, carbs 6, protein 2

Cauliflower and Grapes

Preparation time: 10 minutes
Cooking time: 10 minutes
Servings: 4

Ingredients:
- 1 cup water, for the pressure cooker
- 1 cauliflower head, florets separated
- 1 and ½ cups grapes
- 2 tablespoons capers
- 3 tablespoons olive oil
- 1 teaspoon lemon zest, grated

Directions:
1. Put the water in your pressure cooker, add steamer basket, add cauliflower florets inside, cover, cook on High for 6 minutes, drain and transfer to a bowl.
2. Clean your pressure cooker, set on sauté mode, add oil, heat it up, return cauliflower, stir and cook for 2 minutes.

3. Add grapes, capers and lemon zest, stir, cook for 2 minutes more, divide between plates and serve as a side dish.

Nutrition: calories 114, fat 3, fiber 3, carbs 5, protein 2

Hot Wings

Preparation time: 10 minutes
Cooking time: 10 minutes
Servings: 2

Ingredients:
- 1 and ½ pounds chicken wings pieces
- ½ tablespoon Worcestershire sauce
- 2 tablespoons butter
- 2 tablespoons cayenne pepper sauce
- 1 tablespoon brown sugar
- A pinch of salt
- 3 ounces water

Directions:
5. Put the water in your pressure cooker, add the trivet, add chicken wings, cover and cook on High for 5 minutes.
6. In a bowl, mix butter with Worcestershire sauce, pepper sauce, sugar and salt and whisk really well.
7. Brush chicken pieces with this mix, spread them on a lined baking sheet, introduce in the oven at 400 degrees F and roast for 5 minutes.
8. Serve as an appetizer.

Nutrition: calories 251, fat 5, fiber 3, carbs 6, protein 8

Mango Side Salad

Preparation time: 10 minutes
Cooking time: 8 minutes
Servings: 4

Ingredients:
- 1 shallot, chopped
- 1 tablespoon olive oil
- 4 big mangos, peeled and roughly cubed
- 2 red hot chilies, chopped
- 1 tablespoon balsamic vinegar

Directions:
1. Set your pressure cooker on Sauté mode, add oil, heat it up, add shallot, stir and cook for 3 minutes.
2. Add hot peppers, mangos and vinegar, stir, cover and cook on High for 5 minutes.
3. Divide between plates and serve as a side dish.

Nutrition: calories 120, fat 2, fiber 1, carbs 4, protein 3

Sweet Potato Side Salad

Preparation time: 10 minutes

Cooking time: 5 minutes
Servings: 6

Ingredients:
- 3 green onions, chopped
- 6 sweet potatoes
- 1 cup water
- 3 teaspoons dill, chopped
- 3 ounces mayonnaise

Directions:
1. Put potatoes in your pressure cooker, add the water, cover, cook on High for 5 minutes, transfer them to a cutting board, peel them, roughly chop and transfer to a salad bowl.
2. Add onion, dill and mayo, toss, divide between plates and serve as a side salad.

Nutrition: calories 170, fat 2, fiber 1 carbs 8, protein 4

Sweet Potatoes Mash

Preparation time: 10 minutes
Cooking time: 15 minutes
Servings: 10

Ingredients:
- 3 pounds sweet potatoes, peeled and cubed
- 1 cup milk, hot
- 6 garlic cloves, minced
- 28 ounces veggie stock
- 4 tablespoons butter, melted

Directions:
1. Put potatoes in your pressure cooker, add stock and garlic, stir, cover and cook on High for 15 minutes
2. Drain potatoes, transfer them to a bowl, mash using a potato masher, mix with hot milk and butter, whisk really well, divide between plates and serve as a side dish.

Nutrition: calories 155, fat 4, fiber 2, carbs 9, protein 2

Squash and Apple Mash

Preparation time: 10 minutes
Cooking time: 8 minutes
Servings: 4

Ingredients:
- 1 cup water, for the pressure cooker
- 2 apples, peeled, cored and sliced
- 1 butternut squash, peeled and cut into medium chunks
- 2 tablespoons maple syrup
- A pinch of salt
- 1 yellow onion, roughly chopped

Directions:
1. Put the water in your pressure cooker, add steamer basket, add squash, onion and apple pieces, inside, cover and cook on High for 8 minutes.
2. Transfer all of them to a bowl, mash using a potato masher, add a pinch of salt and maple syrup, whisk well, divide between plates and serve as a side dish.

Nutrition: calories 161, fat 2, fiber 3, carbs 5, protein 3

Italian Dip

Preparation time: 10 minutes
Cooking time: 55 minutes
Servings: 2

Ingredients:
- 1 pound beef roast, cut into medium chunks
- 1 tablespoon Italian seasoning

- 3 ounces beef stock
- 2 tablespoons water
- 4 ounces pepperoncini peppers

Directions:
1. In your pressure cooker, mix beef with seasoning, stock, water and pepperoncini peppers, cover and cook on High for 55 minutes.
2. Shred meat using 2 forks, stir your dip and serve it with sandwiches.

Nutrition: calories 242, fat 4, fiber 4, carbs 6, protein 7

Mussels Appetizer

Preparation time: 10 minutes
Cooking time: 6 minutes
Servings: 2

Ingredients:
- 1 pound mussels, scrubbed
- ½ onion, chopped
- ½ radicchio, cut into strips
- ½ pound baby spinach
- 3 tablespoons white wine
- 4 tablespoons water
- 1 small garlic clove, minced
- 1 tablespoon olive oil

Directions:
1. Set your pressure cooker on Sauté mode, add oil, heat it up, add garlic, wine and onion, stir and cook for 5 minutes.
2. Add the steamer basket inside, add mussels, cover and cook on Low for 1 minute.
3. Divide spinach and radicchio on 2 plates, also divide mussels, drizzle the cooking liquid from the cooker and serve as an appetizer.

Nutrition: calories 65, fat 2, fiber 2, carbs 2, protein 7

Turnips and Chili Pepper Side Dish

Preparation time: 10 minutes
Cooking time: 14 minutes
Servings: 4

Ingredients:
- 20 ounces turnips, peeled and chopped
- 1 cup water
- 2 tablespoons olive oil
- 3 green chili peppers, chopped
- 2 tomatoes, chopped

Directions:
1. Set your pressure cooker on Sauté mode, add the oil, heat it up, add green chilies, stir and cook for 1 minute.
2. Add tomatoes, turnips and water, stir, cover and cook on Low for 13 minutes.
3. Divide between plates and serve as a side dish.

Nutrition: calories 130, fat 2, fiber 2, carbs 5, protein 4

Spinach and Squash Mix

Preparation time: 10 minutes
Cooking time: 20 minutes
Servings: 4

Ingredients:
- 1 butternut squash, cut into medium wedges
- 1 cup water, for the pressure cooker
- 6 cups spinach
- 2 tablespoons balsamic vinegar
- 1 teaspoon Dijon mustard
- 6 tablespoons olive oil

Directions:
1. In a bowl, mix squash with half of the oil and toss.
2. Add the water to your pressure cooker, add the steamer basket, add squash, cover and cook on High for 10 minutes.
3. In a bowl, mix vinegar with the rest of the oil and mustard and whisk very well.
4. Put spinach in a salad bowl, add squash wedges, add salad dressing, toss to coat well, divide between plates and serve as a side dish.

Nutrition: calories 131, fat 3, fiber 2, carbs 6, protein 5

Dessert Recipes

Pumpkin and Yogurt Cake

Preparation time: 10 minutes
Cooking time: 45 minutes
Servings: 12

Ingredients:
- 1 and ½ cups flour
- ½ teaspoon baking powder
- ¾ cup sugar
- ½ cup Greek yogurt
- 8 ounces canned pumpkin puree
- 1 and ½ cups water, for the pressure cooker

Directions:
1. In a bowl, mix flour with sugar, baking powder, yogurt and pumpkin puree, whisk well and pour into a greased cake pan.
2. Add the water to your pressure cooker, add trivet inside, add cake pan, cover and cook on High for 45 minutes.
3. Leave cake to cool down, slice and serve.

Nutrition: calories 201, fat 3, fiber 5, carbs 15, protein 4

Apple Bread

Preparation time: 10 minutes
Cooking time: 1 hour
Servings: 4

Ingredients:
- 1 cup water, for the pressure cooker
- 1 tablespoon baking powder
- 3 eggs
- 2 and ½ cups white flour
- 1 and ½ cups condensed milk, sweetened
- 3 apples, peeled, cored and chopped

Directions:
1. In a bowl, mix baking powder with eggs and whisk well.
2. Add milk, flour and apple pieces, whisk well and pour into a greased loaf pan.
3. Add the water to your pressure cooker, add trivet, add loaf pan inside, cover and cook on High for 1 hour.
4. Leave apple bread to cool down, slice and serve.

Nutrition: calories 211, fat 2, fiber 7, carbs 14, protein 4

Cranberries Dessert Bowl

Preparation time: 10 minutes
Cooking time: 30 minutes
Servings: 2

Ingredients:

For the sauce:
- 2 tablespoons orange juice
- 3 tablespoons sugar
- 1 cup cranberries
- A pinch of cinnamon powder

For the bowls:
- 1 cup milk
- 1 egg, whisked
- 2 tablespoons butter, melted
- 3 tablespoons sugar
- Zest from ½ orange, grated
- ½ teaspoon vanilla extract
- ½ bread loaf, cubed
- ½ cup water

Directions:
1. Set your pressure cooker on sauté mode, add cranberries, orange juice, a pinch of cinnamon and 3 tablespoons sugar, stir, cook for 5 minutes and transfer to a greased pan.
2. In a bowl, mix butter with milk, 3 tablespoon sugar, egg, vanilla extract, bread cubes and orange zest, stir and pour into greased pan as well.
3. Add the water to your pressure cooker, add the steamer basket, add pan inside, cover and cook on High for 25 minutes.
4. Divide into dessert bowls and serve as a dessert.

Nutrition: calories 284, fat 4, fiber 5, carbs 10, protein 4

Sweet Soufflé

Preparation time: 10 minutes
Cooking time: 30 minutes
Servings: 6

Ingredients:
- 1 teaspoon vanilla extract
- ¼ cup sugar
- 8 ounces chocolate, chopped and melted
- 3 egg yolks, beaten
- ¼ teaspoon cream of tartar
- 1 cup water, for the pressure cooker

Directions:
1. In a bowl, mix melted chocolate with vanilla, sugar, egg yolks and cream of tartar, whisk really well and divide into greased ramekins.
2. Add the water to your pressure cooker, add steamer basket, add ramekins, cover and cook on High for 30 minutes.
3. Leave soufflé to cool down just a bit and serve.

Nutrition: calories 190, fat 2, fiber 3, carbs 7, protein 3

Blackberry Pie

Preparation time: 10 minutes
Cooking time: 35 minutes
Servings: 6

Ingredients:
- 1/3 cup tapioca pearls
- 1 cup sugar
- 4 cups blackberries
- 2 tablespoons butter, soft
- A pie crust
- 1 and ½ cups water, for the pressure cooker

Directions:
1. In a bowl, mix tapioca with sugar, blackberries and butter and whisk until sugar melts and pour into pie crust.
2. Add the water to your pressure cooker, add steamer basket, add pie, cover and cook on High for 35 minutes.
3. Leave pie to cool down, slice, divide between plates and serve.

Nutrition: calories 251, fat 3, fiber 7, carbs 7, protein 8

Banana Cake

Preparation time: 10 minutes
Cooking time: 55 minutes
Servings: 2

Ingredients:
- 1 cup water
- ½ cup sugar
- 1 cups flour
- 1 and ½ bananas, peeled and mashed
- 1 egg
- ½ stick butter
- ½ teaspoon baking powder
- ½ teaspoon cinnamon powder
- ½ teaspoon nutmeg, ground

Directions:
1. In a bowl, mix eggs with butter, sugar, baking powder, cinnamon, nutmeg, bananas and flour, stir and pour into a greased cake pan.
2. Add the water to your pressure cooker, add the steamer basket, add cake pan inside, cover cooker and cook on High for 55 minutes.
3. Leave cake to cool down a bit before serving.

Nutrition: calories 293, fat 7, fiber 3, carbs 8, protein 6

Apple Cobbler

Preparation time: 10 minutes
Cooking time: 15 minutes
Servings: 2

Ingredients:

- ½ plum, stone removed and chopped
- ½ pear, cored and chopped
- ½ apple, cored and chopped
- 1 tablespoon honey
- ¼ teaspoon cinnamon powder
- 1 cup water
- 1 and ½ tablespoons coconut oil
- 2 tablespoons pecans, chopped
- 2 tablespoons coconut, shredded
- 1 tablespoon sunflower seeds

Directions:
1. Put plum, pear and apple in a heatproof dish, add coconut oil, cinnamon and honey and toss.
2. Add the water to your pressure cooker, add the steamer basket, add heat proof dish inside, cover, cook on High for 10 minutes and transfer fruits to a bowl.
3. In the same baking dish, mix coconut with sunflower seeds and pecans, stir, return dish to your pressure cooker, cover again and cook on High for 2 minutes more,
4. Sprinkle these over fruits, toss and serve as a dessert.

Nutrition: calories 163, fat 4, fiber 3, carbs 6, protein 7

Peanut Butter Cups

Preparation time: 10 minutes
Cooking time: 4 minutes
Servings: 12

Ingredients:
- 4 cups milk
- 8 ounces chocolate pudding mix
- 10 ounces cake, already prepared and cubed
- 12 ounces whipped cream
- 16 ounces mini peanut butter cups
- 1 and ½ cups water, for the pressure cooker

Directions:
1. In a bowl, mix chocolate pudding mix with milk and whipped cream and whisk.
2. Divide cake cubes in small ramekins, add chocolate mixture and top with peanut butter cups.
3. Add the water to your pressure cooker, add trivet inside, add ramekins, cover and cook on High for 4 minutes.
4. Leave cups to cool down a bit and serve.

Nutrition: calories 177, fat 2, fiber 3, carbs 6, protein 7

Cake Bars

Preparation time: 10 minutes
Cooking time: 20 minutes
Servings: 12

Ingredients:
- 1 and ½ cups water, for the pressure cooker
- 1 yellow cake mix
- ½ cup milk

- 1 egg, whisked
- 1 cup baking chips
- 1/3 cup canola oil

Directions:
1. In a bowl, mix cake mix with milk, eggs, oil and baking chips, stir well, pour into a baking pan and spread well.
2. Add the water to your pressure cooker, add trivet, add baking pan inside, cover and cook on High for 20 minutes.
3. Leave cake to cool down, cut into medium bars and serve.

Nutrition: calories 276, fat 6, fiber 6, carbs 8, protein 3

Pumpkin Granola

Preparation time: 20 minutes
Cooking time: 15 minutes
Servings: 2

Ingredients:
- 1 and ½ cups water
- ½ tablespoon butter
- ½ cup pumpkin puree
- ½ cup steel cut oats
- 2 tablespoons maple syrup
- 1 teaspoon cinnamon powder
- ½ teaspoon pumpkin pie spice

Directions:
1. Set your pressure cooker on Sauté mode, add butter, melt it, add oats, stir and cook for 3 minutes.
2. Add pumpkin puree, water, cinnamon, salt, maple syrup and pumpkin spice, stir, cover the cooker and cook at High for 10 minutes.
3. Divide into 2 bowls and serve as a dessert.

Nutrition: calories 173, fat 2, fiber 3, carbs 8, protein 12

Rice Pudding

Preparation time: 5 minutes
Cooking time: 17 minutes
Servings: 2

Ingredients:
- ½ cup brown rice
- 3 tablespoons coconut chips
- ½ cup coconut milk
- 1 cup water
- 3 tablespoons maple syrup
- 2 tablespoons raisins
- 2 tablespoons almonds, chopped
- A pinch of cinnamon powder

Directions:

1. Put the rice in your pressure cooker, add the water, cover and cook on High for 12 minutes.
2. Add milk, coconut chips, almonds, raisins, salt, cinnamon and maple syrup, stir well, cover the cooker and cook at High for 5 minutes.
3. Divide into 2 bowls and serve.

Nutrition: calories 200, fat 3, fiber 4, carbs 6, protein 8

White Chocolate Mousse

Preparation time: 10 minutes
Cooking time: 3 minutes
Servings: 6

Ingredients:
- 12 ounces white chocolate, chopped
- 2 cups heavy cream
- 1 tablespoon sugar
- 1 teaspoon vanilla extract
- 1 ounce black chocolate, chopped

Directions:
1. In your pressure cooker mix, white and black chocolate with cream, stir, cover and cook on High for 3 minutes.
2. Add sugar and vanilla, stir until sugar melts, divide into bowls and serve cold.

Nutrition: calories 176, fat 4, fiber 4, carbs 12, protein 3

Lemon Pie

Preparation time: 10 minutes
Cooking time: 10 minutes
Servings: 8

Ingredients:
- 1 graham cracker pie crust
- ½ cup sugar
- 8 ounces cream cheese
- 15 ounces canned lemon pie filling
- 8 ounces whipped topping
- 1 and ½ cups water, for the pressure cooker

Directions:
1. In a bowl, mix cream cheese with lemon pie filling and sugar, whisk well, spread into pie crust and top with whipped topping.
2. Add the water to your pressure cooker, add trivet, add pie inside, cover and cook on High for 10 minutes.
3. Leave pie aside to cool down, slice and serve.

Nutrition: calories 233, fat 4, fiber 4, carbs 6, protein 3

Black Rice Pudding

Preparation time: 10 minutes
Cooking time: 35 minutes
Servings: 2

Ingredients:
- 3 cups water
- 3 tablespoons sugar
- 1 cup black rice
- 1 cinnamon stick
- 2 cardamom pods, crushed
- 1 clove
- 3 tablespoons coconut, grated
- 2 tablespoons mango, chopped

Directions:
1. Put the rice in your pressure cooker, add the water, cardamom, clove and cinnamon, cover and cook on Low for 25 minutes
2. Discard cinnamon, clove and cardamom, add coconut, set the cooker on sauté mode, cook rice for 10 minutes, divide between 2 plates, divide mango on top and serve.

Nutrition: calories 118, fat 2, fiber 2, carbs 5, protein 5

Millet Pudding

Preparation time: 10 minutes
Cooking time: 10 minutes
Servings: 2

Ingredients:
- 7 ounces milk
- 3 ounces water
- ½ cup millet
- 4 dates, pitted
- Honey for serving

Directions:
1. Put the millet in your pressure cooker, add dates, milk and water, stir, cover and cook on High for 10 minutes.
2. Divide into 2 bowls, add honey on top and serve.

Nutrition: calories 200, fat 4, fiber 3, carbs 4, protein 7

Chocolate Cookies

Preparation time: 10 minutes
Cooking time: 10 minutes
Servings: 20

Ingredients:
- 17 ounces chocolate cookie mix
- ¼ cup canola oil
- 1 egg
- 1 and ½ cups chocolate covered coffee beans, chopped
- 1 cup macadamia nuts, chopped
- 1 cup water, for the pressure cooker

Directions:

1. In a bowl, mix chocolate cookie mix with oil, egg, coffee beans and nuts, whisk well and divide into small cookies.
2. Add the water to your pressure cooker, add steamer basket, add cookies inside, cover and cook on High for 10 minutes.
3. Leave cookies to cool down and serve them.

Nutrition: calories 200, fat 3, fiber 4, carbs 6, protein 4

Berry Cobbler

Preparation time: 10 minutes
Cooking time: 35 minutes
Servings: 12

Ingredients:
- 40 ounces canned raspberry filling
- 1 package cake mix
- ½ cup canola oil
- 1 and ¼ cups milk
- Vanilla ice cream for serving
- 1 and ½ cups water, for the pressure cooker

Directions:
1. in a bowl, combine cake mix with milk and oil and whisk well.
2. In a pie pan, spread raspberry filling and top and cake mix.
3. Add the water to your pressure cooker, add steamer basket, add cake pan, cover and cook on High for 35 minutes.
4. Leave cobbler to cool down, add vanilla ice cream on top and serve.

Nutrition: calories 227, fat 4, fiber 7, carbs 8, protein 3

Sweet Chia Pudding

Preparation time: 10 minutes
Cooking time: 3 minutes
Servings: 2

Ingredients:
- 4 tablespoons chia seeds
- 1 cup almond milk
- 2 tablespoons almonds
- 2 tablespoons coconut, shredded
- 4 teaspoons sugar

Directions:
1. Put chia seeds in your pressure cooker.
2. Add milk, almonds, sugar and coconut flakes, stir, cover and cook at High for 3 minutes.
3. Divide pudding into bowls and serve.

Nutrition: calories 125, fat 3, fiber 4, carbs 6, protein 8

Lemon Marmalade

Preparation time: 10 minutes
Cooking time: 15 minutes

Servings: 2

Ingredients:
- ½ pounds lemons, washed and sliced
- 1 pound sugar
- ¼ tablespoon vinegar

Directions:
1. Put lemon in your pressure cooker, cover and cook on High for 10 minutes.
2. Add sugar, cover the cooker again and cook at High for 4 more minutes.
3. Pour marmalade into 2 small jars and serve.

Nutrition: calories 73, fat 2, fiber 4, carbs 7, protein 7

Ricotta Mousse

Preparation time: 10 minutes
Cooking time: 8 minutes
Servings: 4

Ingredients:
- ¼ cup pecans, chopped
- 2/3 cup maple syrup
- 1 and ¼ cups ricotta cheese
- ½ cup heavy cream
- ½ cup mascarpone cheese

Directions:
1. In your pressure cooker mix maple syrup with pecans and ricotta, stir, cover and cook on High for 3 minutes.
2. Add heavy cream and mascarpone, stir, divide into bowls, leave aside to cool down and serve.

Nutrition: calories 182, fat 3, fiber 7, carbs 10, protein 4

Baked Custard

Preparation time: 10 minutes
Cooking time: 15 minutes
Servings: 6

Ingredients:
- 2 cups heavy cream, heated
- 3 eggs
- 2 egg yolks
- ¼ cup Irish cream liqueur, heated
- ¾ cup sugar
- 1 and ½ cups water

Directions:
1. In a bowl, mix egg yolks with eggs and sugar and whisk until sugar melts.
2. Add cream and liqueur, whisk really well and divide into ramekins.
3. Add the water to your pressure cooker, add steamer basket, add custard, cover and cook on High for 15 minutes.
4. Leave custards to cool down and serve.

Nutrition: calories 191, fat 3, fiber 8, carbs 9, protein 4

Pumpkin Cake

Preparation time: 10 minutes
Cooking time: 45 minutes
Servings: 2

Ingredients:
- ½ cup white flour
- ½ cup whole wheat flour
- ¼ teaspoon baking soda
- ¼ teaspoon pumpkin pie spice
- 3 tablespoons sugar
- 1 banana, mashed
- ¼ teaspoon baking powder
- ½ tablespoon canola oil
- 2 tablespoons Greek yogurt
- 2 ounces canned pumpkin puree
- Cooking spray
- 1-quart water
- 1 egg
- ¼ teaspoon vanilla extract
- 2 tablespoons chocolate chips

Directions:
1. In a bowl, mix white flour with whole-wheat flour, salt, baking soda and powder and pumpkin spice and stir.
2. Add sugar, oil, banana, yogurt, pumpkin puree, vanilla and egg and stir using a mixer.
3. Add chocolate chips, stir and transfer to a cake pan greased with cooking spray
4. Add the water to your pressure cooker, add the steamer basket, add cake pan inside, cover and cook on High for 35 minutes.
5. Leave cake to cool down, divide between 2 plates and serve.

Nutrition: calories 200, fat 4, fiber 4, carbs 7, protein 2

Apple Cake

Preparation time: 10 minutes
Cooking time: 1 hour
Servings: 2

Ingredients:
- 1 and ½ cups apples, cored and cubed
- ½ cup sugar
- ½ tablespoon vanilla extract
- 1 egg
- ½ tablespoon apple pie spice
- 1 cup flour
- ½ tablespoon baking powder
- ½ stick butter
- 1 cup water

Directions:

1. In a bowl mix egg with butter, apple pie spice, sugar, apples, baking powder and flour stir well and pour into a greased cake pan.
2. Add the water to your pressure cooker, add the steamer basket, add cake pan inside, cover and cook on High for 1 hour.
3. Leave cake pan to cool down a bit, divide between 2 plates and serve.

Nutrition: calories 93, fat 1, fiber 3, carbs 8, protein 6

Rhubarb and Strawberries Mix

Preparation time: 10 minutes
Cooking time: 6 minutes
Servings: 6

Ingredients:
- 3 cups rhubarb, sliced
- ¼ cup orange juice
- 1/3 cup sugar
- 1 cup whipping cream
- 2 cups strawberries, halved

Directions:
1. In your pressure cooker, mix rhubarb with sugar and orange juice, stir, cover and cook on High for 6 minutes.
2. Pulse using an immersion blender, cool down a bit, add strawberries and whipping cream, divide into bowls and serve cold.

Nutrition: calories 222, fat 5, fiber 8, carbs 10, protein 3

Cherry Pie

Preparation time: 10 minutes
Cooking time: 30 minutes
Servings: 16

Ingredients:
- ½ cup butter
- 2o ounces canned cherries
- ½ cup walnuts, chopped
- 1 yellow cake mix
- 2 tablespoons blueberries
- 1 and ½ cups water, for the pressure cooker

Directions:
1. In a bowl, combine cake mix with butter, stir until your obtain a crumbly mixture and press it on the bottom of a pie pan.
2. In a separate bowl, mix cherries with blueberries and walnuts, stir and spread over the crust.
3. Add the water to your pressure cooker, add steamer basket, add pie inside, cover and cook on High for 30 minutes.
4. Leave pie to cool down, slice, divide between plates and serve.

Nutrition: calories 261, fat 3, fiber 7, carbs 12, protein 3

Chocolate Cake

Preparation time: 10 minutes
Cooking time: 6 minutes
Servings: 2

Ingredients:
- 1 egg
- 4 tablespoons sugar
- 2 tablespoons olive oil
- 4 tablespoons milk
- 4 tablespoons flour
- A pinch of salt
- 1 tablespoon cocoa powder
- ½ teaspoon baking powder
- ½ teaspoon orange zest
- 1 cup water

Directions:
1. In a bowl, mix egg with sugar, oil, milk, flour, salt, cocoa powder, baking powder and orange zest, stir very well and pour into 2 greased ramekins.
2. Add the water to your pressure cooker, add the steamer basket, add ramekins inside, cover and cook on High for 6 minutes.
3. Serve warm.

Nutrition: calories 200, fat 2, fiber 1, carbs 7, protein 2

Apples and Wine

Preparation time: 10 minutes
Cooking time: 10 minutes
Servings: 2

Ingredients:
- 2 apples, cored
- ½ cup red wine
- 2 tablespoons raisins
- ½ teaspoon cinnamon powder
- 3 tablespoons sugar

Directions:
1. Put the apples, wine, raisins, sugar and cinnamon in your pressure cooker, cover and cook on High for 10 minutes.
2. Divide between 2 plates and serve as a dessert.

Nutrition: calories 172, fat 1, fiber 2, carbs 7, protein 1

Stuffed Strawberries

Preparation time: 10 minutes
Cooking time: 2 minutes
Servings: 24

Ingredients:
- 24 big strawberries, stems removed and tops cut off
- ¼ teaspoon almond extract
- 11 ounces cream cheese, soft
- ½ cup sugar
- 1 tablespoon chocolate, grated
- 1 cup water, for the pressure cooker

Directions:
1. In a bowl, mix cream cheese with almond extract and sugar, stir until sugar melts and stuff strawberries with this mix.
2. Add the water to your pressure cooker, add steamer basket, arrange strawberries inside, cover and cook on High for 2 minutes.
3. Divide strawberries on dessert plates and serve them cold.

Nutrition: calories 200, fat 4, fiber 2, carbs 6, protein 3

Glazed Fruits

Preparation time: 10 minutes
Cooking time: 12 minutes
Servings: 6

Ingredients:
- ½ cup honey
- ½ cup balsamic vinegar
- 6 peaches, pitted and halved

- A pinch of salt
- Vanilla ice cream

Directions:
1. Set the pressure cooker on sauté mode, add honey and balsamic vinegar, stir and cook for 2 minutes.
2. Add a pinch of salt and peaches, stir, cover and cook on Manual for 10 minutes.
3. Divide into bowls, leave aside to cool down, add vanilla ice cream on top and serve.

Nutrition: calories 169, fat 2, fiber 3, carbs 7, protein 3

Apricots and Cranberries Pudding

Preparation time: 10 minutes
Cooking time: 35 minutes
Servings: 2

Ingredients:
- 2 ounces dried cranberries, soaked in hot water, drained and chopped
- 1 teaspoon olive oil
- 2 cups water
- 2 ounces apricots, chopped
- ½ cup white flour
- 1 and ½ teaspoons baking powder
- ½ cup sugar
- ½ teaspoon ginger powder
- A pinch of cinnamon powder
- 2 eggs
- 7 tablespoons butter
- 1 small carrot, grated
- 1 and ½ tablespoons maple syrup

Directions:
1. In a blender, mix flour with baking powder, sugar, cinnamon, ginger, butter, maple syrup, eggs, carrot, cranberries and apricots, pulse well and spread this mix into a pudding mold greased with the oil.
2. Add the water to your pressure cooker, add the steamer basket, add pudding mix inside, cover and cook on High for 35 minutes.
3. Leave pudding aside to cool down, divide into 2 bowls and serve.

Nutrition: calories 214, fat 3, fiber 3, carbs 8, protein 2

Beans Cake

Preparation time: 10 minutes
Cooking time: 32 minutes
Servings: two

Ingredients:
- ½ cup borlotti beans, soaked and drained
- 2 cups water
- A pinch of almond extract
- 3 tablespoons cocoa powder
- 3 tablespoons sugar
- 1 and ½ tablespoon olive oil

- 1 egg
- 1 teaspoon baking powder
- 2 tablespoons almonds, chopped

Directions:
1. Put beans and water in your pressure cooker, cover, cook on High for 12 minutes, drain, reserve ½ cup cooking liquid, transfer to a blender and pulse well.
2. Add cocoa powder, almond extract, baking powder, egg, sugar and oil and pulse again.
3. Transfer mix to a greased heatproof dish and spread well.
4. Add reserved water from cooking the beans to your pressure cooker, add the steamer basket, add cake mix, cover and cook on High for 20 minutes.
5. Sprinkle almonds on top, divide cake between 2 plates and serve.

Nutrition: calories 172, fat 2, fiber 4, carbs 8, protein 3

Lemon Cookies

Preparation time: 10 minutes
Cooking time: 15 minutes
Servings: 30

Ingredients:
- 1 egg, whisked
- 18 ounces lemon cake mix
- 1 cup crisp rice cereal
- ½ cup butter
- 1 teaspoon lemon peel, grated
- 1 cup water, for the pressure cooker

Directions:
1. In a bowl, mix the egg with cake mix, rice cereal, butter and lemon peel, whisk well, shape cookies out of this mix and arrange on a baking sheet.
2. Add the water to your pressure cooker, add trivet, add baking sheet, cover and cook for 15 minutes.
3. Leave cookies to cool down and serve them.

Nutrition: calories 221, fat 3, fiber 3, carbs 6, protein 3

Chocolate Cake

Preparation time: 10 minutes
Cooking time: 6 minutes
Servings: 3

Ingredients:
- 1 egg
- 4 tablespoons sugar
- 4 tablespoons milk
- 4 tablespoons self-raising flour
- 1 tablespoon cocoa powder
- 1 cup water, for the pressure cooker

Directions:

1. In a bowl, mix the egg with sugar, milk, flour and cocoa powder, stir very well and pour this into a greased cake pan.
2. Add water to your pressure cooker, add steamer basket, add cake inside, cover and cook on High for 6 minutes.
3. Serve your cake warm.

Nutrition: calories 261, fat 5, fiber 5, carbs 20, protein 4

Orange Cream

Preparation time: 1 hour
Cooking time: 15 minutes
Servings: 2

Ingredients:
- 1 cup fresh cream
- ½ teaspoon cinnamon powder
- 3 egg yolks
- 2 tablespoons sugar
- Zest from ½ orange, grated
- A pinch of nutmeg, ground
- 2 cups water

Directions:
1. Heat up a pan over medium high heat, add cream, cinnamon and orange zest, stir, bring to a boil, take off heat and leave aside for half an hour.
2. In a bowl, mix egg yolks with white sugar, whisk well, add to orange cream, stir well, strain this into 2 ramekins and cover them with tin foil.
3. Add the water to your pressure cooker, add the steamer basket, add ramekins inside, cover and cook on Low for 10 minutes.
4. Sprinkle nutmeg on top and leave aside for another half an hour before serving.

Nutrition: calories 200, fat 2, fiber 4, carbs 8, protein 5

Pears with Garlic and Jelly

Preparation time: 10 minutes
Cooking time: 10 minutes
Servings: 2

Ingredients:
- 2 pears
- Juice of ½ lemon
- Zest from ½ lemon, grated
- 13 ounces grape juice
- 6 ounces currant jelly
- 1 garlic clove
- 1/3 vanilla bean
- 2 peppercorns
- 1 rosemary sprigs

Directions:
1. Add currant jelly, grape juice, lemon juice and lemon zest to your pressure cooker.
2. Add pears, garlic, peppercorns, rosemary and vanilla bean, cover cooker and cook on High for 10 minutes.

3. Divide pears between plates and serve with the sauce from the pot.

Nutrition: calories 173, fat 4, fiber 2, carbs 8, protein 10

Apples and Wine Sauce

Preparation time: 10 minutes
Cooking time: 10 minutes
Servings: 6

Ingredients:
- 6 apples, cored
- 1 cup red wine
- 1 teaspoon cinnamon powder
- ¼ cup raisins
- ½ cup sugar

Directions:
1. Put the apples in your pressure cooker, add wine, cinnamon, raisins and sugar, cover cooker and cook on High for 10 minutes.
2. Divide apples on dessert plates and serve warm.

Nutrition: calories 200, fat 3, fiber 7, carbs 34, protein 3

Cream and Cinnamon Puddings

Preparation time: 20 minutes
Cooking time: 15 minutes
Servings: 6

Ingredients:
- 2 cups fresh cream
- 1 teaspoon cinnamon powder
- 6 egg yolks
- 5 tablespoons sugar
- Zest of 1 orange
- 2 cups water, for the pressure cooker

Directions:
1. Set the cooker on sauté mode, heat it up, add cream, cinnamon and orange zest, stir, cook for a few minutes and leave aside for 20 minutes.
2. In a bowl, mix egg yolks with sugar, whisk well, add to cold cream, whisk well again, strain this mix, divide it into ramekins and cover them with tin foil.
3. Clean the pot, add the water, add steamer basket, add ramekins, cover and cook on Low for 10 minutes.
4. Serve puddings cold.

Nutrition: calories 211, fat 8, fiber 5, carbs 20, protein 10

Classic Ricotta Cake

Preparation time: 30 minutes
Cooking time: 30 minutes
Servings: 2

Ingredients:
- ½ pound ricotta
- 3 oz dates
- 1 ounce honey
- 2 eggs
- 1 ounce sugar
- 8 ounces water
- Zest from 1/3 orange, grated
- Juice from 1/3 orange

Directions:
1. In a bowl, whisk ricotta with eggs and whisk really well.
2. Add honey, vanilla, dates, orange zest and juice, stir, pour into a heatproof cake pan, spread well and cover with tin foil.
3. Add the water to your pressure cooker, add the steamer basket, add the cake pan, cover and cook on High for 20 minutes.
4. Divide between 2 plates and serve.

Nutrition: calories 200, fat 4, fiber 3, carbs 8, protein 10

Spicy Tomato Jam

Preparation time: 10 minutes
Cooking time: 30 minutes
Servings: 2

Ingredients:
- ½ pounds tomatoes, chopped
- ½ tablespoons lime juice
- 2 tablespoons white sugar
- 2 teaspoons ginger, grated
- ¼ teaspoon cinnamon powder
- A pinch of cumin, ground
- A pinch of cloves, ground
- 1 jalapeno pepper, minced

Directions:
1. In your pressure cooker mix tomatoes with sugar, lime juice, ginger, cumin, cinnamon, cloves and jalapeno pepper, stir, cover and cook on High for 30 minutes, divide into 2 bowls and serve.

Nutrition: calories 182, fat 0, fiber 2, carbs 9, protein 1

Poached Pears

Preparation time: 10 minutes
Cooking time: 10 minutes
Servings: 6

Ingredients:
- 6 green pears
- 2 teaspoons vanilla extract
- A pinch of cinnamon
- 7 oz sugar

- 1 cup red wine

Directions:
1. In your pressure cooker, mix wine with sugar, vanilla, cinnamon and pears, cover cooker and cook on High for 10 minutes.
2. Leaves pears to cool, transfer them to bowls, drizzle wine sauce all over and serve.

Nutrition: calories 172, fat 5, fiber 7, carbs 20, protein 4

Flavored Pears

Preparation time: 10 minutes
Cooking time: 10 minutes
Servings: 4

Ingredients:
- 4 pears
- Juice and zest of 1 lemon
- 26 ounces grape juice
- 11 ounces currant jelly
- 2 rosemary springs

Directions:
1. Pour currant jelly and grape juice in your pressure cooker, add lemon zest and juice and stir.
2. Add pears and rosemary springs, cover and cook on High for 10 minutes.
3. Arrange pears on plates and serve them cold with the cooking juice on top.

Nutrition: calories 172, fat 4, fiber 7, carbs 17, protein 12

Peach Jam

Preparation time: 10 minutes
Cooking time: 5 minutes
Servings: 2

Ingredients:
- 2 cups peaches, peeled, stones removed and cubed
- 2 cups sugar
- 2 tablespoons ginger, grated
- ¼ box fruit pectin

Directions:
1. In your pressure cooker, mix peaches, ginger, sugar and pectin, stir, set on sauté mode and bring to a simmer.
2. Cover the pot, cook jam on High for 5 minutes, divide into 2 jars and serve.

Nutrition: calories 83, fat 3, fiber 2, carbs 4, protein 3

Lime Pie

Preparation time: 10 minutes
Cooking time: 15 minutes
Servings: 2

Ingredients:

For the crust:
- ½ tablespoon sugar
- 1 and ½ tablespoons butter, melted
- 3 graham crackers, crumbled

For the filling:
- 2 egg yolks
- 6 ounces condensed milk
- 2 tablespoons key lime juice
- 3 tablespoons sour cream
- Cooking spray
- 1 cup water
- ½ tablespoons key lime zest, grated

Directions:
1. In a bowl, whisk egg yolks with milk, lime juice, sour cream and lime zest.
2. In another bowl, mix butter with crackers and sugar, stir well and spread on the bottom of a pie pan greased with cooking spray.
3. Add eggs cream and cover the pan with tin foil.
4. Add the water to your pressure cooker, add the steamer basket, add pie pan inside, cover and cook on High for 15 minutes.
5. Leave pie to cool down completely before dividing between 2 plates and serving.

Nutrition: calories 212, fat 3, fiber 3, carbs 7, protein 8

Dates and Ricotta Cake

Preparation time: 30 minutes
Cooking time: 20 minutes
Servings: 6

Ingredients:
- 1 pound ricotta, softened
- 6 oz dates, soaked for 15 minutes and drained
- 4 ounces honey softened
- Juice of 2 oranges
- 4 eggs
- 17 ounces water, for the pressure cooker

Directions:
1. In a bowl, mix soft ricotta with eggs and whisk well.
2. Add honey, dates, and orange juice, whisk, pour into a cake pan and cover with tin foil.
3. Add water to your pressure cooker, add steamer basket, add cake pan, cover and cook at High for 20 minutes.
4. Allow cake to cool down, slice and serve.

Nutrition: calories 212, fat 7, fiber 1, carbs 20, protein 9

Lemon and Orange Jam

Preparation time: 10 minutes
Cooking time: 30 minutes
Servings: 8

Ingredients:
- Juice of 2 lemons

- 3 pounds sugar
- 1 pound oranges, halved, pulp separated and peel grated
- 1-pint water
- 1 teaspoon vanilla extract

Directions:
1. In your pressure cooker, mix lemon juice with orange juice, vanilla extract, water and peel, cover and cook on High for 15 minutes.
2. Add sugar, set the cooker on sauté mode, cook until sugar dissolves, divide into jars and serve cold.

Nutrition: calories 87, fat 1, fiber 0, carbs 13, protein 2

Peach Compote

Preparation time: 10 minutes
Cooking time: 3 minutes
Servings: 2

Ingredients:
- 3 peaches, stones removed and chopped
- 2 tablespoons sugar
- ¼ teaspoon cinnamon powder
- ¼ teaspoon vanilla extract
- ¼ vanilla bean, scraped
- ½ tablespoons grape nuts cereal

Directions:
1. Put peaches, sugar, cinnamon, vanilla bean and vanilla extract in your pressure cooker, cover and cook on High for 3 minutes.
2. Add grape nuts, stir well, divide compote into 2 bowls and serve.

Nutrition: calories 100, fat 0, fiber 2, carbs 3, protein 1

Carrot Cake

Preparation time: 10 minutes
Cooking time: 30 minutes
Servings: 2

Ingredients:
- 2 ounces flour
- ¼ teaspoon baking powder
- ¼ teaspoon baking soda
- ¼ teaspoon cinnamon powder
- A pinch of nutmeg, ground
- A pinch of allspice
- 1 egg
- 2 cups water
- 1 tablespoon yogurt
- 2 tablespoons sugar
- 2 tablespoons pineapple juice
- 2 tablespoons coconut oil, melted
- 2 tablespoons carrots, grated

- 2 tablespoons pecans, toasted and chopped
- 2 tablespoons coconut flakes
- Cooking spray

Directions:
1. In a bowl, mix flour with baking soda and baking powder, allspice, cinnamon, nutmeg, egg, yogurt, sugar, pineapple juice, oil, carrots, pecans and coconut flakes, stir and pour into a cake pan greased with cooking spray.
2. Add the water to your pressure cooker, add the steamer basket, add the cake pan, cover and cook on High for 32 minutes.
3. Divide between 2 plates and serve.

Nutrition: calories 162, fat 2, fiber 3, carbs 7, protein 3

Ginger and Peach Marmalade

Preparation time: 10 minutes
Cooking time: 5 minutes
Servings: 6

Ingredients:
- 4 and ½ cups peaches, peeled and cubed
- 6 cups sugar
- 3 tablespoon ginger, grated
- ½ teaspoon vanilla extract
- 1 box fruit pectin

Directions:
1. Set your pressure cooker on sauté mode, add peaches, ginger, vanilla extract and pectin, stir, bring to a boil, add sugar, stir, cover and cook on High for 5 minutes.
2. Divide jam into jars and serve.

Nutrition: calories 87, fat 4, fiber 3, carbs 9, protein 2

Peach and Cinnamon Compote

Preparation time: 10 minutes
Cooking time: 5 minutes
Servings: 6

Ingredients:
- 8 peaches, chopped
- 6 tablespoons sugar
- 1 teaspoon cinnamon, ground
- 1 teaspoon vanilla extract
- 2 tablespoons grape nuts cereal

Directions:
3. Put peaches in your pressure cooker, add sugar, cinnamon and vanilla extract, stir well, cover cooker and cook on High for 5 minutes.
4. Add grape nuts, stir, divide into bowls and serve cold

Nutrition: calories 121, fat 4, fiber 2, carbs 17, protein 4

Cheesecake

Preparation time: 15 minutes
Cooking time: 1 hour
Servings: 2

Ingredients:
- 1 tablespoon butter, melted
- 3 tablespoons chocolate graham crackers, crumbled
- 2 tablespoons heavy cream
- 3 tablespoons sugar
- 6 ounces cream cheese, soft
- ½ teaspoon vanilla extract
- 2 tablespoons sour cream
- ½ tablespoon flour
- 1 egg yolk
- 1 eggs
- Cooking spray
- 1 cup water

For the topping:
- 6 caramels
- ½ coconut, shredded
- 2 tablespoons chocolate, chopped

Directions:
1. In a bowl, mix crackers with butter, stir, spread in the bottom of a pan greased with cooking spray and keep in the freezer for 10 minutes.
2. In another bowl, mix cheese with sugar, heavy cream, vanilla, flour, sour cream, egg yolk and egg, whisk well, pour over crust, spread and cover with tin foil.
3. Add the water to your pressure cooker, add the steamer basket, add the pan, cover and cook on High for 35 minutes.
4. Meanwhile, spread coconut on a lined baking sheet, introduce in the oven at 300 degrees F and bake for 20 minutes.
5. Put caramels in a heatproof bowl, introduce in the microwave for 2 minutes, mix them with toasted coconut and spread this on your cheesecake.
6. Put chocolate in another heatproof bowl, introduce in your microwave for a few seconds until it melts and drizzle over your cake.
7. Serve cake really cold.

Nutrition: calories 273, fat 3, fiber 1, carbs 10, protein 6

Chocolate Pudding

Preparation time: 10 minutes
Cooking time: 20 minutes
Servings: 2

Ingredients:
- 3 ounces chocolate, chopped
- 3 tablespoons milk
- 1 cup heavy cream
- 3 egg yolks
- 3 tablespoons brown sugar

- 1 teaspoon vanilla extract
- 1 and ½ cups water
- A pinch of cardamom, ground
- Crème fraiche for serving

Directions:
1. Put cream and milk in a pot, bring to a simmer over medium heat, take off heat, add chocolate and whisk.
2. In a bowl, mix egg yolks with vanilla, sugar and cardamom, stir, strain, mix with chocolate, transfer to 2 small soufflé dishes and cover with tin foil.
3. Put the water in your pressure cooker, add the steamer basket, add soufflé dishes, cover cooker and cook on Low for 18 minutes.
4. Leave chocolate pudding to cool down completely and serve with crème fraiche on top.

Nutrition: calories 212, fat 2, fiber 4, carbs 6, protein 8

Ginger Cookies Cheesecake

Preparation time: 15 minutes
Cooking time: 15 minutes
Servings: 6

Ingredients:
- 2 cups water, for the pressure cooker
- 2 teaspoons butter, melted
- ½ cup ginger cookies, crumbled
- 16 ounces cream cheese, soft
- 2 eggs
- ½ cup sugar

Directions:
1. Grease a cake pan with the butter, add cookie crumbs and spread them evenly.
2. In a bowl, beat cream cheese with a mixer.
3. Add eggs and sugar and stir very well.
4. Add the water to your pressure cooker, add steamer basket, add cake pan inside, cover and cook on High for 15 minutes.
5. Keep cheesecake in the fridge for a few hours before serving it.

Nutrition: calories 394, fat 12, fiber 3, carbs 20, protein 6

Winter Cherry Mix

Preparation time: 10 minutes
Cooking time: 5 minutes
Servings: 6

Ingredients:
- 16 ounces cherries, pitted
- 2 tablespoons water
- 2 tablespoons lemon juice
- Sugar to the taste
- 2 tablespoons cornstarch

Directions:
1. In your pressure cooker, mix cherries with sugar and lemon juice, stir, cover and cook on High for 3 minutes.
2. In a bowl, mix water with cornstarch, stir well, add to the pot, set the cooker on sauté mode, add the rest of the cherries, stir, cook for 2 minutes, divide into bowls and serve cold.

Nutrition: calories 161, fat 4, fiber 2, carbs 8, protein 6

Carrot Pudding and Rum Sauce

Preparation time: 10 minutes
Cooking time: 1 hour and 10 minutes
Servings: 2

Ingredients:
- 1 and ½ cups water
- Cooking spray
- 2 tablespoons brown sugar
- 1 egg
- 2 tablespoons molasses
- 2 tablespoon flour
- A pinch of allspice
- A pinch of cinnamon powder
- A pinch of nutmeg, ground
- ¼ teaspoon baking soda
- 1/3 cup shortening, grated
- 3 tablespoons pecans, chopped
- 3 tablespoons carrots, grated
- 3 tablespoons raisins
- ½ cup bread crumbs

For the sauce:
- 1 and ½ tablespoons butter
- 2 tablespoons brown sugar
- 2 tablespoons heavy cream
- ½ tablespoons rum
- A pinch of cinnamon powder

Directions:

1. In a bowl, mix molasses with eggs and 2 tablespoons sugar, flour, shortening, carrots, nuts, raisins, bread crumbs, salt, a pinch of cinnamon, allspice, nutmeg and baking soda, stir everything, pour into a pudding pan greased with cooking spray and cover with tin foil.
2. Add the water to your pressure cooker, add the steamer basket, add pudding inside, cover and cook on High 1 hour.
3. Meanwhile, heat up a pan with the butter for the sauce over medium heat, add 2 tablespoons sugar, stir and cook for 2 minutes.
4. Add cream, rum and a pinch of cinnamon, stir and simmer for 2 minutes more.
5. Divide pudding into 2 bowls, drizzle rum sauce all over and serve.

Nutrition: calories 261, fat 6, fiber 6, carbs 10, protein 8

Lemon Pudding

Preparation time: 30 minutes
Cooking time: 10 minutes
Servings: 2

Ingredients:
- ½ cup milk
- Zest from ½ lemon, grated
- 3 egg yolks
- ½ cup fresh cream
- 1 cup water
- 3 tablespoons sugar
- Blackberry syrup for serving

Directions:
1. Heat up a pan over medium heat, add milk, lemon zest and cream, stir, bring to a boil, take off heat and leave aside for 30 minutes.
2. In a bowl, mix egg yolks with sugar and cream mix, stir well, pour into your 2 greased ramekins and cover with tin foil.
3. Add the water to your pressure cooker, add the steamer basket, add ramekins, cover and cook on High for 10 minutes.
4. Serve with blackberry syrup on top.

Nutrition: calories 162, fat 2, fiber 2, carbs 8, protein 2

Strawberry and Chia Marmalade

Preparation time: 10 minutes
Cooking time: 4 minutes
Servings: 6

Ingredients:
- 2 tablespoons chia seeds
- 4 tablespoons sugar
- 2 pounds strawberries, halved
- ½ teaspoon vanilla extract
- Zest of 1 lemon, grated

Directions:
1. In your pressure cooker, mix sugar with strawberries, vanilla extract, lemon zest and chia seeds, stir, cover and cook on High for 4 minutes.
2. Stir again, divide into cups and serve cold

Nutrition: calories 110, fat 2, fiber 2, carbs 2, protein 3

Lemon and Maple Syrup Pudding

Preparation time: 10 minutes
Cooking time: 5 minutes
Servings: 7

Ingredients:
- 3 cups milk
- Juice of 2 lemons
- Lemon zest from 2 lemons, grated
- ½ cup maple syrup
- 2 tablespoons gelatin
- 1 cup water, for the pressure cooker

Directions:
1. In your blender, mix milk with lemon juice, lemon zest, maple syrup and gelatin, pulse really well and divide into ramekins.
2. Add the water to your pressure cooker, add steamer basket, add ramekins inside, cover and cook on High for 5 minutes.
3. Serve puddings cold.

Nutrition: calories 151, fat 3, fiber 2, carbs 18, protein 3

Sweet Corn Pudding

Preparation time: 10 minutes
Cooking time: 30 minutes
Servings: 2

Ingredients:
- 6 ounces canned creamed corn
- 2 cups water
- 1 cup milk

- 1 and ½ tablespoons sugar
- 1 egg, whisked
- 1 tablespoon flour
- ½ tablespoon butter
- Cooking spray

Directions:
1. Put the water in your pressure cooker, set on Simmer mode and bring to a boil.
2. In a bowl, mix corn with eggs, milk, butter, salt, flour and sugar, stir well, pour into a heat proof dish greased with cooking spray and cover with tin foil
3. Add the steamer basket into the pot, add the pan, cover and cook on High for 20 minutes.
4. Divide into 2 bowls and serve cold.

Nutrition: calories 162, fat 3, fiber 2, carbs 8, protein 7

Apricot Jam

Preparation time: 10 minutes
Cooking time: 14 minutes
Servings: 2

Ingredients:
- 1 pound apricots, stones removed and halved
- ½ pound white sugar
- 1 orange, peeled and sliced
- 1 teaspoon orange zest, grated
- ½ tablespoon butter
- ¼ teaspoon almond extract

Directions:
5. Put apricots in your food processor, pulse really well, transfer to your pressure cooker, add sugar, orange slices and orange zest, stir, set the cooker on sauté mode and boil the jam for 6 minutes.
6. Add butter and almond extract, cover, cook on High for 8 minutes, divide into 2 jars and serve cold

Nutrition: calories 180, fat 0, fiber 3, carbs 3, protein 8

Banana Cake

Preparation time: 10 minutes
Cooking time: 1 hour
Servings: 4

Ingredients:
- 1 cup water, for the pressure cooker
- 1 and ½ cups sugar
- 2 cups flour
- 4 bananas, peeled and mashed
- 1 teaspoon cinnamon powder
- 1 teaspoon nutmeg powder

Directions:
4. In a bowl, mix sugar with flour, bananas, cinnamon and nutmeg, stir, pour into a greased cake pan and cover with tin foil.

5. Add the water to your pressure cooker, add steamer basket, add cake pan, cover and cook on High for 1 hour.
   6. Slice, divide between plates and serve cold.

Nutrition: calories 300, fat 10, fiber 4, carbs 45, protein 4

Pineapple Pudding

Preparation time: 10 minutes
Cooking time: 5 minutes
Servings: 8

Ingredients:
- 1 tablespoon avocado oil
- 1 cup rice
- 14 ounces milk
- Sugar to the taste
- 8 ounces canned pineapple, chopped

Directions:
1. In your pressure cooker, mix oil, milk and rice, stir, cover and cook on High for 3 minutes.
2. Add sugar and pineapple, stir, cover and cook on High for 2 minutes more.
3. Divide into dessert bowls and serve.

Nutrition: calories 154, fat 4, fiber 1, carbs 14, protein 4

Blueberry Jam

Preparation time: 10 minutes
Cooking time: 11 minutes
Servings: 2

Ingredients:
- ½ pound blueberries
- 1/3 pound sugar
- Zest from ½ lemon, grated
- ½ tablespoon butter
- A pinch of cinnamon powder

Directions:
1. Put the blueberries in your blender, pulse them well, strain, transfer to your pressure cooker, add sugar, lemon zest and cinnamon, stir, cover and simmer on sauté mode for 3 minutes.
2. Add butter, stir, cover the cooker and cook on High for 8 minutes.
3. Transfer to a jar and serve.

Nutrition: calories 211, fat 3, fiber 3, carbs 6, protein 6

Bread Pudding

Preparation time: 10 minutes
Cooking time: 20 minutes
Servings: 4

Ingredients:

- 2 egg yolks
- 1 and ½ cups brioche cubed
- 1 cup half and half
- ¼ teaspoon vanilla extract
- ½ cup sugar
- 1 tablespoon butter, soft
- ½ cup cranberries
- 2 cups water
- 3 tablespoons raisins
- Zest from 1 lime, grated

Directions:
1. In a bowl mix, egg yolks with half and half, cubed brioche, vanilla extract, sugar, cranberries, raisins and lime zest, stir, pour into a baking dish greased with the butter and leave aside for 10 minutes.
2. Add the water to your pressure cooker, add the steamer basket, add the dish, cover and cook on High for 20 minutes.
3. Serve this cold.

Nutrition: calories 162, fat 6, fiber 7, carbs 9, protein 8

Coconut Cream and Cinnamon Pudding

Preparation time: 10 minutes
Cooking time: 10 minutes
Servings: 6

Ingredients:
- 2 cups coconut cream
- 1 teaspoon cinnamon powder
- 6 tablespoons flour
- 5 tablespoons sugar
- Zest of 1 lemon, grated
- 2 cups water, for the pressure cooker

Directions:
1. Set your pressure cooker on sauté mode, add coconut cream, cinnamon and orange zest, stir, simmer for a couple of minutes, transfer to a bowl and leave aside.
2. Add flour and sugar, stir well and divide this into ramekins.
3. Add the water to your pressure cooker, add steamer basket, add ramekins, cover pot, cook on Low for 10 minutes and serve cold.

Nutrition: calories 170, fat 5, fiber 2, carbs 8, protein 10

Plum Jam

Preparation time: 20 minutes
Cooking time: 8 minutes
Servings: 12

Ingredients:
- 3 pounds plums, stones removed and roughly chopped
- 2 tablespoons lemon juice
- 2 pounds sugar

- 1 teaspoon vanilla extract
- 3 ounces water

Directions:
1. In your pressure cooker, mix plums with sugar and vanilla extract, stir and leave aside for 20 minutes
2. Add lemon juice and water, stir, cover and cook on High for 8 minutes.
3. Divide into bowls and serve cold.

Nutrition: calories 191, fat 3, fiber 4, carb 12, protein 4

Cranberry Bread Pudding

Preparation time: 10 minutes
Cooking time: 15 minutes
Servings: 2

Ingredients:
- 2 egg yolks
- 1 and ½ cups bread, cubed
- 1 cup heavy cream
- Zest from ½ orange, grated
- Juice from ½ orange
- 2 teaspoons vanilla extract
- ½ cup sugar
- 2 cups water
- 1 tablespoon butter
- ½ cup cranberries

Directions:
1. In a bowl, mix egg yolks with bread, heavy cream, orange zest and juice, vanilla extract, sugar, butter and cranberries, stir and pour into a baking dish.
2. Add the water to your pressure cooker, add the steamer basket, add baking dish, cover cooker and cook on High for 15 minutes.
3. Divide between 2 plates and serve cold.

Nutrition: calories 189, fat 3, fiber 1, carbs 4, protein 7

Apples and Pears Salad

Preparation time: 10 minutes
Cooking time: 15 minutes
Servings: 2

Ingredients:
- 1 quart water
- 1 tablespoon sugar
- ½ pound mixed apples, pears and cranberries
- 3 star anise
- A pinch of cloves, ground
- 1 cinnamon sticks
- Zest from ½ orange, grated
- Zest from ½ lemon, grated

Directions:
1. Put the water, sugar, apples, pears, cranberries, star anise, cinnamon, orange and lemon zest and cloves in your pressure cooker, cover and cook on High for 15 minutes.
2. Discard cinnamon stick. Divide salad into 2 bowls and serve cold.

Nutrition: calories 83, fat 0, fiber 0, carbs 0, protein 2

Blueberry and Coconut Sweet Bowls

Preparation time: 10 minutes
Cooking time: 6 minutes
Servings: 1

Ingredients:
- 1 cup coconut milk
- 1 cup coconut, unsweetened and flaked
- 1 cup vanilla yogurt
- 1 cup blueberries
- 2 teaspoons sugar
- 1 and ½ cups water, for the pressure cooker

Directions:
1. In a heatproof dish, combine milk with coconut, yogurt, blueberries and sugar, stir well and cover with tin foil.
2. Put the water in your pressure cooker, add trivet, add dish, cover and cook on High for 6 minutes.
3. Divide into bowls and serve cold.

Nutrition: calories 142, fat 2, fiber 3, carbs 4, protein 6

Coconut Pancake

Preparation time: 10 minutes
Cooking time: 40 minutes
Servings: 4

Ingredients:
- 2 cups self-raising flour
- 2 tablespoons sugar
- 2 eggs
- 1 and ½ cups coconut milk
- A drizzle of olive oil

Directions:
1. In a bowl, mix eggs with sugar, milk and flour and whisk until you obtain a batter.
2. Grease your pressure cooker with the oil, add the batter, spread into the pot, cover and cook on Low for 40 minutes.
3. Slice pancake, divide between plates and serve cold.

Nutrition: calories 162, fat 3, fiber 2, carbs 7, protein 3

Apples and Red Grape Juice

Preparation time: 10 minutes
Cooking time: 10 minutes
Servings: 2

Ingredients:
- 2 apples
- ½ cup natural red grape juice
- 2 tablespoons raisins
- 1 teaspoon cinnamon powder
- ½ tablespoons sugar

Directions:
1. Put the apples in your pressure cooker, add grape juice, raisins, cinnamon and stevia, toss a bit, cover and cook on High for 10 minutes.
2. Divide into 2 bowls and serve.

Nutrition: calories 110, fat 1, fiber 1, carbs 3, protein 4

Strawberry Shortcakes

Preparation time: 20 minutes
Cooking time: 25 minutes
Servings: 2

Ingredients:
- Cooking spray
- 3 tablespoons sugar
- 1 cup white flour
- 1 cup water
- ½ teaspoon baking powder
- ¼ teaspoon baking soda
- 3 tablespoons butter
- ½ cup buttermilk
- 1 egg, whisked
- 1 and ½ tablespoons sugar
- 1 cups strawberries, sliced
- ½ tablespoon rum
- ½ tablespoon mint, chopped
- ½ teaspoon lime zest, grated

Directions:
1. In a bowl, mix flour with 2 tablespoons sugar, baking powder and baking soda and stir.
2. In another bowl, mix buttermilk with egg, stir, add to flour mixture and whisk everything.
3. Spoon this dough into 2 jars greased with cooking spray and cover with tin foil.
4. Add the water to your pressure cooker, add the steamer basket inside, add jars, cover cooker and cook on High for 25 minutes.
5. Meanwhile, in a bowl, mix strawberries with 1 tablespoon sugar, rum, mint and lime zest and toss to coat
6. Divide strawberry mix on shortcakes and serve.

Coconut and Avocado Pudding

Preparation time: 2 hours
Cooking time: 2 minutes
Servings: 3

Ingredients:

- ½ cup avocado oil
- 4 tablespoons sugar
- 1 tablespoon cocoa powder
- 14 ounces canned coconut milk
- 1 avocado, pitted, peeled and chopped

Directions:
1. In a bowl, mix oil with cocoa powder and half of the sugar, stir well, transfer to a lined container, keep in the fridge for 1 hour and chop into small pieces.
2. In your pressure cooker, mix coconut milk with avocado and the rest of the sugar, blend using an immersion blender, cover cooker and cook on High for 2 minutes.
3. Add chocolate chips, stir, divide pudding into bowls and keep in the fridge until you serve it.

Nutrition: calories 140, fat 3, fiber 2, carbs 3, protein 4

Cocoa and Milk Pudding

Preparation time: 50 minutes
Cooking time: 3 minutes
Servings: 4

Ingredients:
- 1 and ½ cups water, for the pressure cooker+ 2 tablespoons
- 2 tablespoons gelatin
- 4 tablespoons sugar
- 4 tablespoons cocoa powder
- 2 cups coconut milk, hot
- ½ teaspoon cinnamon powder

Directions:
1. In a bowl, mix milk with sugar, cinnamon and cocoa powder and stir well.
2. In a bowl, mix gelatin with 2 tablespoons water, stir well, add to cocoa mix, stir and divide into ramekins.
3. Add the water to your pressure cooker, add the steamer basket, add ramekins inside, cover and cook on High for 4 minutes.
4. Serve puddings cold.

Nutrition: calories 120, fat 2, fiber 1, carbs 4, protein 3

Caramel Pudding

Preparation time: 20 minutes
Cooking time: 20 minutes
Servings: 2

Ingredients:
- Cooking spray
- ½ teaspoon baking powder
- ½ cup white flour
- 2 tablespoons white sugar
- ¼ teaspoon cinnamon
- 2 tablespoons butter
- 4 tablespoons milk
- 3 tablespoons pecans chopped

- 1 and ½ cups water
- 3 tablespoons raisins
- 3 tablespoons orange zest, grated
- 3 tablespoons brown sugar
- 3 tablespoons orange juice
- Caramel topping

Directions:
1. In a bowl, mix flour with white sugar, baking powder and cinnamon and stir.
2. Add half of butter and milk and stir again well.
3. Add pecans and raisins, stir and pour into a pudding pan greased with cooking spray.
4. Heat up a small pan over medium high heat, add ½ cup water, orange juice, orange zest, the rest of the butter and the brown sugar, stir, bring to a boil for 2 minutes and pour over pudding.
5. Add 1 cup water to your pressure cooker, add the steamer basket, add pudding pan inside, cover and cook on High for 20 minutes.
6. Divide into 2 bowls and serve with caramel topping on top.

Nutrition: calories 194, fat 3, fiber 2, carbs 6, protein 7

Black Tea Cake

Preparation time: 10 minutes
Cooking time: 30 minutes
Servings: 2

Ingredients:
- 2 tablespoons black tea powder
- ½ cup milk
- 1 tablespoon butter
- 1 cup sugar
- 2 eggs
- 1 teaspoons vanilla extract
- 3 tablespoons coconut oil
- 2 cups flour
- ¼ teaspoon baking soda
- 2 cups water
- 1 teaspoon baking powder

For the cream:
- 1 and ½ tablespoons honey
- 1 and ½ cups sugar
- ¼ cup butter, soft

Directions:
1. Put the milk and tea in a pot, warm it up over medium heat, take off the stove and leave aside to cool down.
2. In a bowl, mix 1 tablespoon butter with 1 cup sugar, eggs, oil, vanilla extract, baking powder, baking soda and 2 cups flour, stir everything really well and pour into a greased pan.
3. Add the water to your pressure cooker, add the steamer basket, add the cake pan, cover and cook on High for 30 minutes.
4. Meanwhile, in a bowl, mix honey with 1 and ½ cups sugar and ¼ cup butter and whisk well.
5. Spread this over cake, leave aside to cool down, divide between 2 plates and serve.

Nutrition: calories 150, fat 4, fiber 4, carbs 6, protein 2

Cocoa and Walnuts Sweet Cream

Preparation time: 10 minutes
Cooking time: 2 minutes
Servings: 6

Ingredients:
- 2 ounces avocado oil
- 4 tablespoons cocoa powder
- 1 teaspoon vanilla extract
- 1 cup walnuts, chopped
- 4 tablespoons sugar

Directions:
1. In your pressure cooker, mix oil with cocoa, vanilla, walnuts and sugar, blend using an immersion blender, cover cooker and cook on High for 2 minutes.
2. Divide into small bowls and keep in the fridge until you serve it.

Nutrition: calories 120, fat 4, fiber 3, carbs 9, protein 2

Cream Cheese Pudding

Preparation time: 10 minutes
Cooking time: 20 minutes
Servings: 2

Ingredients:
- 1 and ½ teaspoons caramel extract
- 2 ounces cream cheese
- 2 eggs
- 1 and ½ tablespoons sugar
- ¼ teaspoon vanilla extract
- 1 cup water, for the pressure cooker

Directions:
1. In your blender, mix cream cheese with eggs, caramel extract, vanilla extract and sugar, pulse well and divide into greased ramekins.
2. Add the water to your pressure cooker, add steamer basket, add ramekins inside, cover and cook on High for 20 minutes.
3. Serve your puddings cold.

Nutrition: calories 174, fat 7, fiber 1, carbs 2, protein 4

Green Tea Pudding

Preparation time: 10 minutes
Cooking time: 5 minutes
Servings: 2

Ingredients:
- 7 ounces milk
- 1 tablespoon green tea powder

- 7 ounces heavy cream
- 1 and ½ tablespoons sugar
- ½ teaspoon honey

Directions:
1. In your pressure cooker, mix milk with green tea powder, heavy cream, sugar and honey, stir, cover and cook on High for 3 minutes.
2. Divide into 2 cups and serve cold.

Nutrition: calories 110, fat 2, fiber 2, carbs 3, protein 6

Lemon Curd

Preparation time: 10 minutes
Cooking time: 10 minutes
Servings: 2

Ingredients:
- 2 cups blueberries
- ¼ cup lemon juice
- 2/3 cup sugar
- 2 teaspoons lemon zest, grated
- 4 tablespoons butter, softened
- 3 egg yolks, whisked
- 1 and ½ cups water

Directions:
1. Set your pressure cooker on sauté mode, add lemon juice and blueberries, stir and simmer for 2 minutes.
2. Strain into a bowl, mash, mix with sugar, butter, lemon zest and egg yolks, whisk well and pour into a ramekin.
3. Add the water to your pressure cooker, add the steamer basket, add the ramekin inside, cover cooker and cook on High for 6 minutes.
4. Serve this cold.

Nutrition: calories 140, fat 3, fiber 3, carbs 6, protein 8

Egg and Coconut Cream

Preparation time: 20 minutes
Cooking time: 10 minutes
Servings: 6

Ingredients:
- 2 cups coconut cream, hot
- 1 teaspoon cinnamon powder
- 6 egg yolks
- 5 tablespoons sugar
- Zest of 1 lemon, grated
- 2 cups water, for the pressure cooker

Directions:
1. In a bowl, mix cream with cinnamon and orange zest, stir and leave aside to cool down

2. Add egg yolks and sugar, stir well, strain and divide this into ramekins.
3. Add the water to your pressure cooker, add steamer basket, add ramekins, cover cooker and cook on Low for 10 minutes.
4. Serve cold.

Nutrition: calories 190, fat 4, fiber 2, carbs 12, protein 11

Blueberries and Strawberries Compote

Preparation time: 10 minutes
Cooking time: 7 minutes
Servings: 8

Ingredients:
- 1 cup blueberries
- 2 cups strawberries, chopped
- 2 tablespoons lemon juice
- White sugar to the taste
- 1 tablespoon water

Directions:
1. In your pressure cooker, mix blueberries with strawberries, lemon juice, sugar and water, stir, cover, cook on High for 7 minutes, divide into cups and serve cold.

Nutrition: calories 170, fat 2, fiber 3, carbs 12, protein 2

Apples and Honey

Preparation time: 10 minutes
Cooking time: 20 minutes
Servings: 2

Ingredients:
- 2 big apples, cored
- 1 tablespoon raisins
- ½ tablespoon cinnamon, ground
- 2 tablespoons honey
- 1 and ½ cups water

Directions:
1. Stuff apples with raisins, sprinkle cinnamon and drizzle honey all over.
2. Add the water to your pressure cooker, add the steamer basket, add apples, cover cooker and cook on High for 10 minutes.
3. Divide apples on 2 plates and serve.

Nutrition: calories 160, fat 2, fiber 3, carbs 4, protein 5

Strawberries Dessert

Preparation time: 5 minutes
Cooking time: 10 minutes
Servings: 2

Ingredients:

- 1/3 cup rolled oats
- 2 tablespoon strawberries, chopped
- 2 cups water
- 2/3 cup whole milk
- 2 teaspoons white sugar

Directions:
1. Put the water in your pressure cooker, add strawberries, oats, milk and sugar, stir, cover and cook on High for 10 minutes.
2. Divide into 2 bowls and serve.

Nutrition: calories 160, fat 2, fiber 2, carbs 12, protein 8

Sweet Zucchini Bread

Preparation time: 10 minutes
Cooking time: 20 minutes
Servings: 6

Ingredients:
- 1 cup milk
- 3 eggs, whisked
- 4 tablespoons sugar
- 2 cups zucchini, grated
- 2 and ½ cups self-raising flour
- 2 cups water, for the pressure cooker

Directions:
1. In a bowl, mix milk with eggs, sugar, flour and zucchini, whisk well and pour into a loaf pan.
2. Add the water to your pressure cooker, add steamer basket, add cake pan, cover and cook on High for 20 minutes.
3. Slice and serve cold as a dessert.

Nutrition: calories 200, fat 3, fiber 6, carbs 12, protein 3

Poached Figs

Preparation time: 10 minutes
Cooking time: 4 minutes
Servings: 4

Ingredients:
- 1 cup grape juice
- 1 pound figs
- ½ cup pine nuts, toasted
- 4 tablespoons brown sugar
- ¼ teaspoon vanilla extract

Directions:
1. In your pressure cooker, mix grape juice with figs and sugar, cover cooker and cook on High for 4 minutes.

2. Divide this into bowls, sprinkle pine nuts on top and serve cold.

Nutrition: calories 140, fat 0, fiber 2, carbs 10, protein 3

Peaches and Cream

Preparation time: 10 minutes
Cooking time: 3 minutes
Servings: 2

Ingredients:
- 2 peaches, stones removed and chopped
- 1 cup whole milk
- 2 teaspoons sugar
- 1 cup steel cut oats
- ½ vanilla bean
- 2 cups water

Directions:
1. Put the peaches in your pressure cooker, add milk, oats, vanilla bean and water, stir, cover and cook on High for 3 minutes.
2. Divide into 2 bowls and serve.

Nutritional value: 130, fat 1, fiber 2, carbs 6, protein 3

Pumpkin and Coconut Sweet Mix

Preparation time: 10 minutes
Cooking time: 14 minutes
Servings: 6

Ingredients:
- 2 cups water
- 1 tablespoon butter, melted
- 1 cup pumpkin puree
- 1 cup coconut flakes
- 3 tablespoons sugar

Directions:
4. Set your pressure cooker on sauté mode, add butter, heat up, add coconut flakes, pumpkin, water and sugar stir, cover and cook on High for 14 minutes.
5. Divide into bowls and serve cold.

Nutrition: calories 202, fat 2, fiber 4, carbs 8, protein 3

Apricot Marmalade

Preparation time: 10 minutes
Cooking time: 15 minutes
Servings: 4

Ingredients:
- 2 pounds apricots, stones removed and halved
- 1 pound sugar
- 2 oranges, peeled and sliced
- 1 tablespoon butter
- ½ teaspoon vanilla extract

Directions:
7. Put apricots in your food processor, pulse, set the pressure cooker on sauté mode, add apricots mix to the pot, also add sugar and orange slices, stir and boil the jam for 6 minutes.
8. Add butter and vanilla extract, cover, cook on High for 8 minutes, divide into jars and serve cold

Nutrition: calories 200, fat 0, fiber 2, carbs 7, protein 3

Stuffed Peaches

Preparation time: 10 minutes
Cooking time: 4 minutes
Servings: 2

Ingredients:
- 2 peaches, tops cut off and insides removed
- 2 tablespoons flour
- 2 tablespoons maple syrup
- 2 tablespoons butter
- ½ teaspoon cinnamon powder
- ½ teaspoon almond extract
- 1 cup water

Directions:
1. In a bowl, mix flour with maple syrup, butter, cinnamon and almond extract, stir well and stuff peaches with this mix.
2. Add the water to your pressure cooker, add the steamer basket, add peaches inside, cover and cook on High for 4 minutes.
3. Arrange peaches on 2 plates and serve.

Nutrition: calories 140, fat 2, fiber 2, carbs 8, protein 3

Milk and Cream Pudding

Preparation time: 10 minutes
Cooking time: 5 minutes
Servings: 4

Ingredients:
- 14 ounces milk
- 2 tablespoons matcha powder

- 14 ounces heavy cream
- 3 tablespoons sugar
- 1 teaspoon honey

Directions:
1. In your pressure cooker, mix milk with green tea powder, heavy cream, sugar and honey, stir, cover and cook on High for 5 minutes.
2. Divide into dessert cups and keep in the fridge until you serve it.

Nutrition: calories 220, fat 1, fiber 2, carbs 5, protein 2

Fall Pear Cake

Preparation time: 10 minutes
Cooking time: 35 minutes
Servings: 4

Ingredients:
- 2 cups self-rising flour
- 8 tablespoons milk
- 5 tablespoons maple syrup
- 2 tablespoons vegetable oil
- 1 cup pear, cored and chopped
- 1 and ½ cups water, for the pressure cooker

Directions:
1. In a bowl, mix flour with milk, maple syrup, oil and pear, stir and pour into a greased cake pan.
2. Add the water to your pressure cooker, add the steamer basket, add cake pan, cover and cook on High for 35 minutes.
3. Leave cake to cool down, slice and serve.

Nutrition: calories 150, fat 2, fiber 2, carbs 10, protein 2

Cranberry and Pear Cake

Preparation time: 10 minutes
Cooking time: 35 minutes
Servings: 2

Ingredients:
- 1 cup flour
- ¼ teaspoon baking powder
- ¼ teaspoon baking soda
- ¼ teaspoon cardamom, ground
- 4 tablespoons milk
- 3 tablespoons maple syrup
- 1 tablespoon flax seeds
- 1 tablespoon vegetable oil
- ½ cup pear, cored and chopped
- 4 tablespoons cranberries, chopped
- 1 and ½ cups water

Directions:
4. In a bowl, mix flour with baking soda and powder, cardamom, milk, flax seeds, maple syrup and oil and stir well.
5. Add chopped pear and cranberries, stir and pour into a greased cake pan.
6. Add the water to your pressure cooker, add the steamer basket, add cake pan, cover cooker and cook on High for 35 minutes.
7. Divide between 2 dessert plates and serve.

Nutrition: calories 140, fat 3, fiber 2, carbs 9, protein 3

Chocolate Fondue

Preparation time: 5 minutes
Cooking time: 2 minutes
Servings: 2

Ingredients:
- 2 cups water
- 1.5 ounces dark chocolate, cut into chunks
- 1.5 ounces coconut milk
- ½ teaspoon Amaretto liquor

Directions:
1. In a ramekin, mix chocolate pieces with coconut milk and liquor.
2. Add the water to your pressure cooker, add the steamer basket, add ramekin, cover and cook on High for 2 minutes.
3. Stir chocolate mix well and serve.

Nutrition: calories 180, fat 2, fiber 3, carbs 7, protein 3

Pear and Maple Dessert

Preparation time: 10 minutes
Cooking time: 10 minutes
Servings: 2

Ingredients:
- 1 pear, cored and chopped
- ½ teaspoon maple extract
- 2 cups milk
- ½ cup steel cut oats
- ½ teaspoon vanilla extract
- 1 tablespoon stevia
- ¼ cup walnuts, chopped for serving

Directions:
1. In your pressure cooker, mix pear with maple extract, milk, oats, vanilla extract, sugar and walnuts, stir, cover and cook on High for 10 minutes.
2. Divide into 2 bowls and serve.

Nutrition: calories 150, fat 1, fiber 2, carbs 4, protein 4

Cherry Bowls

Preparation time: 10 minutes

Cooking time: 10 minutes
Servings: 2

Ingredients:
- 1 cup milk
- 1 cup water+ 1 tablespoon
- ½ cup steel cut oats
- 1 tablespoon cocoa powder
- 1 cup cherries, pitted + 3 tablespoons
- 2 tablespoons maple syrup
- ½ teaspoon almond extract

Directions:
1. Put the milk in your pressure cooker, add 1 cup water, oats, cocoa powder, 3 tablespoons cherries, maple syrup and half of the almond extract, stir, cover and cook on High for 10 minutes.
2. Meanwhile, in a pot, mix 1 tablespoon water with 3 tablespoons cherries and the rest of the almond extract, stir and simmer for a few minutes over medium high heat.
3. Divide cherries mix into 2 bowls, drizzle the sauce all over and serve.

Nutrition: calories 120, fat 1, fiber 2, carbs 4, protein 4

Cold Pineapple and Cherries Mix

Preparation time: 10 minutes
Cooking time: 10 minutes
Servings: 10

Ingredients:
- 3 cups canned pineapple chunks, drained
- 3 cups canned cherries, drained
- 3 cups natural applesauce
- 2 tablespoons sugar
- 1 teaspoon cinnamon powder

Directions:
1. Put pineapples, cherries, applesauce, cinnamon and sugar in your pressure cooker, cover and cook on High for 10 minutes.
2. Divide into dessert bowls and keep in the fridge until you serve.

Nutrition: calories 140, fat 0, fiber 2, carbs 2, protein 1

Fall Plums Mix

Preparation time: 10 minutes
Cooking time: 6 minutes
Servings: 4

Ingredients:
- 12 plums, stones removed and halved
- 1 tablespoon cornstarch
- 2 cup sugar
- 1 teaspoon vanilla extract
- 6 tablespoons water

Directions:
1. In your pressure cooker, mix plums with sugar, cornstarch, vanilla and water, stir, cover and cook on High for 6 minutes.
2. Divide into bowls and serve cold.

Nutrition: calories 150, fat 2, fiber 1, carbs 6, protein 5

Sweet Blueberry Butter

Preparation time: 10 minutes
Cooking time: 10 minutes
Servings: 2

Ingredients:
- 1 cup blueberries puree
- ½ teaspoons cinnamon powder
- Zest from 1/3 lemon, grated
- 2 tablespoons sugar
- A pinch of nutmeg, ground
- ¼ teaspoon ginger, ground

Directions:
1. In your pressure cooker, mix blueberries with cinnamon, lemon zest, sugar, nutmeg and ginger, stir, cover and cook on High for 10 minutes.
2. Divide into jars and serve cold.

Nutrition: calories 133, fat 1, fiber 2, carbs 4, protein 6

Sweet Quinoa Dessert

Preparation time: 10 minutes
Cooking time: 20 minutes
Servings: 2

Ingredients:
- ½ cup apricots, dried and chopped
- ½ cup red quinoa
- ¼ cup steel cut oats
- 1 tablespoon sugar
- ¼ teaspoon vanilla bean paste
- ¼ cup hazelnuts, toasted and chopped
- 3 cups water

Directions:
1. In your pressure cooker, mix quinoa with apricots, oats, sugar, vanilla paste, hazelnuts and water, stir, cover and cook on High for 20 minutes.
2. Divide into 2 bowls and serve.

Nutrition: calories 151, fat 3, fiber 5, carbs 6, protein 5

Notes

RECIPE INDEX

A

Acorn Squash Side Dish 33
Appetizer Egg Spread 30
Apple Bread 229
Apple Butter 93
Apple Cake 240
Apple Cobbler 232
Apple Steel Cut Oats 71
Apples and Honey 273
Avocado Spread 112

B

Baby Back Ribs Appetizer 212
Baby Carrots Snack 8
Baked Custard 239
Baked Sweet Potatoes 177
Banana Cake 232
Banana Cake 261
BBQ Chicken Wings 209
BBQ Ribs 125
BBQ Ribs 162
BBQ Square Ribs 15
Bean Casserole 155
Beans and Avocado Salsa 191
Beans and Chorizo 182
Beans Cake 245
Beans Chili 157
Beef and Artichokes 140
Beef and Broccoli 132
Beef Curry 139
Beef Dip 206
Beef Dish 131
Beef Meatballs 209
Beef Sandwiches 61
Beef Stew 121
Beef Stew 128
Beet Appetizer Salad 13
Beet Soup 146
Beets Cakes 36
Beets Side Dish 185
Beets Spread 110
Bell Peppers and Sausages 195
Bell Peppers Stir Fry 194
Berry Cobbler 237
Black Bean Salsa 51
Black Bean Soup 129
Black Bean Soup 148

Apples and Pears Salad 264
Apples and Red Grape Juice 266
Apples and Wine 243
Apples and Wine Sauce 247
Apricot Jam 260
Apricot Marmalade 276

Black Beans Patties 27
Black Rice Pudding 236
Black Tea Cake 269
Blackberry Pie 231
Blue Cheese Dip 48
Blueberries and Strawberries Compote 272
Blueberry and Coconut Sweet Bowls 265
Blueberry Breakfast Bowl 78
Blueberry Breakfast Delight 86
Blueberry Jam 262
Boiled Peanuts 215
Bok Choy and Rice 197
Bok Choy Side Dish 196
Braised Collard Greens 43
Braised Endives 196
Bread Pudding 89
Bread Pudding 262
Breakfast Apple Dish 96
Breakfast Apple Dumplings 115
Breakfast Arugula Salad 99
Breakfast Bacon Potatoes 86
Breakfast Banana Bread 84
Breakfast Banana Bread 87
Breakfast Beans 99
Breakfast Butter 115
Breakfast Cake 80
Breakfast Cheese Spread 113

Apricots and Cranberries Pudding 244
Arborio Rice Side Salad 216
Artichokes and Citrus Sauce 157
Artichokes Side Dish 183
Artichokes Spread 47
Asian Wings 13

Breakfast Chestnut Butter 117
Breakfast Chickpeas Spread 113
Breakfast Cobbler 95
Breakfast Couscous Salad 117
Breakfast Egg Salad 105
Breakfast Meat Soufflé 71
Breakfast Oatmeal 79
Breakfast Orange Marmalade 107
Breakfast Potatoes 108
Breakfast Rice and Chickpeas Medley 98
Breakfast Rice Pudding 81
Breakfast Rice Pudding 93
Breakfast Tortillas 83
Broccoli and Bacon Appetizer Salad 38
Broccoli and Cheese Soup 152
Broccoli and Garlic 187
Broccoli Appetizer Salad 37
Broccoli Pasta 178
Brown Rice Mix 97
Brown Rice Salad 218
Brussels Sprouts and Apples Appetizer 35
Brussels Sprouts and Broccoli Appetizer Salad 34
Brussels Sprouts and Chestnuts 217
Brussels Sprouts and Potato Bowls 102

Brussels Sprouts and Potatoes Appetizer Salad 32

C

Cabbage and Cream 184
Cabbage Rolls 22
Cabbage Side Dish 181
Cajun Sausage Mix 159
Cake Bars 233
Calamari Salad 63
Calamari Stew 170
Caramel Pudding 268
Carrot Breakfast Salad 116
Carrot Cake 253
Carrot Pudding and Rum Sauce 257
Carrots and Kale 184
Carrots and Walnuts Salad 64
Carrots Mix 62
Cashew Spread 26
Cauliflower and Barley Bowls 104
Cauliflower and Grapes 224
Cauliflower Dip 40
Cauliflower Salad 65
Cauliflower Salad 165
Celeriac Breakfast Mix 105
Cheddar Quiche 72
Cheesecake 254
Cheesy Broccoli Appetizer Salad 39
Cheesy Cauliflower Bowls 108
Cherry Bowls 279
Cherry Pie 241
Chestnut Mushrooms 17
Chicken and Fennel Soup 147
Chicken and Kale Soup 146
Chicken and Potatoes Mix 159
Chicken and Red Cabbage Soup 149
Chicken and Salsa 174
Chicken and Tomatillo Salsa 137

Brussels Sprouts Side Salad 218
Buckwheat Porridge 82
Buckwheat Porridge 91

Chicken and Veggie Soup 144
Chicken Appetizer Salad 53
Chicken Curry 121
Chicken Dip 47
Chicken Dish 130
Chicken Fall Stew 161
Chicken Sandwiches 65
Chicken with Dates 138
Chicken Wrap 133
Chickpea Curry 130
Chickpeas Appetizer 29
Chickpeas Cakes 177
Chili Beef 125
Chili Dip 20
Chili Mahi Mahi 137
Chinese Fish 166
Chinese Mustard Greens 33
Chinese Style Peanuts 11
Chocolate Bread Pudding 90
Chocolate Cake 242
Chocolate Cake 246
Chocolate Cookies 237
Chocolate Fondue 278
Chocolate Oatmeal 69
Chocolate Pudding 255
Chunky Warm Salsa 48
Cinnamon Pho 128
Clams Appetizer 9
Classic Ricotta Cake 248
Cocktail Boiled Peanuts 10
Cocoa and Milk Pudding 267
Cocoa and Walnuts Sweet Cream 270
Coconut and Avocado Pudding 267
Coconut Cabbage 202
Coconut Cream and Cinnamon Pudding 263
Coconut Pancake 265
Coconut Quinoa 133

Bulgur Appetizer 58
Burrito Casserole 76
Buttery Potatoes 206

Cod and Beer 164
Cod and Orange Sauce 138
Cold Pineapple and Cherries Mix 280
Collard Greens and Bacon 198
Collard Greens and Peas 44
Collard Greens Side Dish 198
Collard Greens Stew 166
Corn Dip 20
Corn on the Cob 203
Corn Side Dish 210
Cornmeal Porridge 81
Cornmeal Porridge 95
Couscous and Mint 117
Crab Spread 19
Cranberries Dessert Bowl 230
Cranberry and Pear Cake 278
Cranberry Beans Salad 100
Cranberry Bread Pudding 264
Cranberry Side Dish 190
Cream and Cinnamon Puddings 248
Cream Cheese Pudding 270
Cream of Spinach 154
Creamy Broccoli Appetizer 38
Creamy Corn 187
Creamy Endives Appetizer Salad 21
Creamy Spinach 52
Creamy Squash Bowl 114
Crispy Chicken 124
Crispy Chicken 214
Crunchy Brussels Sprouts Salad 34
Cumin Dip 49

D
Dates and Ricotta Cake 251
Delicious and Simple Octopus 143

E
Egg and Coconut Cream 272
Egg Bake 70
Egg Muffins 90
Eggplant and Cashews Mix 220
Eggs and Bacon Breakfast Risotto 76
Endives Platter 24
Espresso Oatmeal 92
Espresso Steel Cut Oats 68

F
Fall Pear Cake 277
Fall Plums Mix 280
Fast Salmon 132
Fast Shrimp Scampi 141
Fennel and Shallots 200
Fennel Cream 163
Fish and Orange Sauce 175
Fish Balls 8
Fish Soup 136
Flavored Parmesan Mushrooms 205
Flavored Pasta 156
Flavored Pears 250
French Eggs 75
French Toast 74
Fresh Peach Jam 106
Fruit Cobbler 91

G
Garlic Beets Salad 223
Garlic Green Beans 55
Garlic Shrimp 139
Ginger and Peach Marmalade 254
Ginger Cookies Cheesecake 256
Glazed Fruits 244
Grated Carrot Appetizer Salad 15
Greek Meatballs 10
Green Beans and Bacon 191
Green Beans and Blue Cheese 59
Green Beans and Cranberries Side Dish 59
Green Beans Appetizer Salad 16
Green Beans Fries 208
Green Beans Stew 175
Green Cabbage and Tomatoes Side Dish 222
Green Olive Pate 45
Green Tea Pudding 271

H
Ham and Cheese Dip 18
Ham and Egg Casserole 69
Haricots Verts Side Salad 67
Honey Chicken Appetizer 220
Hot Wings 224
Hulled Barley Appetizer 55

I
Italian Dip 227
Italian Eggplant Breakfast Mix 114
Italian Eggplants Bowls 104
Italian Mussels 9

J
Jambalaya 162
Juicy Roast 122

K
Kale and Carrots Salad 42
Kale and Wild Rice Appetizer Salad 42
Kale Sauté 56
Kidney Beans 219

L
Lamb Casserole 160
Lamb Ribs 67
Lamb Ribs and Sauce 170
Lemon and Maple Syrup Pudding 259
Lemon and Olive Chicken 136
Lemon and Orange Jam 252
Lemon Cookies 245
Lemon Curd 271
Lemon Lamb Chops 174
Lemon Marmalade 238
Lemon Pepper Salmon 134
Lemon Pudding 258
Lemony Endives Appetizer 23
Lentils Patties 27
Light Lemon Dip 45
Lime Pie 251

M
Mac and Cheese 123
Mango Salsa 37
Mango Side Salad 225
Maple Acorn Squash Dish 25

Mashed Potatoes 189
Mexican Breakfast 74
Mexican Corn on the Cob 14
Mexican Zucchini Side Dish 192
Milk and Cream Pudding 277
Millet and Oats Porridge 85
Millet Porridge 110

O
Octopus Appetizer 53
Onion Cream 147
Onion Dip 14

P
Pancake 83
Parmesan Zucchini Fries 212
Parsnip and Quinoa Breakfast Mix 102
Pasta and Spinach 158
Pasta Appetizer Salad 219
Pasta with Salmon and Pesto 171
Pea and Ham Soup 160
Pea Rice 201
Peach and Cinnamon Compote 254
Peach Breakfast 88
Peach Compote 252
Potato and Salmon Breakfast 119
Potato and Spinach Hash 87
Potato Salad 103
Potato Soup 152

Q
Quince Jam 118
Quinoa and Tomatoes Breakfast Mix 97

R
Radishes Side Salad 222
Ranch Spread 51
Red Onions and Apples Mix 25
Red Pepper Dip 46
Red Pepper Hummus 12
Red Pepper Soup 151
Refried Beans 179

S
Salmon and Chili Sauce 169

Meatloaf 153
Millet Pudding 236
Minestrone Soup 150
Minty Carrots 62
Minty Kale Salad 43
Mixed Veggies 208
Mixed Veggies Side Dish 195
Mushroom Appetizer Salad 26
Mushroom Cakes 30

Onion Soup 148
Onion, Celery and Bread Side Dish 190
Peach Jam 250
Peaches and Cream 275
Peaches Oatmeal 71
Peanut Butter Cups 233
Pear and Maple Dessert 279
Pearl Onions Side Dish 66
Pears with Garlic and Jelly 247
Pepper Frittata 73
Pineapple and Peas Breakfast Curry 101
Pineapple Pudding 261
Pinto Bean Dip 44
Pinto Beans Breakfast Salad 112
Potato Soup 153
Potato Wedges 207
Potatoes and Shrimp Appetizer Salad 31
Pumpkin and Coconut Sweet Mix 275

Quinoa Bowls 78
Quinoa Breakfast 80
Quinoa Salad 98

Rhubarb and Strawberries Mix 241
Rhubarb Breakfast Spread 120
Rice and Beans 126
Rice and Black Beans Breakfast Dish 101
Rice and Edamame 199
Salmon and Risotto 167
Salmon and Veggies 171
Salmon Casserole 169

Mediterranean Cod 173
Mushroom Dip 40
Mushrooms and Asparagus 189
Mushrooms and Rosemary 17
Mushrooms Side Dish 188
Mussels and White Wine Sauce 145
Mussels Appetizer 227
Mussels Bowls 156

Orange and Beet Appetizer 54
Orange Cream 246
Plum Jam 263
Poached Fennel 200
Poached Figs 274
Poached Pears 249
Pomegranate Oatmeal 107
Pork and Lemon Sauce 163
Pork and Pineapple Delight 142
Pork Burritos 60
Pork Cakes 68
Pork Chops and Tomato Sauce 129
Pork Roast 142
Pork Tenderloin and Pomegranate Sauce 173
Pumpkin and Yogurt Cake 229
Pumpkin Cake 240
Pumpkin Granola 234
Pumpkin Oatmeal 82

Quinoa with Sausages 111

Rice and Quinoa 188
Rice Pudding 234
Rice with Fennel 201
Rich Chicken Salad 168
Ricotta Mousse 239
Roasted Hummus 216
Roasted Potatoes 180

Salmon with Lemon 164
Sautéed Escarole 204
Scallion Spread 19

Scotch Eggs   79

Shiitake Mushrooms Mix   221
Shredded Chicken   127
Shrimp 176
Shrimp and Tomatoes Appetizer Mix 46
Spinach and Salami   52
Spinach and Squash Mix   228
Spinach Pasta 176
Spinach Side Dish   217
Squash and Apple Mash   226
Squash and Apple Soup   144
Squash Porridge   84
Squash Porridge   92
Squash Risotto   180
Steamed Leeks   203
Steamed Tilapia   134
Stir Fried Okra 204
Strawberries Dessert 273
Strawberry and Chia Marmalade   259
Strawberry and Rhubarb Breakfast Compote   120

Shrimp Boil   141
Soup   155
Southern Peanuts   11

Spaghetti Squash Delight   183
Spanish Frittata   77
Spanish Rice   182
Strawberry Jam   105
Strawberry Quinoa Bowl   94
Strawberry Shortcakes   266
Stuffed Bell Peppers Appetizer   32
Stuffed Chicken Breasts   211
Stuffed Peaches   276
Stuffed Strawberries   243
Summer Lentils Appetizer   58
Sweet and Sour Side Salad   64
Sweet Baked Plums   282
Sweet Blueberry Butter   281
Sweet Brussels Sprouts   179

Spicy Chicken Wings 167
Spicy Collard Greens 199
Spicy Salmon 172
Spicy Tomato Jam   249
Spicy Zucchini 192

Sweet Brussels Sprouts Appetizer   35
Sweet Chia Pudding   238
Sweet Corn Pudding   260
Sweet Pearl Onion Mix   215
Sweet Potato Hash   85
Sweet Potato Puree   186
Sweet Potato Side Salad   225
Sweet Potatoes Casserole   109
Sweet Potatoes Mash 226
Sweet Quinoa Dessert   281
Sweet Soufflé 230
Sweet Zucchini Bread 274
Swiss Chard Salad   110
Swiss Chard Soup   150

T
Tapioca Pudding 116
Teriyaki Scallops 143
Tikka Masala 135
Tofu and Sweet 96
Tofu Appetizer 23
Tomatoes and Salad 214
Tomatoes and 213

Tomatoes and Garlic Dip 29

V
Vegetarian Lentils Soup 123
Veggie and Couscous Breakfast 118

W
Watercress Appetizer Salad 18
Western Omelet 73
Wheat Berries Appetizer 56

Tomatoes Appetizer Salad 41
Tomatoes Side Salad 210
Tortillas 49
Turkey Breast Breakfast Mix 106
Turkey Meatballs 126
Turkey Mix 161
Turkey Soup 150

Turnip Mash 223

Veggie Breakfast Casserole 88
Veggie Dumplings 28
Veggie Quiche 94

White Beans Dip 50

White Chocolate Mousse 235
Wild Rice Breakfast Salad 100

Turnips and Chili Pepper Side Dish 228
Turnips Spread 63

Veggies and Wheat Appetizer Salad 57

Vidalia Onions Mix 211

Winter Cherry Mix 257
Yellow Squash and Zucchini 194
Zucchini and Mushrooms 193
Zucchini Spread 22

Made in the USA
Columbia, SC
05 November 2019